Frederick W. Taylor
and the
Rise of Scientific Management

Special Collections, S. C. Williams Library, Stevens Institute of Technology

Frederick W. Taylor

as President of the American Society of Mechanical Engineers, 1906

Frederick W. Taylor
and the
Rise of Scientific Management

Daniel Nelson

The University of Wisconsin Press

Published 1980

The University of Wisconsin Press
114 North Murray Street
Madison, Wisconsin 53715

The University of Wisconsin Press, Ltd.
1 Gower Street
London WC1E 6HA, England

First printing

Printed in the United States of America

For LC CIP information see the colophon

ISBN 0-299-08160-5

To Catherine and Debra

Contents

Preface

This is the story of an unlikely revolutionary and his role in the transformation of American industry. Frederick W. Taylor was a member of the nineteenth-century economic and social elite, the principal beneficiaries of the American industrial revolution. He was also a creative technician, the single most important contributor to the rise of a "new factory system" and of an aristocracy based on technical knowledge, education, and organizational skills rather than inherited wealth, social and familial ties, or business acumen. At one level Taylor's story is an account of an enormously influential innovator; at another it is a case study of the evolving structure of American society in the years before World War I.

Two themes dominated Taylor's innovative activities. The first was his interaction with contemporary business and managerial developments, particularly the growth of big business and "systematic management."[1] This was the essential relationship of Taylor's career, the key to his creativity and the gauge by which his contributions should be measured. Not only did it provide an essential setting for Taylor's contributions; it made his career a prism through which the revolutionary changes of his era can be examined and understood. The second theme, inescapable because of the literature of scientific management, is Taylor's relationship to the worker. In his approach to labor and labor problems Taylor also reflected his environment, though in a radically different way. Rather than a creator, he was a captive of his milieu. In dealings with subordinates, employees, and clients' employees he was invariably a traditionalist, even a reactionary. With certain limited exceptions he neither innovated nor was sympathetic to innovators in the labor-management and personnel field.[2] He was, however, an acute, if often cynical, student of public anxiety over the "labor problem," the continuing, possibly escalating, phenomenon of labor unrest. For twenty years he worked assiduously to associate his reform of the factory system, a subject of modest appeal, with the elimination of the labor problem. His enduring fame is in large measure a testament to his success in that endeavor.

In retrospect the story of Taylor's career is a study in paradox. Few men of his generation were as familiar with contemporary economic developments or worked with as many of the men who played vital roles in shaping the modern American economy. Yet Taylor responded to these men and events in ways that are difficult to understand three-quarters of a century later. Sensitive in the extreme to relations among businessmen, he was indifferent, often ruthless, in his relations with workers, particularly those workers who were least able to defend themselves. A man of uncompromising principle in dealings with his economic and social equals, he was a man of expediency in dealings with his social inferiors. A reformer in one sphere, he was a reactionary in others.

Taylor's work also reflected this duality. His management system, both as symbol and substance of the factory revolution, profoundly affected American industry, but its impact in practical terms consisted mostly of changes in machine operations, plant layout, and managerial activities. Despite Taylor's apparent preoccupation with the worker, scientific management had little direct effect on the character of factory work or the lot of the worker. Taylor's labor "reforms" were introduced *in toto* in only a handful of firms. And even in piecemeal form they had far less impact than his technical and organizational innovations. Taylor's claims and reputation notwithstanding, a different and often antagonistic group of labor reformers revolutionized the worker's role in the twentieth-century factory.

A second paradox compounds the first. Having shown little regard for the employees in the plants where he developed scientific management in the 1880's and 1890's, Taylor made his relationship with them the basis for his immensely successful promotional campaign after 1895. As long as Taylor's audiences consisted of engineers and businessmen, this contradiction was not apparent. After 1910, however, his audience and his reception changed. At the height of his career as a reformer he became, ironically, the object of concerted attacks by other groups of reformers.

Taylor's paradoxical use of the workers in his promotional campaign and the ensuing conflict left an indelible stamp on the literature of scientific management and the public perception of his contributions. Among Taylor's most successful promotional tools were his writings, particularly "A Piece Rate System" (1895), "Shop Management" (1903), and *The Principles of Scientific Management* (1911). Together with his authorized biography, Frank Barkley Copley's *Frederick W. Taylor, Father of Scientific Management* (1923), they form a large and potentially valuable resource. They must, however, be used with the utmost caution. Like all primary sources they reflect their author's setting; but they have an additional complicating feature. Taylor viewed his professional papers as technical treatises and as educational tracts. As a result, they are part factual report and part polemical essay. They supply information unobtainable elsewhere, but they also convey inaccurate, often misleading, impressions of Taylor's interests and contributions.

Since 1911 students of Taylor's career have operated within the intellectual framework created by these works. The one major exception, C. Bertrand Thompson, Taylor's scholar-disciple, had little influence.[3] The best of the books written in the Taylor-Copley tradition, like Milton Nadworny's *Scientific Management and the Unions, 1900–32* (1955) and Hugh G. J. Aitken's *Taylorism at Watertown Arsenal* (1960), focus explicitly on Taylor's labor "reforms" and their impact. The least helpful discuss scientific management in general from such a perspective. In recent years, unfortunately, the volume of publication has increased in inverse proportion to the volume of meaningful research. Aitken's *Taylorism at Watertown Arsenal* was the last work based on extensive use of original sources. The chapters on scientific management in three recent imterpretative volumes could have been written in 1915, and a 1970 psychohistory reduces Taylor to a caricature figure.[4]

A more realistic approach requires greater attention to chronology and the dynamics of Taylor's professional life. To appreciate his contribution, it is necessary to view his activities in sequence and in the proper historical context—the last quarter of the nineteenth century, not the years after 1910, when Taylor, his work, and his ideas became well known. The following account, then, begins with an examination of the traditional factory system and the origins of the second or "new" factory system, the organizational and intellectual milieu in which Taylor operated. Chapters 2 through 4 reassess Taylor's business career between the 1870's and 1901, the truly creative years of his life. Chapters 5 and 7 reexamine Taylor's "second" career as a publicist and interpreter of the factory revolution, and Chapter 6 summarizes the effects of his activities on contemporary industry. Fortunately, Taylor's significance derived primarily from his reactions to economic, technical, and ultimately political events. When personal or psychological factors affected his work I have described that impact as fully as the available evidence permits. The absence of reliable sources and an overabundance of speculative assessments probably make a more complete account of his personal life and character impossible.

In preparing this book I have acquired numerous debts. Undoubtedly the most important are to Robert P. A. Taylor, who discussed his stepfather's life and career at length with me, and the staffs of the Stevens Institute of Technology and the University of Akron libraries. The Stevens librarians, notably Frances Duck, were unfailingly helpful during my many visits. The Akron librarians expeditiously handled innumerable interlibrary loan requests and in other ways facilitated my research. I am also grateful to the University of Akron Faculty Research Committee, which financed my travel, and the staffs of the Franklin D. Roosevelt Library, the Library of Congress, the Baker Library of the Harvard Business School, the New York Public Library, the National Archives, the Purdue University Library, and the Friends Library at Swarthmore College. Charles P. Wrege discussed his work with me, and Edward A. Coates supplied background information on Atherton B. Wadleigh. Elizabeth Madeira, Harris Ebenbach, Bayard S. Clark, and Frederick W. Clark helped me trace Taylor's Germantown ties. David Kyvig and James Laux read the entire manuscript and offered many valuable suggestions. The editors of *Business History Review, Pennsylvania Magazine of History and Biography,* and *Journal of Arizona History* permitted me to use material that had appeared originally in article form. My wife, Lorraine, encouraged me throughout the preparation of the manuscript.

Frederick W. Taylor
and the
Rise of Scientific Management

1

The Factory Revolution

The second half of the nineteenth century was a time of far-reaching change in the structure and operation of the business firm. The best known of these innovations, the creation of large national and multinational enterprises in transportation and manufacturing, intrigued and often outraged contemporaries.[1] A product of the mid-century expansion of the railway industry, the modern big business appeared in the industrial sector in the 1870's and became the dominant institution in much of industry between 1897 and 1902, the years of the first great merger movement. From the beginning it was an object of public scrutiny and comment.[2] The railroads were the most controversial institutions of their age; their creators and managers, and those of the large industrial firms of the late nineteenth century, were the best-known businessmen of the time, perhaps of any time. Though assessments varied widely, big business corporations had few uncritical defenders. By the early twentieth century they had generated a current of apprehension that became the central theme of the progressive reform movement in the years before World War I.

By contrast, another late-nineteenth-century development, the transformation of the factory, was less auspicious and, for many years, less controversial. A response to the apparent deficiencies of mid-nineteenth-century manufacturing operations, the factory revolution occurred slowly, almost imperceptibly. It had no obvious institutional manifestation; its most prominent figure, Frederick W. Taylor, the "father of scientific management," worked in comparative obscurity until 1910. And though it occurred during the same period as the rise

3

of the big business corporation, reflected the same underlying forces of technology and economics, and also spawned a new managerial elite, many contemporary observers, including Taylor, viewed it as a separate, distinct, remedial development, an antidote to the rise of big business. Only after World War I did large numbers of Americans perceive the "new factory system" with the same fascination and anxiety they had long exhibited toward the large corporation.

The First Factory System

The advent of modern machines and industrial processes in the first quarter of the nineteenth century marked the beginning of a new phase in the organization of American industry, a radical departure from the household-handicraft-mill complex of the eighteenth century.[3] An extension of earlier English developments, the first factory system appeared in Waltham and Lowell in the 1810's and 1820's, spread to the chemical and metallurgical industries in the 1840's, and embraced virtually all market-oriented industry by the 1860's and 1870's.[4] For the next half century it remained the dominant mode of organization in manufacturing. To contemporaries the first factory system was a technological and economic achievement of the first order, a symbol of modernity in economic life. Only its social impact, its association with industrial unrest in particular, created as much argument as adulation.

The first factory system was the product of interrelated developments in technology, management, and the utilization of labor. Of these elements the first was by far the most influential. Machine processes gave rise to the factory; they remained its *raison d'être* and the chief link between the manufacturer and production. Never again would technology play such a dominant role in determining the day-to-day activity of the factory. Yet this most crucial feature of the nineteenth-century manufacturing plant was also its most elusive element. For while all factories operated in a common technical milieu, they differed widely in mechanical detail. Men who were familiar with one industry or group of industries assumed, with some justice, that they had no claim to expertise in others. By comparison, managerial practice was less influential and diverse. The basis of shop management in a textile mill, machinery plant, or an ironworks was the delegation of power and authority. For most purposes the foreman was the manufacturer. Personnel and labor relations also varied little from plant to plant. Analysts of the "labor problem" could generalize with little fear of contradiction.

Despite their complexity and variability, machine processes had two common effects on the operation of the factory. First, they dictated the nature and organization of production. Though the exact effects varied by industry and product, there were major temporal distinctions. In one group of industries—cotton and woolen textiles were the most notable examples—the advent of power-driven machinery almost immediately created a sequential manufacturing process that remained characteristic of the industry throughout the nineteenth century. Invention altered specific machines and processes, but had little impact on the organization of the factory.[5] In a second group—iron and steel or shoe manufacture, for example—machinery created a standard factory design and layout but only after an extended transition period. Technical innovation was either more (iron and steel) or less (shoe manufacture) disruptive than in textiles. In either case there was little uniformity in factory organization until the end of the nineteenth century.[6] In a third category—the machinery makers were the pre-eminent case—mechanization never imposed a specific pattern or sequence of production. Apart from common functions such as metal forming, metal cutting, and final assembly, the organization of the machinery works remained a tribute to the manufacturer's imagination and creativity.

It is not surprising, then, that machinery manufacturers became the most assiduous students of internal shop operations and the proponents of more rational plans of factory organization. For decades they debated the best arrangement for a machinery plant: the hollow square, the H, or the L form; the multi-floor versus the single-floor machine shop; and the "group" versus the "output" (emphasizing product rather than machine function) plan of machine shop layout. Most manufacturers came to favor the other forms over the hollow square, the single-story plant over the multi-story shop, and the "output" over the "group" plan. They also concluded that for improved safety and sanitation, foundry and blacksmith shops should be segregated from the rest of the plant.[7]

Second, machinery decisively influenced the social environment of the factory. Obviously it had a major effect on working conditions. But there was also a close association between production techniques, managerial authority, and labor-management relations. The essential division was between the heat-using industries—iron and steel, glass, oil, food processing, and others based on chemical processes—and the mechanical industries that relied on discrete machine operations.[8] In the former, machines were the dominant factor in defining relations between managers and workers; in the latter they were not. In heat-using factories, chemical processes governed the activities of employees, who facilitated production or performed essential subsidiary tasks. In the short term, at least, technology determined the pace of work, the length of the work period, and the sequence of jobs. As a result there was relatively little contact and presumably little opportunity for conflict between supervisors and workers. The work in the heat-using plants, however, was so unpleasant and dangerous that the potentially positive social implications of the production process often were not apparent. Skilled metal workers were among the earliest and most persistent adherents of trade unionism of all American industrial employees.[9]

Technology played a similar role in precision machinery manufacture, the most complex and demanding of the mechanical industries. Mass production techniques based on specialized machine tools and interchangeable component parts first appeared in armories and gun factories in the 1830's; spread to related industries, such as watch and sewing machine manufacture after mid-century; and became characteristic of locomotive, steam engine, and other heavy machinery manufacture in the late nineteenth century.[10] By the climactic years of the first factory system the "American System of Manufacturers" had become a synonym for American technical virtuosity and for a material culture based on widespread familiarity with machinery. Mass production was only possible, however, when the factory was organized like an iron or glass plant and the production of hundreds or thousands of discrete components occurred in a semiautomatic flow pattern. Successful machinery manufacturers necessarily mastered the intricacies of factory organization and machine layout; yet because of the specialization and undeviating attention to detail necessary for simulated flow production, they did not develop a generalized approach or a larger view of their activities.[11]

For managers and workers the stringent demands of mass production created a unique social climate. Except for the foundry, where the customary problems of the heat-using industries prevailed, precision machinery plants were clean and well maintained. As an expert observer noted, technical and commercial success demanded that "neatness and order" be given the "highest consideration."[12] Moreover, a high percentage of the employees, often 50 percent or more, worked at machine tool and assembly operations, the cleanest and safest areas of the factory.[13] And that characteristic, in turn, meant there was an unusually large number of highly skilled, well-paid workers. In the typical American System factory of the 1870's the skilled contingent ranged from 25 to 60 percent of the total. In an iron mill the comparable figure was 20 to 25 percent, and in a cotton textile factory it was only 10 to 15 percent.[14] Finally, the multiplicity of functions and jobs in the precision machinery factory created unprecedented opportunities for advancement.[15] By any measure the employees of such factories were an elite element, the little-noticed aristocrats of American industrialism.

On the other hand, the mechanical industries generally operated in a radically different environment. In the years after the Civil War textile, shoe, and related manufactures employed nearly two-thirds of all industrial employees.[16] In those factories machines performed discrete functions, but neither the raw materials nor the final product required the same degree of precision as in metal machinery manufacture. As a consequence, technology influenced plant design and working conditions, but managers determined the character and pace of work. In the competitive atmosphere of nineteenth-century industry, plant officials often embraced the "driving" method of supervision, a combination of authoritarian rule and physical compulsion. As an observer of the Fall River textile mills reported, the "agent drives the superintendent, he drives the overseer, and the overseer drives the operative."[17]

Whether technology permitted little (iron and steel) or much (textiles) managerial discretion, the tendency in all plants was to delegate authority and to rely on the first-line supervisor for a wide array of functions.[18] Within the limits set by the manufacturing process, the foreman was usually responsible for production management, quality control, cost accounting, and all phases of personnel management except the negotiation of union contracts. In nearly all industries he was held accountable for what, in fact, the employees did. And he typically had complete control over the hiring, training, supervising, and disciplining of the workers. Understandably, his social standing was second only to that of the highest executives. At the Reed and Barton Company, not an unusual case, the foremen "deported themselves with great dignity and . . . customarily reported for work attired in silk hats, cutaway coats, and attendant accessories.[19]

In the heat-using and precision machinery industries, where the intricacy or complexity of the manufacturing process required maximum decentralization, a remarkable group of factory entre- preneurs appeared. In the iron, glass, pottery, and foundry industries skilled workers operated their machines and managed assistants with minimal supervision. In the precision machinery factories they had even greater authority. Under the "internal contract" system they worked as semi-independent businessmen. The firm provided "contractors"—the most skilled and reliable workers—with raw materials, tools, and power. The "contractors" manufactured a particular component for an agreed-upon price. Their profit, the difference between the contract price and the cost of production, depended on their ability to innovate and control costs. To maximize their profit, they demanded complete control over the production process, including the selection and the management of the labor force.

In the other mechanical industries, where machine processes permitted a larger managerial role, the supervisor had less freedom. In the textile industry it was customary for an overseer to head a department or several similar departments in different mills. Though he might be responsible for a large number of machines and several hundred workers, including subforemen called "second" and "third" hands, his managerial prerogatives were limited. He did not decide what to produce or when to do it. At a typical mill "the overseers are limited as to . . . the number of people they shall employ, and in other directions, but they are held responsible for the amount and character of the work they shall turn out."[20]

Whatever the relationship between the manufacturer and the foreman, the latter exercised near-absolute authority over the workers. He hired and fired, promoted and demoted, provided whatever training the worker received, handled grievances (until they resulted in strikes), and enforced the manufacturer's personnel policies regarding hours of work, personal appearance, and decorum. Where hourly or daily wage rates were the rule, the foreman often had the power to vary rates for individuals. Where the piecework system prevailed, he usually acted as rate-setter. His technique was the time-honored rule-of-thumb approach.

> We take all but the very slow . . . and get the average [time] of the lot. Then we deduct about ten per cent for loafing and go to some factory in our town that has a piece price on that work. If no one in our town has a piece price we compare it with factories in other towns, and if we are not much too low or too high we put it in.[21]

Still, the foreman's power was not absolute. The manufacturer closely watched the payroll and was tempted to interfere whenever piece-workers' incomes exceeded the day work rate. In such situations he often cut the rate so the employee earned the equivalent of the day rate despite his higher output. This practice soon destroyed the piecework incentive: after experiencing rate cuts, the workers learned to produce only enough to make the equivalent of the day wage. Perceptive employers concluded that the solution to this problem lay in two areas:

more care in rate fixing and a guarantee against rate cutting. By the 1890's leading firms, such as Brown and Sharpe, Baldwin Locomotive, and William Sellers and Company, guaranteed rates unless the job changed.[22]

The combined effect of difficult working conditions in the heat-using industries, the "driving" method in the mechanical industries, and the favoritism, physical abuse, and insecurity everywhere associated with the foreman's control of the labor force was a more or less permanent state of antagonism and strife.[23] The first half century of the factory was a half century of unrest, a fact that the vicissitudes of the business cycle, union organizing, reform, and war tended to obscure.[24] The advent of "industrial discipline," while possibly making industrial workers more conscious of the time clock, did little to make them more agreeable or subservient to their employers. Nor did the vaunted advantages of American society—high wages, the promise of mobility, and the absence of a rigid pre-industrial class system—immunize them against strikes, violence, the blandishments of trade union organizers, or a sense of class or occupational consciousness.[25]

The most obvious manifestations of the "labor problem," as contemporaries referred to this situation, were strikes and violence, the classic hallmarks of discontent.[26] But there was another dimension to the labor problem, less dramatic but no less important. This was covert resistance expressed in various forms of noncooperation or outright sabotage. Most prevalent was artificially restricted production, the result of informal collusion among the workers.[27] Although the practice was common to many industries, it evoked the greatest interest and comment among machinery makers.[28] They noted that "soldiering" occurred when manufacturers cut wage rates, when foremen drove noncontract workers, or when the work was not sufficiently complex to require a contract but too demanding for close managerial control. It was the one manifestation of the labor problem common to the machinery plants.

By the 1880's the benefits and costs of the first factory system had sparked widespread debate among managers and workers. Clearly, it could be argued, the factory system facilitated rapid technological change, permitted mass production without a large organization or elaborate planning, and allowed the manufacturer to devote his attention to finance, marketing, and technical innovation. In an age of short-lived, intensely competitive manufacturing firms, it was in many respects an ideal arrangement. Yet there were also flaws. Technological innovation could place enormous strains on the decentralized management system. In some heat-using industries a shift from large batch to genuine flow production produced demands for better scheduling and coordination and, inevitably, for a larger managerial staff.[29] The growing size of the plant had a similar effect. No matter how the manufacturer sought to insulate himself from day-to-day affairs, his role in the factory, particularly in labor-management relations, inevitably increased. The obvious response was to recruit a corps of specialists. The most common complaints, however, concerned the role of the foreman, especially his treatment of the worker. In Philadelphia, Chicago, and Cincinnati, but even more so in Fall River, Lynn, and other communities where the mechanical industries dominated the local economy, there was an ominous correlation between the rise of the factory and the fragmentation of society along class and occupational lines. To many observers, including many manufacturers, the labor problem threatened to outweigh the technological and economic advantages of the factory.

Origins of the New Factory System

In the following decades the factory revolution obliterated most features of the nineteenth-century manufacturing plant. While labor leaders, social critics, and many businessmen bemoaned the deficiencies of the factory system, technological and economic change and the activities of two groups of innovators gradually transformed the character of American manufacturing. Before 1900 this development was confined to a small number of plants and was apparent to only the most careful students of American industry.[30] By 1915, the year of Frederick W. Taylor's death, the outline of a new and different factory system had become clearer. By the mid-1920's observers hailed the new factory environment as a prominent feature of the "New Era" economy and a social innovation comparable in significance to the earlier rise of the big business corporation.

Of the many interrelated facets of the factory revolution, technological change is perhaps the least well known because it was seldom directly related to the efforts of critics and reformers. Nevertheless, machine processes remained the heart of the factory, and mechanical innovation played a major role in the transformation of the manufacturing system. In the early nineteenth century, technology had freed the manufacturer from the burdens of day-to-day production and personnel management. In the latter years of the century it encouraged the opposite tendency, enlarging the realm of the manager and enhancing the possibilities for managerially defined social relationships.

Unquestionably, the most important technical innovations of the
quarter century before World War I were outgrowths of the advent of
electric power. In the 1880's manufacturers began to replace gas or oil
with arc and then incandescent bulb lighting, a trend that led to the use
of electricity for other ends. The first important application of electric
power to drive machinery occurred in 1890 when the Baldwin Locomotive Company remodeled its erecting shop and installed electric
motors.[31] In 1893 the Ponemah Mills at Taftville, Connecticut, and the
Columbia Mills at Columbia, South Carolina, introduced electric power
to the textile industry. In the next two decades the use of electrical
machinery became widespread.[32] Supposedly Building No. 60 of the
General Electric Schenectady works, with thirty-five electric cranes and
1,000 motor-driven tools, was the first shop to dispense with shafts and
belts altogether.[33]

The potential effects of electric power on the factory setting were
almost limitless. It reduced transmission costs, and, with the growth of
public utilities and the shift from "group" to "unit" drive (the installation
of motors in each tool or machine), electric power eliminated the
expense of maintaining the traditional system of steam engines, shafts,
and belts. By freeing manufacturers to build plants in any shape, it
undoubtedly speeded the adoption of steel and concrete construction.
By permitting the use of improved cranes, conveyors, railways, and
other transportation devices, it facilitated the handling of materials. By
allowing the removal of the maze of belts that was characteristic of most
machinery plants, it permitted natural lighting to an unprecedented
extent. Its impact on working conditions notwithstanding, electric
power greatly increased the manufacturer's ability to control the factory
environment.[34]

Other changes had similar effects. The technical breakthroughs that
revolutionized production methods in the iron and glass industries
between 1880 and 1910 eliminated intricate hand procedures which had
been essential to those industries since the industrial revolution and
reduced dependence on highly skilled workers. Technology remained a
determinant of social relationships in the factory, but the managers'
ability to control the manufacturing process increased. In the
mechanical industries, particularly the auto industry after 1900, steel
and concrete buildings, electrical power, and materials-handling
devices likewise created a new and distinctive industrial setting.

The other critical element in the rise of the new factory system was
the advent of two groups of innovators who responded to the apparent
shortcomings of the traditional factory. Seeking solutions to specific
problems, these men, mostly executives of manufacturing companies,

developed new conceptions of management and the manager's role. Though they spoke and wrote in particularistic, often technical terms, their analyses and prescriptions were revolutionary in implication. Before 1900 their appearance was the most obvious manifestation of the new factory system. The transformation of the manager preceded the transformation of the manufacturing plant.

One group consisted of professional mechanical engineers. As Monte Calvert and others have noted, nineteenth-century engineers suffered the frustrations of a new and poorly defined calling.[35] They also benefited from the increased size of the manufacturing plant.[36] But these factors alone do not explain their behavior. Versed in the scientific principles of machine building and operation and in the flexible arrangement of the machine shop, they became profoundly dissatisfied with the managerial status quo, particularly the decentralized management system and the role of the "contractor" or foreman. To them contemporary shop management was like some ingenious mid-nineteenth-century machine, an ad hoc reaction to the needs of the moment rather than the result of careful design and systematic application of science to utilitarian ends. Their answer to this apparent defect was what might be called the "machine model." If shop management were undertaken with the same knowledge and forethought as the building of a complicated machine, the plant would run with similar efficiency. Because of their positivistic outlook and their background in the relatively trouble-free machinery industry, engineers tended to downplay the severity of labor unrest and to see public outcries as the result of the naive or self-serving efforts of professional social reformers and trade unionists. To them the most important and immediate problem was restricted output, a problem they attributed largely to the haphazard leadership of the over-worked and underqualified foreman.[37]

The second group, larger and more influential, was the labor reformers. They included manufacturers, as well as businessmen from other industries and conservative social critics.[38] Most manufacturers who became involved were from the mechanical industries, where the larger sphere of managerial discretion had resulted in "driving" and widespread unrest. Whatever their background, they were united in their determination to alleviate the labor problem without surrendering authority to outsiders.[39] Whereas the engineers were sensitive to production problems but indifferent to labor unrest, the labor reformers were preoccupied with employer-employee relations. Textile manufacturers in particular revealed little anxiety about the organization of their plants or the foreman's role except in the personnel area. On the other hand, they were keenly sensitive to the specter of conflict, union organization, and social revolution that confronted them.

In their statements, writings, and activities the engineers expressed the outlook and concerns of machinery manufacturers. Reflecting the perspective of men who were increasingly sensitive to the organizational demands of mass production, they emphasized that traditional factory administration was "increasingly chaotic, confused and wasteful."[40] They stressed the lack of coordination between functions and departments in the plant and the need, to use Joseph Litterer's phrase, for "organizational recoupling."[41] Their interpretations of this need were diverse, but reflected a common assumption: the desirability of more systematic management. The hallmarks of their reform proposals were orderly procedures, careful organization, and attention to detail.

Predictably, the engineers sought to make accounting a tool for identifying real or potential problems in the shop.[42] Their accounting plans provided for more detailed statements and comparative cost data. By using job cards and time clocks, they were able to allocate prime costs (materials and direct labor) to specific jobs. The cards also provided a convenient system of inventory control. By 1905 or 1910 prime cost accounting had assumed its twentieth-century form.[43]

Equally important were their methods for determining and allocating overhead costs. The quantity of writing on this subject increased rapidly after 1885; many so-called management systems were really accounting systems with special attention to "burden" costs. There were major debates over the types of costs to consider—specifically whether office and selling charges should be included in manufacturing costs—and over the handling of idle time. Probably the most important innovation of the period was the "machine hour" method of allocating costs by which overhead costs were related to machine use. A. H. Church's "scientific production center" plan of 1901, an elaboration of this approach, was the most influential cost plan of the period.[44]

The engineers adopted a similar approach to the control of materials and production. They advocated centralized purchasing, standardized materials, and efforts to integrate the various steps of the manufacturing process.[45] Their production management systems included the specification of major operations, restrictions on the movement of parts and materials, and methods for recording direct costs and allocating overhead costs to specific jobs.[46]

The effect of these proposals was to reduce the foreman's area of discretion and in some cases to eliminate his auxiliary duties. The routing of orders, scheduling of jobs, moving and storing of materials and finished parts, and recording of production costs were either subjected to explicit policy statements or delegated to specialists. The formerly autonomous foreman ceased to be the all-round manager that he had been since the beginning of the factory system.

While engineers divested the supervisor of his ad hoc managerial functions, they also revised his powers vis-à-vis the workers. With few exceptions they did not question his authority to hire, fire, train, and discipline. Their concern was his traditional control of wage rates and his inability to prevent restrictions on production. Their answer to both problems was the incentive wage. A leading engineer, Henry R. Towne of Yale and Towne, devised the first important incentive plan, the "gain-sharing" system. Towne's contribution was part of a far-reaching effort to improve the operation of his plant. He introduced a production control system, a combination cost and time card plan, and a "first class foundry which is systematically managed," and he maintained the building and yards in immaculate condition.[47] Lavatories abounded, and the "use of the well-appointed washing facilities is not optional with hands, but obligatory."[48]

Towne's most noteworthy innovations, however, applied to the workers. He wrote that "some readjustment of the relations of labor and capital has got to be made." Yet his proposals were consistent with his professional background. The proper motive, he argued, was not fear of unions or considerations of "philanthropy or sympathy," but the "self-interest . . . of the employer. Some better method of bringing out . . . the best that is in [the men] in doing their work must be adopted."[49]

Towne's solution embraced a variety of measures. He abolished the contract system, introduced piece rates which he guaranteed for a year, and established systematic procedures for dealing with grievances. On new work Towne set minimum and maximum earnings levels so that the piece rates, if incorrect, would not unduly punish or reward the workers.[50] In 1887 Towne introduced his best-known innovation, the gain-sharing plan. This he defined as "savings sharing" rather than "profit sharing," since it divided part of any reduction in production costs with the employees who were responsible for the saving.[51] Though the plan seemed to work at first, Towne soon discovered a serious defect: there was no direct relationship between an individual's effort and his reward. As a result he ended gain sharing 1893 and 1895 and introduced an executive profit-sharing plan.

The next important incentive system was Frederick W. Halsey's "premium" plan. Like Towne, Halsey was troubled by the labor turmoil of the mid-1880's.[52] But his remedy was different from Towne's; indeed, he explicitly rejected anything that resembled profit sharing. "It is wrong in principle," he wrote, "and cannot be in any large sense a solution of the wages problem."[53] Instead, Halsey proposed the premium, a corrective to the piece rate that offered fractionally higher pay for substantially higher output. If, for example, the rate was $.50

per piece and the worker produced four pieces per day, Halsey might add a premium of $.25 for each additional piece. If the worker then produced six pieces per day, his output increased by 50 percent while his income increased by only 25 percent ($2.50 rather than $2.00).[54] The premium was less than the piece rate to discourage rate cutting, but high enough to presumably encourage greater effort and improved techniques.

The premium, Halsey believed, would end restrictions on production and reduce labor conflict since the managers' interest in lower unit costs would be reconciled with the workers' interest in higher pay. To make the premium attractive to workmen, Halsey urged employers not to cut the base rate (usually the traditional piece rate for a particular job) and make the plan "voluntary"—meaning that employees would not have to earn the premium or face discharge—in order to avoid charges of "driving." "Surely," he wrote, "a system which increases output, decreases cost, and increases workmen's earnings simultaneously, without friction, and by the silent force of its appeal to every man's desire for a larger income, is worthy of attention."[55]

Despite these advantages the premium plan made little progress until the turn of the century. Though Halsey first developed his ideas in 1884 and explained the plan to friends in 1888, he did not publish a description of it until 1891. At that time three firms, including his own, had introduced it. Halsey did not publish another account of his plan until 1899, supposedly waiting for independent verification of his experience.[56] After that time, however, he promoted it widely and successfully. As a consequence the premium became a popular incentive plan on both sides of the Atlantic for several decades and the basis for many related bonus schemes.[57]

The premium was similar to the other features of systematic management not only in its designer's primary objective, but also in its underlying assumptions about the workers' motives. Halsey believed, as did most proponents of systematic management, that "every man's desire for a larger income" was the essential consideration. He and the others tended to dismiss as romantic or unrealistic the notion that noneconomic factors might affect the workers' behavior. This view of motivation resulted in numerous disputes, especially when workers—including the foremen—refused to respond to incentive plans in ways the engineers anticipated.

The conflict began almost immediately when the craft unions of the metal trades, particularly the Machinists, signaled their opposition to the premium. The unions had long opposed piecework; the Machinists had even forbidden members to work under piece rates, a prohibition

that was unenforceable but indicative of the unionists' sentiments.[58] To
such men Halsey's plan was simply another form of piecework, more
insidious because of its novel features. A crucial battle occurred in
1899 when the union machinists at the Bickford Tool and Drill Company
of Cincinnati struck rather than accept the premium plan. After a conference with the plant superintendent, the Machinists' president agreed
to present the plan to the union convention. The delegates rejected it
overwhelmingly.[59] Their reaction, based on a misinterpretation of the
purpose of the premium, was nevertheless prophetic. To Halsey and
most employers who adopted his plan, the premium was merely a
corrective to defects in the piecework method of wage payment. To the
employees, however, it was an unwelcome attack on the status quo.
They viewed the union as the proper antidote to the foreman's abuses,
while Halsey and the engineers sought to curtail the union's real or
potential power, as well as the foreman's empire. During the next
decade employers often assumed the unionists' opposition was merely
an example of obstructionist tactics and would have no more practical
effect than their opposition to piecework. The union leaders, however,
reaffirmed their stand and waited for opportunities to renew their
attack.[60]

The labor reform movement, on the other hand, reflected radically
different perceptions of the strengths and weaknesses of the first factory
system. It grew out of earlier, less systematic efforts to recruit workers
and to counteract the inevitable tensions of industrial life.[61] Because of
this tie and the involvement of nonindustrialists, the labor reformers
tended to define their objectives narrowly. They devoted little attention
to production methods and the foreman's powers, except perhaps for
his ability to hire and discharge. Instead, they focused on the factory
environment and the social and cultural life of the operative class. To
eliminate unrest, they advocated programs that appeared paternalistic
or demeaning to men like Halsey and Taylor. Increasingly they
emphasized a complex of employee assistance programs designed to
improve morale, increase productivity, and bridge the apparent gap
between the employer and the employee. As the National Civic Federation explained, systematic "welfare work"—as the new approach was
known—involved "special consideration for physical comfort wherever
labor is performed; opportunities for recreation; educational advantages; and the providing of suitable sanitary homes, . . . plans for saving
and lending money, and provisions for insurance and pensions."[62]

By the turn of the century labor reform had attracted adherents in
nearly every industry and region.[63] In general, businessmen who had
large numbers of women employees were most sensitive to the labor

problem and likely to respond with benefit programs. In manufacturing, employers in the mechanical industries were the leading proponents of welfare work. Textile firms, where managerial prerogatives were substantial, women workers prevalent, and the foreman's empire unchecked by technology, labor unions, or workers' skills, accounted for more welfare plans than any other group of manufacturers. Lowell, Willimantic, and other New England textile towns were early centers of labor reform activity, but the proprietors of the new mill communities in the South Atlantic states were the most vigorous advocates of benefit programs. By the turn of the century they had established an enduring tie between the industry and welfare work. In the Carolina Piedmont, welfare work became the principal defense against labor unrest, strikes, unions, and government interference.

The tie between women workers, the mechanical industries, and labor reform was a central feature in the rise and subsequent transformation of welfare work at the National Cash Register Company (N.C.R.), the most important and innovative practitioner of labor reform. In many respects N.C.R. was an unlikely candidate for the leader's mantle. "The Cash" was a manufacturer of mass produced precision machinery, the type of firm that had mastered the intricacies of simulated flow production. Although the internal contract system was not used, N.C.R. operations were otherwise typical of late-nineteenth-century precision machinery plants. Wages were high and workers had abundant opportunities for advancement. Unrest presumably should have been minimal. Yet there were problems, most notably, incompetent and arbitrary managers in certain departments, that undermined quality control and made the social environment of the Dayton plant more like that of a textile mill than a machinery works.[64] In the mid-1890's the iconoclastic president and principal owner, John H. Patterson, responded to these difficulties by introducing systematic management procedures *and* a varied welfare program. Patterson's benefit plans, which he intended mostly for the women workers, approximately one-sixth of the total work force, included an insurance association, a medical department, baths, a dining area and "rest rooms" for the women workers, a library and reading room, a Sunday School, choral societies, musical groups, a theater, a kindergarten, and neighborhood clubs. The women worked only eight hours and arrived and left at different times from the men to minimize "unpleasantness and danger."[65] To oversee these activities, Patterson hired a Dayton woman, Lena Harvey, in 1897.

Patterson's programs operated successfully for five years, though not without opposition. Some of the executives thought he was spending too much money, particularly for Miss Harvey's work. Like other employers, they had reservations about Patterson's frequent assertion that "it pays." Apparently some workers also resented the company's heavy-handed efforts to "persuade" them to participate in the welfare programs. One observer who visited the plant in 1901 reported that the welfare programs had been "overdone."[66] Whatever the validity of these observations, it was widely—and mistakenly—believed that welfare work was responsible for the strike and lockout that closed the plant in the summer of 1901 and led Patterson to reassess his commitment to welfare work.

At the same time he had introduced welfare work, Patterson had permitted local unions to organize his skilled employees. Petty disputes and bickering among the organizations may have led him to regret his decision, but he took no action until 1901. In May of that year the brass foundry foreman, a "driver" and antiunion militant, fired the union molders in his department, provoking a strike by 150 brass molders and metal polishers. Fearful that a union "victory" would undermine discipline, Patterson refused to reinstate the discharged men and, when it appeared that the conflict might spread, locked out the rest of his 2,400 employees.[67] When he reopened the plant six weeks later, he announced major changes in the management. He fired the controversial foreman and adopted an open-shop policy. He also dismissed Miss Harvey and discontinued some of her activities. Most important, since the conflict made it clear that welfare work did not necessarily alter the way the plant operated at the shop level, Patterson introduced an additional innovation. Soon after the lockout he appointed a young executive, Charles U. Carpenter, to head a new labor department.

The N.C.R. labor department was the first modern personnel department in American industry. Before the lockout N.C.R. had had an employment department, but it, like many such offices in other firms, served as little more than a hiring and record-keeping bureau.[68] Under Carpenter and his successors the labor department assumed a variety of other functions. It handled grievances and discharges, promoted sanitation and shop safety, kept the management informed of legislation and court decisions pertaining to labor matters, and conducted foremen's meetings to bring the supervisors "into sympathy with its aims and purposes."[69] Designed to curtail the powers of the foremen and to increase the management's influence over the workers, the N.C.R. labor department anticipated the personnel management movement of the World War I period and after.

At N.C.R. and elsewhere one of the major features of systematic welfare work was the introduction of a specialist manager, the welfare with the most dramatic period of American industrial growth; his economic background assured him a degree of economic security; range of social contacts that less favored youths did not enjoy; and, least, the location of his home brought him into contact with many he most influential manufacturers of his era. Taylor's early career he story of a privileged young man who made the most of his many portunities.

Taylor's parents were "Proper Philadelphians," members of the aker aristocracy that formed an important component of the Philadelphia elite. Franklin Taylor, his father, came from a prominent Bucks ounty, Pennsylvania, Quaker family. A Princeton graduate of 1840, he as admitted to the Philadelphia bar in 1844 but practiced only briefly. ranklin's resources were sufficient to permit him, like other affluent hiladelphians of his age, to escape the workaday world; indeed, he as, in Nathaniel Burt's phrase, "born retired."[2] But whereas the vicissides of the late-nineteenth-century economy often wreaked havoc on hese occupationless gentlemen, the Taylors prospered. Franklin's nvestments in Bucks County mortgages, his simple but elegant lifestyle, and the price deflation of the last quarter of the nineteenth century enhanced rather than diminished his inheritance. By the time of his death in 1910 he was a near-millionaire.[3]

Emily Winslow, Taylor's mother, was the daughter of a wealthy New England Quaker merchant and Revolutionery era Loyalist émigré. The Winslows returned to Massachusetts in the 1820's and moved to Philadelphia in the 1840's. Emily and Franklin met there and were married in 1851. They made their home in Germantown, an upper-middle-class, predominantly Quaker suburb noted for its "elegant cottages and villas . . . delightfully shaded."[4] They had three children in the following years: Edward Winslow, in 1854; Frederick Winslow, in 1856; and Mary Newbold, in 1859. Shortly after Frederick's birth the family moved to Cedron, a substantial estate owned by a member of the Taylor family in the undeveloped southwest corner of Germantown. In 1872 the Taylors bought a home on Ross Street, on the east side of Germantown, where they lived for the rest of their lives. Edward and Mary eventually married into other prominent Germantown families. Mary's future husband was Clarence M. Clark, son of Edward W. Clark, the richest man in Germantown, whose estate at School Lane and Wissahickon Avenue was only a few blocks from Cedron.

Economically secure, the Taylors devoted themselves to activities that befitted responsible members of their class. If Franklin and Emily Taylor knew little of the burgeoning Philadelphia working class, they were intimately acquainted with the plight of the recognizably under-

secretary. By 1906 there were more than twenty professional welfare secretaries of both sexes. The women were teachers or nurses or had had experience in religious or philanthropic work. The men came from similar vocations; many had training as doctors or clergymen. Charles Henderson, a prominent reformer, accurately described the situation when he wrote that "employers must decide for themselves . . . what they wish to do. . . . There is no one science or art which can be mastered in preparation for all kinds of welfare work."[70] The common denominator was an interest in improving the lives of working people in ways consistent with the employer's economic objectives.

The duties of welfare secretaries were equally diverse. Some had explicit administrative responsibilities; others were merely "advisors." Secretaries trained as teachers, doctors, and nurses devoted most of their time to their respective specialties but were expected to perform other duties as well. Besides operating one or more welfare programs, the secretaries normally acted as ombudsmen and, in subtle ways, as disciplinarians. Depending on the firm, they took over some or most of the personnel functions that foremen had traditionally performed and that personnel departments and labor unions later assumed. These were demanding, perhaps impossible tasks, and the welfare secretary led a precarious existence. Those who performed specialized functions, like the operation of clinics or schools, and avoided controversy often enjoyed a lengthy tenure; but the more outspoken and ambitious secretaries, like Lena Harvey, soon ran afoul of their colleagues. The overt and covert opposition of superintendents or foremen, occasional charges of interference by workers, and changes in the management frequently made the secretary's position untenable.

The number of labor reformers and personnel management programs grew rapidly in the decade before World War I—a reflection of increased public interest in the "labor problem" and of the belief that welfare work reduced or eliminated it. The National Civic Federation's welfare department, established in 1904 to promote employee benefit programs, had 250 employer members in 1906 and 600 in 1911.[71] These figures, indicators of growth on one hand, also suggest the comparatively modest inroads of the new factory system on the real world of machines and men. Personnel management, like the engineers' revisions of traditional production management, underwent a substantial gestation period. Businessmen often accepted the reformers' arguments long before they were prepared to attack the status quo.

The first factory system and the dynamics of the factory revolution had profound effects on the career of Frederick W. Taylor. The distinctive characteristics of the nineteenth-century machinery plant, the values of the engineering profession, and the conflicting approaches of the engineers and the labor reformers were essential determinants of his approach to industrial and later social change. They explained his perception of contemporary business developments and the particular features of scientific management. Ultimately they accounted for the ironies that marked his work. More than most prominent men, Taylor was a product of his environment. That it could simultaneously serve as a stimulus to creativity and to misunderstanding was perhaps the most important paradox of his career.

2
Formative Years, 1856–188

In the 1870's and 1880's no American communi
abundant opportunities for observing the strengths an
the first factory system than Philadelphia. Long an indu
a disproportionate share of the nation's leading manufa
also retained much of the intellectual vitality that had n
of scientific and rationalist thinking early in the century
phia "fraternity of mechanicians"—to use Anthony F.
phrase—continued to influence young men of technical b
to adulthood in such an environment was to acquire an a
the force of tradition and the promise of creativity. So
Frederick W. Taylor. As a member of the Philadelphia
novice engineer at the Midvale Steel Company, he de
outlook and values that colored his thinking for the rest of
the early 1880's he began to alter the operation of the Midv
By 1889, when he left Midvale, his innovations—scientific m
—had become an identifiable entity, incomplete, unrefine
some respects ineffectual, but nonetheless a potentially radic
tive to the status quo.

A Proper Philadelphian

Taylor was born in 1856 into a prominent Philadelphia fa
combination of circumstances that gave him a substantial advan
later years. The timing of his birth insured that his career would

privileged. Franklin was an active trustee of a school for retarded children for more than half a century; Emily was an outspoken feminist and abolitionist. An adherent of the extremist antislavery faction headed by William Lloyd Garrison, she was one of a group of women who shocked the reform establishment by attempting to participate in the deliberations of the World Anti-Slavery Convention in London in 1840.[5] In subsequent years she was a fervent supporter and confidant of Lucretia Mott, the most prominent Philadelphia abolitionist. Birge Harrison, who lived near Cedron as a boy in the 1850's, believed that the Taylors harbored fugitive slaves.[6] There is no indication of the Taylors' involvement in the Civil War, but Germantown was the site of several army camps and three military hospitals, which offered numerous opportunities for humanitarian service.[7]

Most of all, the Taylors were committed to the cultural life of their community and times. Franklin, a lifelong devotee of literature and history, read Greek and Latin for pleasure. On a typical evening he would recite to the family, often in French or German. Emily was an expert linguist; "frequently she would entertain the ladies of her literary circle with such feats as offhand translations from Italian into German."[8] After leaving the Friends Meeting in the early 1850's, she, the Clarks, and other religious liberals founded the Unitarian Society of Germantown, which became the source of most of the Taylors' social ties.[9] She also "established at her home something of a salon for those devoted to plain living and high thinking," especially "innovators and reformers."[10] In 1869 the Taylors began a three-year tour of Europe so their children might have first-hand exposure to the cultural heritage they cherished.

It is testimony to the precarious nature of parental expectations that Franklin's and Emily's preoccupations had relatively little effect on Frederick. He was, of course, the beneficiary of their wealth and connections, but, unlike Edward, who became a nonpracticing physician devoted to travel and the arts, he had little interest in his parents' social or intellectual concerns. As an adult he made few charitable gifts and was active only in professional societies. To his parents' chagrin he soon adopted the racial and ethnic stereotypes common to industrialists of the late nineteenth century. Fluent in French and German, he had little interest in languages. Literature was simply a diversion, a way of relaxing after a hard day's work. Taylor remained a member of the Unitarian Society, but seldom attended services or took an active role in the church.

Frederick's independence was apparent as early as 1869-70, when the Taylors lived in Europe. In a journal he dutifully recorded his visits to museums and galleries, but he revealed more enthusiasm for his lessons in mathematics, his collections of stamps and birds' eggs, and his mountain climbing experiences.[11] In his later autobiographical writings he always dismissed European travel as an unsatisfactory background for a practical life.

Still, Taylor's early years were happy and eventful. The family was secure; Franklin and Emily were devoted, affectionate, and responsible parents. "Honesty, honor and self-respect," Franklin wrote his son, were all-important qualities. "A true gentleman scorns to do a mean action."[12] Within these constraints the children had abundant opportunities for self-fulfillment. Frederick in particular developed two interests that profoundly affected his later life. The first was athletics. Cricket (the preeminent Germantown sport), baseball, football, hiking, and skating were the chief absorptions of his adolescent years. From all accounts, Taylor played fiercely and successfully, though always within the rules, as his father insisted. The second interest was mechanical invention, at which he likewise excelled.

Taylor's early inventions were ad hoc responses to problems that arose in his daily activities. They revealed an inquiring mind, mechanical aptitude, tenacity, and a tendency, which became pronounced in later years, to assume that personal and social problems were amenable to better organization and improved mechanical devices. Birge Harrison recalled that "even . . . croquet was a source of study and careful analysis with Fred, who worked out carefully the angles of the various strokes, the force of impact, and the advantages and disadvantages of the understroke, the overstroke, etc."[13] In addition to athletic equipment—a special bobsled brake, for example—he developed gadgets to help overcome nightmares and insomnia, two seemingly persistent afflictions from which he suffered. He analyzed his problem, tested several theories, and devised apparatus to enable him to sleep properly. A special harness designed to wake him when he lay on his back fascinated his friends—and continues to intrigue his biographers.[14]

Taylor's interests became more clearly defined during the two years he spent at Phillips Exeter Academy after the family's return from Europe. Apparently he enrolled at the New Hampshire school because of family tradition and Exeter's close ties with Harvard, where Franklin hoped Frederick would prepare for a legal career. Few other Proper Philadelphians of the 1870's traveled so far from home for their secondary education or thought of any college except the University of Pennsylvania.[15] Nevertheless, Taylor profited from the experience, though not in the ways Franklin and Emily had anticipated.

Like other preparatory schools of the period, Exeter was undergoing important changes at the time Taylor attended. Growing pressure from students, parents, and the universities resulted in the modification of the traditional curriculum with its emphasis on Latin, Greek, and mathematics. In 1873, Taylor's second year, English, French, geography, and physics were taught for the first time. There was also widespread pressure from faculty for a greater voice in school policy, a demand that led to the upgrading of institutions such as Phillips Andover, Exeter's traditional rival.[16] At Exeter the faculty soon emerged triumphant. When the long time principal retired in early 1873, the two most important teachers, George A. Wentworth and Bradbury L. Cilley, took charge of the school for the rest of the year. Though the trustees appointed a new princip. i for the fall of 1873, Wentworth and Cilley never really relinquished their position. Wentworth, known to the students as "Bull" or "Bull Dog" for his "burly frame and roaring habit in the classroom," was the dominant force at Exeter for the next twenty years. His repute as a teacher and his influence as an author of popular mathematics texts placed him beyond reproach; he was, as the school's historian has written, "a law unto himself."[17]

Taylor was probably oblivious to these developments during his first year at Exeter. If his parents' letters of 1872-73 are any measure, he was almost wholly preoccupied with more pedestrian, but from his viewpoint no less important, concerns. Almost immediately he committed offenses—reading a book during church and cheating on an exam—that might have led to his expulsion. His parents were naturally shocked, and a series of long, admonitory letters issued from the Taylor household.[18] In contrast, Taylor's athletic career at Exeter was one of unblemished success. He was a member and later the captain of the crew, a pitcher on the intramural baseball team, and an accomplished skater and gymnast.

By the spring of 1873 there were signs of change. Taylor was more circumspect, he improved his academic performance, and he joined the debating society. He also gradually realized that his chief interest lay in mathematics and its applications. Franklin, undoubtedly pleased with his son's new sense of purpose, wrote in April 1873 that if he intended "to become an engineer" he could not "master too thoroughly the elementary branches of mathematics."[19] As early as September 1873 Emily Taylor suggested that he enroll at Rensselaer Polytechnic Institute or the Massachusetts Institute of Technology.[20]

During his second year at Exeter, Taylor became an outstanding student, the leader of his class. His natural competitiveness, his new

interest in a career, and Wentworth's rigorous methods all contributed
to this change. Taylor recalled with affection his mentor's classroom
technique.

> The moment he [Wentworth] found that such and such men were
> not working . . . He would call them up, stand them up in front
> and ask them all kinds of questions in his tremendously sarcastic
> manner. The whole class was familiar with this roughing operation,
> and it was sport for all the rest of us. Whenever "Old Bull" would
> ask a fellow a sarcastic question, the whole class would get up
> and howl.[21]

It is also likely that Taylor devoted more time to his studies. How much
more is impossible to ascertain, though his parents believed that he was
working very hard and that his exertions, rather than his career interest,
regard for Wentworth, or other factors, were responsible for his
improved performance. As Emily Taylor wrote in December 1873: "I
am afraid you have been studying too hard or you would not be likely
to get high grades in Greek or Latin."[22]

This assumption had an important impact on Taylor's subsequent
activity. At the same time his grades were improving, he began to
experience problems with his vision, probably a result of an astigma-
tism. By 1874, when he passed the entrance examinations to Harvard,
he suffered frequent headaches, and Franklin and Emily had become
deeply concerned about his health. They presumed, logically in view of
their earlier assumption that his high grades reflected excessive study,
that the headaches were a result of his academic endeavors. Not
surprisingly, they soon convinced him that too much study had damaged
his eyesight. We now know that their reasoning was erroneous:
Taylor's problem was physiological in nature and probably would have
had similar manifestations if he had been a farmer or a factory laborer.
The proper remedy was appropriate medical treatment (i.e., corrective
eyeglasses) not a change of environment or activity.[23]

Acting on their mistaken interpretation of his problem, Franklin and
Emily urged him to reconsider his college plans. In February 1874
Franklin cautioned his son to "weigh carefully the pros and cons . . .
[of] obtaining a classical education at the expense of one's eyesight or
perhaps permanently injuring the eyes. . . . I do not want you to suffer
hereafter for your present ambition of standing high in your class or
because you want to go to college."[24] By the spring of 1874 these arguments seemed irrefutable. Taylor was undoubtedly ambivalent about
forsaking Harvard; many of his classmates enrolled there and a Harvard

degree would help him in any career he chose. On the other hand, he had little interest in a traditional collegiate education. His decision to forego any additional study, including the engineering course at Rensselaer or MIT was of greater significance than his decision not to enroll at Harvard. Indeed, Taylor soon recognized his error. As soon as his eye problem had been properly treated (he wore eyeglasses for the rest of his life), he enrolled at the Stevens Institute of Technology.[25]

Yet Taylor's return to Germantown in 1874 in no way altered or frustrated his immediate vocational goal. Though the number of college-trained engineers was increasing rapidly in the 1870's, most manufacturers, machinery designers, and engineering executives still obtained their training on the job. They were products of the "shop culture" which had supplied the bulk of American mechanics and engineers during the preceeding half century. Hard-headed, practical, and pragmatic, these men often disdained theory and questioned the value of formal education.[26] In the Philadelphia area, long a center of textile and machinery manufacture, the shop culture tradition was especially strong. Although the apprenticeship system had declined and an ambitious boy could not reasonably expect to work his way to the top of a large manufacturing concern without specialized study, it was still not unusual for a potential executive to spend his early career in the shop, to learn the business "from the ground up."[27]

In the fall of 1874 Taylor became an apprentice machinist and patternmaker at the Enterprise Hydraulic Works in downtown Philadelphia. In later years he made several statements about his apprenticeship that indicated that neither he nor his parents viewed his new job as a sign of failure or social embarrassment. He recalled, for example, that before starting at the Enterprise Works, he visited his father's older brother, Caleb N. Taylor, a bank president and accomplished businessman. Caleb Taylor gave him a lecture on success in business, emphasizing long hours and the subordination of personal to company interests.[28] Taylor later acknowledged that he had been something more than an ordinary apprentice:

> my father had some means and owing to the fact that I worked during my first year of apprenticeship for nothing, the second year for $1.50 a week, the third year for $2.50 a week, and the fourth year for $3.00 a week, I was given, perhaps, special opportunities to progress from one kind of work to another; that is I told the owners of the establishment that I wanted an opportunity to learn fast rather than wages.[29]

In 1876 when the Centennial Exhibition was held in Philadelphia, Taylor left his job at the Enterprise Works for six months to represent a group of machinery manufacturers at the exhibition grounds.[30]

Nor did Taylor's lowly occupation affect his social position. As Proper Philadelphia began to move from the crowded Rittenhouse Square area to Chestnut Hill and the Main Line suburbs in the 1870's and 1880's, new avocations occupied the leisure hours of the wealthy. Though cricket became the sport of rich and poor alike in the 1870's, only the elite could afford the exclusive cricket clubs that flourished in the western suburbs. As a member of the Young America Cricket Club, a group noted for athletic distinction, Taylor moved freely among the social establishment, at least during his nonworking hours. Besides athletics he enjoyed amateur theatrical performances in which he played "a broken-English speaking German doctor" and female parts. Frank Barkley Copley reported that on one occasion Taylor and a male friend disguised themselves as women and went to a photographer who had agreed to photograph two young men. "Now look here," Taylor supposedly said in a masculine voice after the deceived photographer insisted that he had an appointment with two men, "why the hell can't you take our pictures?"[31]

By the mid-1870's many cricket club members, including Taylor, were attracted to the new game of lawn tennis. Utilizing the Cricket Club's facilities, Taylor and his closest friends, Clarence M. and Joseph S. Clark, became expert players and tournament champions. Taylor and Clarence M. Clark won the first United States Lawn Tennis Association doubles championship in 1881. To improve his game, Taylor constantly tinkered with his equipment. Among his inventions were an improved tennis net, which Spaulding and Company marketed for him with some success, and a spoon-shaped racket that evoked considerable ridicule, particularly at Newport.[32] Taylor also installed a tennis court at his Ross Street home, which became the scene of lively competition and even livelier dinner parties during the early 1880's.

Despite his special status and many diversions Taylor was deeply affected by his experiences at the Enterprise Works. In later years he believed that the "first six months of my apprenticeship as a pattern maker [were] on the whole, the most valuable part of my education. Not that I gained much knowledge during that time . . . but the awakening as to the reality and seriousness of life was complete, and I believe, of great value."[33] His experiences seemed to confirm the lessons of his Exeter years and the advice of Caleb Taylor.

In 1878 Taylor completed his apprenticeship. He had mastered the trades of machinist and patternmaker and had become familiar, he believed, with the outlook of the workmen. He had also acquired a series of beliefs about the types of behavior that would benefit himself and others.

> Your knowledge will avail you nothing [he recalled] without energy, grit, pluck, determination, ability to stick to it, character.
>
> Of all the habits and principles which make for success in a young man, the most useful is the determination to do and do right all those things which come his way each day, whether they are agreeable or disagreeable.[34]

These beliefs were hardly original; indeed, they were shared (or given lip service) by most businessmen and engineers of the time and were indicative of the prevailing entrepreneurial conception of opportunity and success. In the long term they influenced Taylor's perception of both his achievements and the deficiencies of the new social order he helped create. In the short term they aided his business career, which began at the Midvale Steel Company in the fall of 1878.

The Making of a Mechanical Engineer

For the next decade Taylor continued to enjoy the advantages of his time and station. He finished his apprenticeship at an auspicious moment, both in terms of the general economic climate and of his immediate situation. He exploited his family's social position and contacts to enhance his opportunities. Most of all, perhaps, he profited from close association with an able and influential group of industrialists and co-workers.

At the time Taylor emerged from the relative isolation of suburban Germantown, Philadelphia was the second largest city in the United States and one of the nation's industrial centers. In the previous half century "the endless grid streets, the scattering of churches, stations and factories, [and] the flood of immigrants" had obliterated most vestiges of the eighteenth-century city.[35] Philadelphia's expansion, moreover, had certain novel features which affected Taylor's career and outlook. More than Boston, New York, or Baltimore, it had become an industrial city. Since the early nineteenth century, Philadelphia had been a center of textile, particularly woolen, worsted, and carpet, manufacture. By the 1870's textiles, plus the "iron triangle" of Philadelphia enterprise—iron, coal, and railroads—made it the nation's preeminent industrial metropolis. To serve the needs of this burgeoning complex, the city also developed important banking, machinery, and machine tool firms.

By the 1880's its reputation as a site of machinery production was unsurpassed.[36]

Three men who, directly or indirectly, had a substantial impact on Taylor's career symbolized these changes. Enoch W. Clark (1802–56) came to Philadelphia in 1837 and founded one of the first important American investment banking concerns. By the mid-1840's E. W. Clark and Company had become the city's most prestigious financial institution. Though Enoch Clark died in 1856, his partners, notably his son Edward W. Clark and Jay Cooke, maintained the firm's position among the city's banks, and the Clark family remained prominent in Philadelphia financial and social circles for several generations thereafter. Edward W. Clark and his sons were the wealthiest Germantown residents, the principal benefactors of the Unitarian Society, and leading members of the cricket clubs. The Clark and Taylor families had developed close ties by the 1850's, and the marriage of Clarence M. Clark and Mary Taylor made the bond permanent.[37]

William Sellers (1824–1905) was the most notable nineteenth-century American machine tool builder and a vital force in the emergence of Philadelphia as a center of machinery manufacture. A member of a distinguished family of mechanics and the larger "fraternity of mechanicians," Sellers formed his firm in Philadelphia in 1847 and for a half century pioneered the manufacture of stronger, more durable tools with interchangeable parts. In the 1860's he devised standards for screw threads and bolt sizes which "came into use throughout America within the next ten years."[38] As a result of these and other achievements, Sellers attracted outstanding young mechanics and engineers, including Henry R. Towne, Wilfred Lewis, and Carl G. Barth, who were to play important roles in the development of scientific management. Sellers also controlled and operated several other large metal-working plants. One of these, the Midvale Steel Company, which he and Edward W. Clark purchased in 1873, was to become the largest Philadelphia steelworks.

Joseph Wharton (1826–1909), a member of one of Philadelphia's oldest and most distinguished Quaker mercantile familes, symbolized the shift from commerce to industry that characterized Philadelphia's economy in the nineteenth century. Starting as a bookkeeper in a dry goods house, Wharton had become the manager of a zinc mining and smelting firm at South Bethlehem, Pennsylvania, and a pioneer in the American nickle industry in the 1860's.[39] In the next decade he became the largest stockholder of the Bethlehem Iron Company, one of the first integrated steel mills. In the 1870's and 1880's Wharton helped make Bethlehem one of the nation's largest defense contractors. By the 1890's he was probably the most important figure in the eastern iron and steel industry and one of the richest men in Philadelphia.[40] Though primarily a financier, Wharton played an active role in the operation of his properties. His influence was to be a crucial factor in the rise of scientific management.

As a home for industrial workers Philadelphia also differed from other big cities of the late nineteenth century. It had a relatively high proportion of West European, particularly British, workers. The latter dominated the managerial and skilled positions in the textile industry and in many metal-working firms. They also formed a substantial element of the middle class and contributed to the city's image as a conservative, home-owning community, relatively immune to the industrial conflict and class differences so evident in New York and Chicago.[41] Philadelphia industrialists often boasted of their close relations with their workmen and of their ability to thwart union organizers. The Baldwin Locomotive Works, Cramp Shipyard, Midvale, and most other large industrial plants were known for their commitment to the open shop.

The Midvale Company was a product of the expansion of Philadelphia industry that followed the Civil War. Formed in 1867 by Sellers, Clark, and other Philadelphia capitalists to provide a local source of steel, the company was at first unsuccessful. Its principal product, crucible steel railroad tires, "proved as unreliable as they were costly," and Midvale failed in 1873.[42] According to Russell W. Davenport a superintendent in later years:

> The works had been brought into this condition by the grossest carelessness, if not ignorance, in the direction of the details of manufacture. . . . There had only been needed, to make the enterprise a success, a more accurate chemical knowledge of the difference between good and bad steel and a common sense conscientious application of it in the direction of the work.[43]

Davenport may have been unduly critical; Midvale was a pioneer in the development of steel castings, and its initial failure may have been due as much to the primitive state of the art as to bad management.[44] In any event Sellers and Clark bought out their associates, provided additional funds, and employed new managers. Charles A. Brinley, a Yale graduate who had specialized in metallurgical chemistry, was hired as superintendent, and Davenport, his college classmate, as general manager and chief chemist. Under their stewardship the firm prospered and expanded.

Two factors accounted for Midvale's improved performance. The first was Brinley's and Davenport's scientific expertise. When they arrived,

> something like 3000 tons of various kinds and in various conditions
> of manufacture were piled about the yard regarding which little or
> nothing was known. The only stock record book in existence was
> in the brain of old Miky Kelly and to him Mr. Brinley would go for
> information, such as it was. The question of assorting this mass of
> material and determining its usefullness had to be solved by the
> laboratory.[45]

Working in the "laboratory," an old house across from the plant, Brinley
and Davenport identified and reclassified the steel. "By careful selection
and mixing with high grade pig iron . . . all this old stuff was successfully worked into rail[s]."[46] Brinley and Davenport then applied their
skills to the development of new products. At that time the Pennsylvania Railroad was buying its car axles from an English firm for 13½¢ a
pound. After extended negotiations Brinley obtained an order from the
railroad for one hundred axles. Davenport recalled

> how carefully we considered the subject and analyzed a piece of
> an English axle; how many trial heats we melted, and how anxiously
> we watched the result of the drop tests, shivering in the cold those
> winter days. Finally we succeeded, and have since made many
> thousand of these axles for the Pennsylvania Road, and have been
> selling them for several years past for about 4½ cents per pound.[47]

The second factor in Midvale's rise was the growth of the late-
nineteenth-century defense industry. In 1875 Midvale received an order
for gun forgings from the Navy, apparently the first such order given a
U.S. firm. "We grappled with the subject with great doubts of our success," Davenport later wrote. "The tests demanded were very severe
and our facilities very limited, but Mr. Brinley's careful, scientific mind
directed our first efforts and we obtained promising results from the
start."[48] This success led to a gradual reorientation of the company's
activities. In the 1880's, when government ordnance expenditures increased rapidly, Midvale was able to satisfy the new demand. By the
1890's it had become one of the largest defense contractors.

By the time Taylor joined Midvale the company's prospects had
improved considerably. In 1873 Midvale had had less than seventy-five
employees. "One small open-hearth furnace was in operation; No. 1
hammer ran a few days a week; some tool steel was melted in the
crucibles and hammered at old No. 3 hammer." During the next five
years "additional hammers and rolls were put in and the production of
miscellaneous forgings, tool and spring steel, etc., constantly in-

creased."[49] By 1878 Midvale had four hundred employees and "five or six buildings—a small open-hearth furnace, a hammer or forge shop, a machine shop, a small rolling-mill, a blacksmith shop, and a carpenter and pattern shop." Still, the plant was unimpressive in appearance. The buildings were "dilapidated" and "so dark that they continuously called for artificial lighting . . . furnished by Kerosene torches that filled the place with a foul odor."[50]

Taylor's decision to join Midvale was a logical conclusion to his apprenticeship. Brinley and Davenport had made the company attractive to aspiring engineers, and Edward W. Clark's influence gave him entree to the management. Clarence M. Clark started to work in the laboratory at approximately the same time Taylor began in the machine shop; until 1886 the two men looked forward to eventually controlling Midvale. Finally, the plant was located in Nicetown, on the southern edge of Germantown, less than a mile from the Clark estate and two miles from Taylor's Ross Street home. There was no immediate executive opening for Taylor, so he worked briefly as a laborer, a clerk, and a machinist. But with the business recovery of 1878 the plant was soon "full of work," and Taylor became a subforeman in the machine shop, his first managerial position.[51]

Soon afterward he precipitated an incident which he later associated with the beginning of scientific management. As an executive trainee eager to demonstrate his ability, Taylor announced that he expected the machinists to increase their output.[52] This was the kind of demand that workers in the mechanical industries had learned to expect from aggressive supervisors, and they resisted. Apparently they were not sufficiently aggrieved or united to form a union or oppose Taylor in any overt way, so they relied on informal, covert techniques. Taylor wrote that for "two or three years" he did everything in his power to increase output, "while the men were absolutely determined that the output should not be increased."[53] He discharged some men and lowered the wages of others. Even sabotage did not deter him.[54] With Brinley's support he finally forced the workers to increase production—to do a "fair day's work." As a consequence of this struggle, Taylor wrote, he devised a "scientific" piecework system that reconciled the managers' desire for increased production and the workers' desire for a higher wage.[55]

Taylor's account of the incident surely distorted its significance. A conflict of this type was neither unusual nor particularly notable. Taylor may have recalled it with special vividness because it was his first encounter with industrial workers, but there is no indication that his superiors or employees shared his estimation of its importance. The workers' only recorded response to his "driving" methods was to oppose a fining system he had introduced to punish men who broke tools or spoiled work. The fines, rather than time study or any other aspect of scientific management, were their principal grievance in subsequent years.[56] Similarly, the confrontation cannot be associated literally with the development of a "scientific" wage system. Taylor's innovations in that area occurred several years later, after he left his supervisory position, and are properly associated with his more mundane but important activities of the post-1880 period.

Nevertheless the "fight" marked an important step in Taylor's development as a manager and reformer. His unusual position in the Midvale plant had enabled him to examine at first hand the decentralized, unsystematic managerial methods that were the hallmark of the first factory system. The contrast between Brinley and Davenport's rational, scientific approach to technical problems and the foreman's capricious, often destructive approach to production problems, including the workers' behavior, made a strong impression on him. There must be a better method, he reasoned, a way to apply the engineer's scientific perspective to management, as well as machinery. Taylor thus arrived at the juncture many other engineers would reach in the latter years of the nineteenth century. When he associated his "confrontation" with the rise of scientific management, he was describing his intellectual growth, not the actual events of 1878–80. From this point on he would adopt a more critical attitude toward the operation of both the Midvale plant and the factory generally.

While supposedly forcing the managerial viewpoint on the machinists, Taylor completed his personal preparations for advancement. Realizing that he had little chance to succeed Brinley or Davenport without additional training and professional standing, he continued his studies at home. At first he took correspondence courses.[57] But in late 1879 or early 1880 he entered an unorthodox arrangement with the Stevens Institute of Technology in Hoboken, New Jersey. He would remain in Philadelphia and study in his spare time but take final examinations with the regular students. Perhaps the Stevens officials agreed to this plan because he was older and had served a machine shop apprenticeship; or perhaps his parents' influence was the decisive factor. In any case, he approached his engineering courses with the same diligence he had shown during his second year at Exeter. During one period, according to Copley, he studied from two to five a.m.[58] Wilfred Lewis later doubted "if he had more than five hours of sleep out of the twenty-four."[59] Still, "without . . . having been [at the Stevens campus] except for the purpose of passing all of the entrance examinations and finally one after another of the examinations required throughout the course" and apparently without having paid any tuition or fees, Taylor received a mechanical engineering degree from Stevens in June 1883.[60] The haphazard nature of his formal education troubled him in later years, but in the early 1880's the generosity of the Stevens officials was a major boon to his career. He signaled his new status by joining the American Society of Mechanical Engineers (ASME). In the following years he became an active member, an acquaintance of the leading engineers, and a keen observer of the nascent systematic management movement.

Despite his hectic schedule, Taylor did not devote himself entirely to his work. He found time for tennis (including championship tournament play) and social events appropriate to his station. In the early 1880's he courted Louise M. Spooner, the daughter of friends the Taylors had met through the Unitarian Society. Louise was outgoing and vivacious, devoted to music, her circle of friends, and the social life of Proper Philadelphia. On May 3, 1884, after Taylor had been promoted at Midvale, they were married. For more than a decade their life together was stable and happy, marred only by the absence of children. Copley reported that Taylor never discussed his business affairs with his wife.[61] Louise, in turn, took little interest in Taylor's work, at least until it took them away from Philadelphia and subjected her to a new and alien regimen.

In the meantime Taylor's career was progressing rapidly. He was given new responsibilities, first as machine shop foreman, then, in 1884, as master mechanic, and shortly afterward as chief engineer in charge of maintaining and improving machinery in the plant.[62] These jobs greatly enlarged his knowledge of Midvale and its operations. As machine shop foreman Taylor became more familiar with machine tools and metal-cutting operations; as chief engineer he became acquainted with the machinery in other departments. The nature of the engineer's work, moreover, gave him a broader perspective. He was in daily contact with the different departments of the plant and thus in a position to observe, to study, and to experiment. It was an ideal situation for a creative technician. Taylor began to indulge his talent for invention.

Taylor later recalled that his "enthusiasm for invention" created friction with Brinley and especially Davenport, who had become plant superintendent in 1882.

> My head was full of wonderful and great projects to simplify the processes, to design new machines, to revolutionize the methods of the whole establishment. . . . I was devoting every minute of my spare time, at home and on Sunday, and entirely too much of my time at the works, to developing these wonderful and great

projects. Now the superintendent of the works . . . wanted me to keep all the machines going with the minimum loss of time, and kept telling me this over and over again. . . . He stood this as long as he could . . . and finally came into my office one day and swore at me like a pirate. This had never happened before, and I, of course, at once made up my mind that I should get right out; wouldn't stand any such treatment. I, however, waited 48 hours before doing anything. By that time I had greatly cooled off, but for two or three weeks at regular intervals my friend, the superintendent, repeated this process of damning me up and down hill, until he finally beat it into my dumb head that I was there to serve him.[63]

Taylor intended this account as an illustration of the importance of loyalty and cooperation to the operation of the factory, but it also illuminated his relationship with Brinley and Davenport. The latter did not condemn his "projects," only his tendency to give them precedence over his routine duties. From all indications, both men generally adopted an indulgent attitude toward Taylor's "projects," an approach consistent with their long-standing commitment to technological innovation.

Once he had clarified his function at Midvale, Taylor became an enormously creative technician. Invention, he later confessed, was "a very great amusement rather than a labor."[64] In earlier years his impulse to improve the physical environment had manifested itself in his tennis equipment; during his retirement years it would be expressed in his gardening experiments. In the 1880's, when his attention was focused on Midvale, it took the form of machine improvements. He devised a railroad car wheel for use with Midvale tires[65] and an elaborate set of forging equipment, including an unusual steam hammer.[66] For several years Taylor had collected information on other hammers, noting their strong and weak points. He

> then copied the design of each of the parts that had broken, collecting the one element from one machine, another from another. . . . There was, however, one portion of the machine which he could find no single instance of a design which had not, at some time or other, broken. He devoted his special energy and ingenuity to the study of this element, and finally evolved what he believed would be a principle which would prevent it from breaking.[67]

By using flexible components he was able to build a powerful and reliable hammer. For twelve years his Midvale hammer operated without serious difficulty.[68]

Since Taylor devoted most of his time to the machine shop, the largest Midvale department, the majority of his inventions pertained to the operation of metal-cutting machines. They included a tool grinder, a machine tool table, a chuck, a tool-feeding device for lathes, a work carrier for lathes, a boring-bar puppet, and two boring and turning mills.[69] The grinding machine was a notable achievement, which Taylor manufacturered and sold for several decades. But all of Taylor's machine shop inventions had a transcendent importance; they were products of the investigation of the "art of cutting metals" that he began in 1880 or 1881. This study, a meticulous trial and error search for "laws" that governed the application of cutting tools, the small metal objects that performed the actual cutting operations, precipitated a revolution in machine shop practice. It also helped signal a new era when the scientific method would be applied to practical ends. Not least, it marked the beginning of scientific management. Taylor, the consummate engineer, soon discovered that technical advance demanded organizational innovations of comparable significance.

Unfortunately, the origins of Taylor's metal-cutting experiments are obscure, and the "mysterious disappearance" of the relevant records virtually prohibits any interpretation except the one Taylor advanced in his writings.[70] He first described his investigations in 1903 and published detailed accounts of them in 1906, 1911, and 1912. In 1903 he simply dated his work without amplification. In the subsequent accounts he associated his experiments with his efforts to end restrictions on production, a rather strange connection, since he had supposedly already eliminated that problem (or at least learned how to eliminate it) by traditional driving methods. It is more likely that a variety of duties, including his efforts to drive the workers to greater output, alerted him to the fact that he had only a general idea of the optimum rates of machine performance. As he explained in his 1906 paper, his "knowledge of just what combination of depth of cut, feed, and cutting speed would in each case do the work in the shortest time was less accurate than that of the machinists."[71] And the machinists' knowledge was rudimentary as well. Here was an area of machine development that was no more precise or advanced than the techniques of the factory manager. For Taylor it was an irresistable challenge. As a consequence,

> he obtained the permission of the management to make a series of experiments to investigate the laws of cutting metals. . . . He expected that these experiments would last not longer than six months. . . . Mr. Sellers, in spite of the protests which were made against the continuation of this work, allowed the experiments to proceed; even, at first, at a very considerable inconvenience and loss to the shop.[72]

Taylor's experiments began between late 1880 and late 1881, very likely at the former date. In either case he was far in advance of his contemporaries.[73] Sellers probably approved his actions personally, as Taylor recalled. The Midvale president was an inventor himself and had been responsible for the establishment of the laboratory and a research program at Midvale. In addition he permitted Wilfred Lewis, assistant chief engineer at the Sellers Company, to leave his work to help Taylor at Midvale.[74] Finally, since Sellers often spent "months and months in making a design for a machine, without doing it," it is understandable that he was willing to allow Taylor to devote additional time and money to the project when six months proved inadequate.[75]

If the experiments did not immediately provide the answers that Taylor sought, they did produce (in addition to the inventions) new information about the relationships between the "speed" or rate at which the metal in a lathe revolved, the "feed" or application of the tool, the depth of the cut, the power required for various processes, and external factors, such as the use of water to cool the cutting tool.[76] By 1884 Sellers was sufficiently impressed to permit Taylor to hire an assistant, George M. Sinclair, a former acquaintance at Stevens. In 1887, when Sinclair resigned, Taylor replaced him with Henry L. Gantt, another Stevens classmate. Gantt, who supposedly devoted "about 1½ years exclusively to this work," later managed the Midvale steel foundry and was responsible for important improvements in foundry machinery.[77] In the following years he became one of Taylor's closest friends and disciples.

There were three other results of the metal-cutting experiments that Taylor noted in 1906: in 1883, "the starting of a set of experiments on belting;" in 1884, "the construction of a tool room for storing and issuing tools ready ground to the men;" and in the period 1885 to 1889, "the making of a series of practical tables for a number of machines . . . [by] which it was possible to give definite tasks each day to the machinists who were running machines."[78] These developments were logical outgrowths of Taylor's technical work. They showed the many possible ramifications of the metal-cutting investigation. Equally important, they suggested the close ties between Taylor's technical virtuosity and his solutions to the apparent deficiencies of the factory.

The Genesis of Scientific Management

Despite his "wonderful and great," and presumably costly, projects, Taylor considered himself primarily a businessman and acted accordingly. As gang boss and machine shop foreman he had adopted policies that benefited the company; as master mechanic and chief engineer he worked assiduously to advance his employer's interests. Even his inventive activities were usually compatible with his role as junior executive and apprentice shop superintendent; he undertook the metal-cutting experiments to improve the operation of the shop, as well as to satisfy his curiosity. It is not surprising that Taylor soon began to experiment with the organization, as well as the machinery, at Midvale, or that he attacked problems that first became apparent as a result of his day-to-day duties. By the mid-1880's he had independently duplicated important features of the systematic management plans of Towne and others. In the process he had also devised an approach to the incentive wage that would ultimately make him the most famous—and controversial—engineer of his time.

As a manager Taylor adopted the authoritarian style characteristic of late-nineteenth-century executives. Charles W. Shartle, who worked as a repairman at Midvale from 1884 to 1887, recalled how Taylor, like Brinley and Davenport, would not tolerate excuses or imperfect work: "When he would give us a job he would tell us when he expected it finished, and there was no reason to ask questions about it, or argue the matter, and it was up to us to finish it even if we had to work all night to get it done."[79] Taylor was equally insistent that his men follow orders.[80] Yet like many contemporary executives, he combined his authoritarianism with a friendly and sympathetic personal manner. He spoke to the men in their own language, tempered his criticisms with "a touch of human nature and feeling," and encouraged the workers to discuss their problems with him. He adopted this approach in part as a hedge against unrest and unions.[81] From all accounts, he was personally popular. Despite widespread resentment of his fining system, most Midvale workers respected him and his work.[82]

By 1883 Taylor's critique of the plant management, Sellers's or Davenport's demands for cost reductions, and most of all the dynamics of the metal-cutting experiments led him to broaden his efficiency campaign.[83] If machine performance could be improved by careful study, reorganization, and innovation, he reasoned, could not the quality of the management and the workers' efforts be improved by a similar process?

Unfortunately, the precise chronology of Taylor's administrative reforms is not clear from his writings and papers, and his rapid advancement from machine shop foreman to chief engineer in 1883 and 1884 makes it virtually impossible to reconstruct his work during those years. Apparently he hired additional clerks, devised a system of production controls, and introduced stopwatch time study and an incentive wage, the "differential piece rate," before 1885. His greatest impact was in the machine shop, but he reorganized other departments as well. Though crude by later standards, Taylor's plans were innovative, perhaps even unique.[84] In any case they established Taylor as a leader of the systematic management movement.

Taylor's most ambitious initiative was a complicated production control system for coordinating the work of the functional departments. The "chief idea," he explained in 1886, was that "authority for doing all kinds of work should proceed from one central office." In each department a clerk controlled the flow of orders and records between the central office, the supervisors, and the workers. "The clerk or clerks . . . write . . . under the direction of the foremen . . . orders stating that work is to be done; what order number to charge it to, and what drawings and tools are to be used, etc." The clerk posted the orders on a bulletin board and sent each worker "a note or card . . . which refers him to the more elaborate order." When the worker completed the job, he or the foreman entered "all desired information" on the note and returned it to the clerk. The clerk compiled the data from the notes and sent to the central office "such data . . . as is . . . needed to keep them posted as to the cost and progress of the work and the men's time."[85]

Two distinctive features of Taylor's system were the bulletin board and written orders or instruction cards, innovations that struck at the foremen's traditional prerogatives of scheduling work and determining the method of production. But Taylor's initiatives, if advanced in comparison to most systematic management plans, were exceedingly crude by his later standards; as he admitted, the instruction card clerks worked under the foreman. After analyzing the forms Taylor used at Midvale, Carl Barth concluded in 1933 that the effort to "get the ball rolling at Midvale was still largely left to the shop, a practice later soundly condemned and abandoned."[86]

Taylor's approach to supervision was equally uncertain and incomplete. Like other engineers, he was dissatisfied with the foremen's powers and methods. His production control plan attacked their authority indirectly; even in this primitive form the planning office and departmental clerks stripped them of much of their ability to plan and to control production. But Taylor also anticipated a later innovation by assigning some of the foremen's remaining powers to specialized supervisors who would perform only one of their major functions, but perform it carefully and systematically. In the mid-1880's he apparently introduced three "functional" foremen: the "gang boss," the "disciplinarian," and the "inspector." Yet his gang boss appears to have differed little from the conventional subforeman, and the shop foreman doubled as disciplinarian—hardly an innovation. Only when he introduced the independent inspector "with orders to go straight to the men rather than to the gang boss," did he break with the customary approach to supervision.[87]

Taylor's other managerial reforms of the mid-1880's were closely related to his technical work. A reorganized tool room and standardized tools were direct results of the metal-cutting studies. One investigator later found "that the grinding was all done by two young boys and that the tools were uniformly ground. The tools are all numbered and the shop foreman describes the style of tools to be used on each job."[88] Standardized maintenance procedures for machines and belts and a "tickler" or maintenance schedule were likewise products of Taylor's efforts to achieve optimum machine performance. His rules for oiling machinery (coupled with the fines he levied for violating them) evoked strong opposition from the workers.[89] Charles W. Shartle, who paid several fines during his years at Midvale, recalled:

> He had all the oil holes in every machine fitted with a plug. In fact, there were two sets of plugs, one of them had round heads and the other one square heads. It was the duty of each man starting his day's work to remove the round plug, oil the hole, and insert a square plug. To show how absolute he was in his orders, that is, to have his orders obeyed, he did not allow any variation from this rule. For instance, if one man was started on a machine one hour, during which time he would spent fifteen minutes in changing plugs and oiling the machine, and another man would take up the machine for an hour[']s work, it was just as necessary for the second man to spend fifteen minutes in oiling the machine the second time.[90]

Taylor later wrote that he devised stopwatch time study in 1883 and established a time study or "rate fixing" department—presumably an adjunct to his "central office" or planning department—in 1884.[91] Copley concluded, probably correctly, that Taylor's initial goal was "simply that of improving the statistics long used in the shop in connection with setting piece rates for . . . a new job."[92] Taylor's contributions were the substitution of a stopwatch for the foreman's conventional timepiece, and, more significantly, the division of the work into basic steps or elements, each of which he timed separately. He then combined his figures to find a time for the entire job.[93] By dividing this figure into the workday, he arrived at an optimum production rate. Sellers soon approved his request to employ a clerk, Emlen Hare Miller, to conduct the time studies. Yet "it was several years before the full benefits of the system were felt," since "the best methods of making and recording time observations" and of "determining the maximum capacity of each of the machines" and "of making tables and time tables, were not at first adopted."[94]

In 1884 Taylor applied his "differential piece rate" to "part of the work in the machine shop."[95] Unlike Halsey, who retained the existing piece rate as his base wage, Taylor set a high bonus rate for workers who completed their assignment in the allotted time and a low penalty rate for all others. Thus the Midvale machinists earned either a high wage or a very low wage, one designed to discourage "even an inferior man." On one job, for example, the machinist had received a rate of 50¢ per piece and usually turned out four or five finished pieces per day. After time studies Taylor concluded that the man should produce ten pieces per day.[96] He set a new rate of 35¢ per piece if the machinist finished ten acceptable pieces per day (or a wage of $3.50 rather than $2.00 to $2.50 per day), and 25¢ if he completed nine or fewer pieces (or a maximum of $2.25 per day). Taylor claimed that he established his high or bonus rate by adjusting the piece rate upward until the men agreed to cooperate.[97] In reality he was probably somewhat less gentle. According to George F. Steele, a close friend and associate, he fired several machinists who refused to increase their pace.[98]

Between 1884 and 1889 Taylor supposedly extended the differential piece rate to many, perhaps most, of the Midvale workers.[99] Yet his records and published statements mention only the yard laborers and plant maintenance men, and there are several reasons why the records probably suggest the actual thrust of his work. First, as chief engineer he was a staff rather than a line executive and had no direct control over the employees with the possible exception of the machinists. Davenport was certainly amenable to his suggestions, but, other things being equal, the superintendent was probably more receptive to radical plans that applied to the eminently replaceable, powerless laborers than to the valuable machine workers. Second, after 1884 Taylor viewed the differential piece rate as a cheap and easy way to increase output. Yet some types of output were easier and cheaper to increase than others. Because of his personal interest in metal cutting, Taylor fully understood the complexities of rate setting for machine workers, particularly machinists. Laborers presented no such problems and were therefore obvious targets for his efficiency campaign. By 1889 he had applied the differential piece rate to such diverse tasks as unloading pig iron and sand, whitewashing walls, painting, and even changing light bulbs.[100] It seems reasonable to conclude that his wage plan—a plan he customarily described as a spur to machine production and an answer to the restriction of machine output—was in practice primarily an answer to the inefficiencies of workers performing manual, mostly unskilled tasks.

Whatever the exact reason, Taylor's emphasis on the laborers marked the beginning of an ambitious experimental project. Believing that the laborers posed fewer obstacles than the machinists, he began a search for "what constituted a day's work." As he later wrote, "what we hoped ultimately to determine was . . . how many foot-pounds of work a man could do in a day."[101] He assigned an assistant, probably Miller, to review the published literature for possible answers. When the assistant failed to find anything of value, Taylor proceeded with his time studies.[102] Though the work proved difficult and the solution elusive, Taylor remained optimistic. For at least fifteen years he expected to discover an appropriate rule or formula that would enable him to set bonus rates for all such workers. Indeed, it is unlikely that he ever fully reconciled himself to the notion that men could be as complicated as machines.

From Taylor's viewpoint the attractive features of his labor measures were the ease with which they could be implemented and their immediate results. Apart from the determination of metal-cutting times, "rate fixing" and the differential piece rate required neither concerted attention nor technical expertise. In "A Piece Rate System," Taylor assured his readers that in most plants both activities could be undertaken by one man working part-time. Moreover, the rate fixer "soon becomes so familiar with the time required to do each kind of elementary work performed by the men, that he can write down the time from memory."[103] This was in fact what happened at Midvale. As one of Taylor's colleagues reported in 1894:

> [Time study originally] necessitated a considerable clerical force, and they had in the thick of it, about 8 clerks in the estimating department, and some of them were first class men. At the present time their files are full of data on which to base estimates, and the entire work of the estimating office is done by a man. . . . It hardly seemed to me that it was safe for them to have but one rate clerk, as his unavoidable absence or sickness would be likely to embarrass them.[104]

Nevertheless the results were impressive. Taylor argued that output had doubled or tripled, that the quality of the work had improved, and, despite initial opposition to time study, that the "labor problem" had been eliminated.[105] Unfortunately there is no other assessment of the workers' response to time study and the differential piece rate. The most that can be said is that they did not strike or resist in any demonstrative way. Apparently they either welcomed the opportunity to earn higher wages or went elsewhere.

Though the least demanding of his Midvale innovations, time study and the differential piece rate were important steps in the evolution of scientific management and in Taylor's career as a factory manager. By 1890 he recognized that time study could be a potent managerial tool. He was even more confident about the incentive wage. His Midvale experiences indicated that it could be a powerful force in stimulating workers to greater output. In this respect his thinking was similar to that of Halsey and other innovative engineers. But there was also a basic difference. Taylor's conclusions derived wholly from his pragmatic effort to increase production rather than from anxiety over the "labor problem," the state of American society, the workers' welfare, or some combination of economic and social concerns. His single-minded emphasis on production became more apparent in the 1890's when he introduced the differential piece rate in other factories.

Taylor's management innovations, intimately related to his technical achievements, thus made him a pioneer in the management movement. His production control and supervisory methods were as thorough as those of other management reformers, and his wage system was an important refinement of the most advanced practice. But if Taylor profited from his intimate knowledge of the shop, he was also a captive of his Midvale experiences. A master of machine techniques, he had little familiarity with other aspects of management at Midvale. His neglect of purchasing and stores procedures and cost accounting, not to mention corporate finance and marketing, was the most obvious evidence of his limited perspective.

In one other important area Taylor was less advanced than many of his contemporaries. At a time when personnel work was emerging as a distinctive function, Taylor clung to the "rule of thumb" methods that he condemned in other spheres. He was indifferent to new methods of handling workmen and hostile to welfare work and collective bargaining. This lapse, like most aspects of his work, was a product of his background and professional associations. Sellers was known for his rough treatment of subordinates. Brinley and Davenport were somewhat kinder, but, like Sellers, had little or no interest in personnel management as a specialized activity.[106] Midvale had a mutual benefit insurance society by the late 1870's and a haphazard apprenticeship program, but nothing else. The foremen hired and fired and, except for Taylor's limited use of functional supervisors, controlled their subordinates in the traditional fashion. The management discouraged union membership but did not deliberately exclude or discharge union men. There were no strikes until the 1890's.[107]

Taylor's approach to personnel management was essentially the

Midvale approach. He was convinced that men worked for money and that anything that obscured or confused this basic fact was unsound.[108] Forestalling or eliminating the "labor problem" was an engineering problem, a facet of the larger challenge of systematic production management. Beyond this he had nothing to offer; indeed, in most respects he was a reactionary. In later years he proclaimed the "scientific selection and progressive development of the workmen" as one of his "principles" of scientific management, but these were largely meaningless phrases.[109] Taylor's methods of "selection" and "development" were to offer bonuses to able and cooperative workers. Those who succeeded "selected" and "developed" themselves. His only concession to personnel work was the "disciplinarian" who, he later explained, might also serve as an employment manager.[110] Welfare work, he believed, was a "joke."[111] And under scientific management, labor unions were irrelevant.

Taylor's debt to his colleagues is apparent from a comparison of a speech Davenport made in 1888 and Taylor's "A Piece Rate System," his initial description of scientific management.[112] Davenport first ventured an explanation for the absence of the labor problem, or at least its more dramatic manifestations:

> the fact that gives me more pleasure and satisfaction than any I have mentioned to you is that during all these 14 years [at Midvale] . . . we have never had a serious disagreement and work has never been stopped by a strike. And what has been the cause of this most desirable condition of affairs? It is, I think, chiefly because we have been able to trust one another.

Taylor started with a similar explanation, though he emphasized his rather than Davenport's contribution to labor-management harmony:

> I attribute a great part of this [Midvale's] success in avoiding strikes to the high wages which the best men were able to earn with the differential rates, and to the pleasant feeling fostered by this system; but this is by no means the whole cause. It has for years been the policy of that company to stimulate the personal ambition of every man in their employ by promoting them either in wages or position whenever they deserved it, and the opportunity came.

Davenport then elaborated on his initial theme:

> They [the managers] have come among you . . . not with an overbearing importance of the theoretical knowledge they had acquired, but with a high appreciation of the practical knowledge and skill acquired by you in years of hard work and with a desire to

learn from you and give what they could in exchange. They have tried, I think, not to take undue advantage of the power accompanying their position, and not to make promises that they could not carry out. They have endeavored to know you personally; to meet you as man to man; to make you trust them and their efforts have not failed.

Taylor made the same point, though in more general terms:

The employer who goes through his works with kid gloves on, and is never known to dirty his hand or clothes, and who either talks to his men in a condescending or patronizing way, or else not at all, has no chance whatever of ascertaining their real thoughts or feelings. . . .

Above all it is desirable that men should be talked to on their own level by those who are over them. Each man should be encouraged to discuss any trouble which he may have . . . with those over him. . . .

It is not the large charities . . . so much as small acts of personal kindness and sympathy, which establish a bond of friendly feeling between them and their employers.

Personnel policy was the one area of Midvale management that Taylor was involved in but did not revise. Rather than a stimulus to innovation, his experiences in this case became a deterrent to change.

With this exception Taylor's career at Midvale was a triumph of creative enterprise. Emotionally wedded to the status quo, Taylor applied his knowledge and talents to a novel endeavor, the improvement of the Midvale technology in the broadest sense of the term. He devised new salable products such as the railroad wheel and the grinding machine. But most of his innovations were neither marketable nor separable from the Midvale environment—or so it seemed at the time. They were not only objects, but ideas and procedures. Under the best of circumstances their value was difficult to measure; ultimately it depended on the observer's values and biases. Nevertheless, Taylor's innovations won him a considerable reputation in and out of the plant. As one observer noted in 1894, Midvale employees from the president to the "humblest piece rate worker are heart and soul believers in the Midvale system."[113] However, it was Taylor's professional reputation that was of greater immediate importance. In the late 1880's a change in the Midvale management unrelated to his work brought the first phase of his career to a premature close. Temporarily, at least, Taylor's ambition triumphed over his devotion to Midvale, Philadelphia, and scientific management.

3

Years of Revelation, 1890–1898

Contrary to his expectations, the years between Taylor's departure from Midvale in 1889 and his arrival at South Bethlehem, Pennsylvania, in 1898 were among the most difficult of his adult life. A variety of pressures, frequent moves, and limited resources probably caused him to question his decision to leave Midvale on more than one occasion.[1] But these experiences, however unpleasant, were among the most important of his career. Taylor's interests did not change, nor did his conception of systematic management. But his view of society, particularly the business system, and the place of his work in that larger setting underwent major alterations. If the 1870's and 1880's were years of discovery, the 1890's were years of maturation and revelation. Had it not been for the severe industrial depression of the mid-1890's, scientific management might have appeared as an integrated management system as early as 1897, and Taylor as a spokesman for managerial and social reform by the turn of the century. Yet there was also a less positive side to Taylor's revelation. It was during this period that he fully realized his labor measures had applicability and appeal apart from the other features of scientific management. Though he was too preoccupied with day-to-day activities to understand the implications of this perception, it is apparent in retrospect that his discovery marked the first step toward a new career in which he would exploit time study and the incentive wage to promote scientific management.

The Manufacturing Investment Company, 1890–1893

In 1890 Taylor became general manager of the Manufacturing Investment Company, a wood pulp and paper manufacturing firm that had plants in Madison, Maine, and Appleton, Wisconsin. Though this forced him to leave Germantown, his friends, and associates, the move was a logical step for a man of his position and ambitions. It gave him responsibility he did not have and was unlikely to obtain at Midvale. Ultimately it affected scientific management, his conception of its utility, and his notion of the roles of the manufacturer and the engineer in society. While Taylor continued to think of himself as a technician—a designer and manager of machinery—he was ready by 1893, when he left the Manufacturing Investment Company, to advertise himself as a consulting engineer, "systematizing shop management and cost systems a specialty."

Taylor's association with the Manufacturing Investment Company was a direct outgrowth of his Midvale successes. In 1885 William C. Whitney, the Secretary of the Navy, had assigned Commander Caspar F. Goodrich to find a new manager for the Navy's Washington gun works. Goodrich logically turned to Midvale, which did similar work, and decided, apparently with the concurrence of the naval inspectors stationed there, that Taylor was the best choice.[2] Taylor, however, turned down the offer; government service seemed a poor alternative to Midvale.

Several events of the following years led Taylor to reconsider his commitment to Midvale. In 1886 Edward W. Clark sold his Midvale holdings to Charles J. Harrah, a self-made millionaire merchant. Harrah died in 1888, but his property passed to his son, Charles, Jr., who, like his father, was able and headstrong. The Harrahs' emergence resulted in Sellers's withdrawal in 1887 and in Davenport's decision the following year to accept an offer from the Bethlehem Iron Company to head its new armor plate department. Charles J. Harrah, Jr., also circumscribed Taylor's opportunities. In 1888 the younger Harrah became the manager of the Midvale works, ending or at least diminishing Taylor's long-term prospects. Though the two men got along well, the attraction of Midvale lessened for Taylor. In 1889 when Whitney offered him a position with the Manufacturing Investment Company, he accepted.[3]

The Manufacturing Investment Company had been organized in the late 1880's by a group of prominent politicians and financiers to exploit the so-called Mitscherlich patent for manufacturing wood pulp from lumber mill by-products.[4] Its promoters included New York financiers, Democratic party leaders, and several members of President Grover Cleveland's cabinet. J. P. Morgan, the investment banker, was the largest investor, followed by men like Oliver H. Payne, the Standard Oil millionaire, Don M. Dickinson, a lumber tycoon and Cleveland's Postmaster General, and Whitney. Taylor, who was the tenth largest stockholder, invested $45,000 when he took the job of general manager.[5] In 1889 Whitney arranged leaves of absence for Captain Robley O. Evans and Commander Goodrich to build mills for the company at Appleton and Madison; Taylor's job was to operate the mills and realize the potential of the Mitscherlich process. In one step he thus fulfilled his ambition, enhanced his chances for a personal fortune, and entered the larger world of business and finance that had emerged in the latter years of the nineteenth century.

By March 1891 the Taylors had settled in Madison, a small, isolated community on the Kennebec River.[6] Apparently they chose Madison because the mill there required more attention and because it was closer to Philadelphia and Plymouth, Massachusetts, where many of Louise's relatives lived. To alleviate Louise's loneliness and to counter the antipathy of the local French-Canadian population, they soon adopted a busy social schedule. Old acquaintances and relatives often visited Madison.[7] The Taylors also entertained the mill supervisors, all of whom were new to the area.[8] Commander Goodrich and Sanford E. Thompson, a young civil engineer who joined the company in 1890, were frequent guests. Goodrich, a man of unusual charm and sophistication, became a lifelong friend.[9] Thompson, more reserved and intellectual, became Taylor's most valued subordinate at Madison and his first disciple.[10]

Taylor soon realized that his expectations for the Manufacturing Investment Company were overly sanguine. Neither the Mitscherlich process (Taylor called it an "enormous fraud") nor the patent rights that Dickinson and his associates had secured was as valuable as he had anticipated. In addition, the mills had been built quickly and haphazardly. What Goodrich had called the "finest and best arranged [mill] . . . in the country" proved to be hopelessly inadequate.[11] The investors' insistent demands for profits further complicated Taylor's role. Compared to their relentless pressure for immediate returns, Davenport's reprimands became happy memories. Taylor's work increasingly became a desperate and exhausting attempt to satisfy their expectations.

Some of Taylor's activities at Madison undoubtedly fascinated him. Copley reports that he invented several devices for the plant, including an exotic safety mechanism that evoked widespread comment.[12] He also conducted more belting experiments and installed an auxiliary power plant and additional shafting to eliminate delays. In general, however, he had to leave this work to Thompson. He recalled, with more than a touch of bitterness, that "owing to the many calls upon [my] time, I was unable to give more than a few hours each month to this work."[13]

As Taylor implies, he devoted most of his time to the continuing struggle to increase production and earnings. In mid-1892 he wrote that "the running of this mill contains so many problems . . . that it seems impossible to leave here."[14] An unidentified associate recalled:

> My first important contact with Mr. T. was at Madison, Maine, and while waiting for my turn in conference . . . it was impossible not to overhear conversation with those who preceded me, it all sounded very business-like and imperative, each man must make his every move count, and the work as a whole must proceed in spite of all obstacles. A superintendent came in while I sat there and reported that some work would have to stop, as a pulley had split, and although a new one had been ordered, it would take a week to get there. Now this would not do at all, the work must proceed, clamp the broken pulley together, replace it with some sort of spare pulley, make a wooden one, no matter what or how, but keep that shaft revolving.[15]

Taylor was never entirely satisfied, but by early 1893 the operation of the Madison plant had become sufficiently routine and successful for him to reconsider his ties to the Manufacturing Investment Company.

In the meantime the Appleton mill had posed a far different type of challenge. It too had been hastily constructed and required extensive alteration. There was too little water; the saws in the sawmill did not operate properly; and the belting was inadequate.[16] Equally serious was the labor situation. Appleton was an important manufacturing center, and mill workers, particularly foremen, were in short supply.[17] To achieve the production levels demanded by Taylor and the New York officers, the plant manager, A. L. Smith, Jr., and Taylor's Midvale repair boss, William A. Fannon, drove the employees. The results were unrest, strikes, and an exodus of experienced men. In the summer of 1892, when Taylor sought to transfer several of the Appleton foremen to Madison, Smith bemoaned the scarcity of supervisors and the continuous influx of new workers.[18]

Taylor's response was predictable, but significant. Improvements in the mill and machinery would require time, but a piecework system that reconciled the manager's demand for greater production with the workers' desire for higher pay would have an immediate impact on output and morale. At Appleton, Taylor reasoned, the differential piece rate would have the same beneficial effect it had had at Midvale. With this expedient step he distinguished between the incentive wage and scientific management. Beginning in late 1891 or early 1892, Smith and his subordinates conducted time studies and installed the differential rate. By the spring of 1893, except for

> some few trifling things . . . mostly of the nature of repairs . . . every operation in the mill [is] done on the differential rate system from the time our materials arrive in the yard until they are shipped in the cars. For example, all the coal, wood, sulfur and limestone, . . . are unloaded from the cars and piled on piece work. They are then transported to the rooms in which they are worked up on piece work and the wood is barked and sawed on piece work. Our digesters are filled, emptied and cooked on piece work . . . and the pulp . . . runs on to a paper machine and is bundled into rolls, weighed, sampled and shipped all on piece work.[19]

The results of this innovation, according to Taylor, were precisely what he had expected:

> we have reduced the cost of manufacture from $75 to $85 per ton to $35 per ton. . . . We have increased the product from 20 tons per day [in early 1892] to 36 tons per day. . . . Some days we have made as high as 46 tons. The cost of labor, including superintendence, was reduced between $30 to $40 per ton to about $8 per ton, and we use from 75 to 100 men less in turning out 30 tons per day than when we only turned out 10 tons [mid-1891]. Our men, of course, are earning higher wages per man than they were when we were turning out only 10 tons.[20]

The differential piece rate also "gives us the pick of all the men throughout a large radius about the mill."[21] Without "piece work in the Western mill," Taylor concluded, the company would have failed by 1893.[22] As soon as possible, probably in early 1893, he also introduced time study and the differential piece rate at Madison.

Nevertheless, the piecework system introduced at Appleton in 1892 and 1893 and presumably at Madison in 1893 differed in important respects from the Midvale system. First, it was installed without the other features of scientific management that Taylor had implemented at Midvale. In part this was because the manufacturing process was simpler; the Appleton workers were more like the Midvale laborers than the Midvale machinists. In part, however, Taylor's abbreviated approach was simply a reflection of his desire to earn a profit at the first possible moment. Second, piece rates at Appleton were based on time study, but hardly the type of time study Taylor had developed in the 1880's. Smith described his rate setting techniques for filling and emptying digesters:

> After the digesters had been run for some time and by trying different methods of placing men . . . the most economical method was decided upon . . . [and] a large number of observations were taken and reported. . . . These figures were taken by the foreman

while the men were under his direct supervision, and the work was done steadily and with no interruption.[23]

Except for the use of the stopwatch, this technique differed little from the "rule of thumb" methods that competent foremen had traditionally used to set piece rates.

This approach had an important impact on Taylor's conception of his labor measures. At Midvale he had realized that a manager could increase the output of unskilled laborers without major organizational changes or additional investment; at Appleton he saw that this principle applied potentially to workers in a wide range of occupations. In essence he had arrived at the position that other engineers of the Halsey school would reach in the 1890's. If this marked a partial retreat from his earlier view which had emphasized the interdependence of technology, management, and labor, it moved him closer to the mainstream of contemporary engineering thinking on the "labor problem" and enhanced his chances for professional recognition. He first became alert to this possibility in 1895 when he read "A Piece Rate System: A Step Toward Partial Solution of the Labor Problem" to an ASME meeting. To his amazement the commentators were so preoccupied with the incentive wage that they neglected time study and the other features of his work.[24]

In the short term, however, Taylor's innovations produced only a marginal improvement in the financial performance of the Manufacturing Investment Company. He acknowledged in 1893 that, despite his "driving" management and differential piece rate system, "profits are not what they should be."[25] He attributed this problem to the Mitscherlich process, which was neither an effective method of papermaking nor a deterrent to competition. Fannon later blamed the mistakes of Evans and Goodrich, the mill designers, and Taylor's inexperience.[26] Whitney and his associates probably believed that Taylor's lack of business expertise was a major reason for the company's disappointing performance.[27] Taylor readily admitted his weakness in this area; in late 1891 he hired "a good paper man," George F. Steele, to handle the company's marketing operations.[28] Finally, the depression of 1893 reduced the demand for paper and the prospect of improved profitability in the foreseeable future. As a consequence, Taylor was forced to take a pay cut and to agree to purchase an additional $30,000 of common and preferred stock.[29]

These problems exacerbated tensions that had developed between Taylor and the other investors. To Payne, Whitney, or R. D. Hayes, a railroad executive who was installed as president in April 1892 to bring greater financial acumen to the management, Taylor was an engineer, a technician unfamiliar with the larger world of corporate business.

Competent in his field, he lacked the perspective to rise above production management. Taylor, in turn, increasingly viewed the stockholders as irresponsible manipulators. Their insistent demands for profits, regardless of the long-term interests of the enterprise, and their indifference to manufacturing shocked and antagonized him. Their readiness to summon him, a Proper Philadelphian, to New York or Newport for conferences did not help the situation.[30] The fact that they were Democrats tended to confirm his worst suspicions.[31]

The contrasting ways in which Goodrich and Taylor approached Whitney suggest the differences of outlook and style that separated the financiers and Taylor. A consummate bureaucratic politician, Goodrich actively cultivated Whitney; his letters to the financier are a mixture of flattery, subtle boasts of his own achievements, and requests for additional favors.[32] Apparently these tactics were successful. Despite his unsatisfactory performance at Madison, he retained the friendships of both Whitney and Taylor and rose rapidly in the Navy. In contrast, Taylor's letters are formal and businesslike. They contain information and opinions but nothing to ingratiate him with the financier.[33]

By the spring of 1893 Taylor had decided to leave. On the one hand, his original expectations were shattered; on the other, as he explained, "our western mill is now doing finely . . . and our Madison mill, mechanically speaking, is all straightened out and we are progressing fairly with the piece work system."[34] There was a third factor as well. The success of the differential piece rate at Appleton had convinced Taylor that his managerial reforms were indeed transferable and marketable. They, rather than his engineering training or managerial experience, could be the basis for a satisfying career. Whitney, according to Copley, relieved him of his $30,000 stock purchase obligation and offered additional concessions if he would stay.[35] But Taylor was adamant, despite a substantial loss on his original investment and the bleak economic prospects of the period.[36] By June he was "entirely out of the M. I. Company." He had not "felt so well and free from care for a great many years."[37]

Taylor's experiences between 1890 and 1893 had a profound effect on his thinking. His former indifference to marketing and finance and the men who were responsible for those activities changed to contempt; in later years he would often contrast finance and manufacturing as if they were competing and irreconcilable functions. To Taylor a firm was run either by financiers or engineers. The former might make a profit, but little else. They were "looking merely for a turnover." They had "absolutely no pride of manufacture." To the financier "it is all a question of making money quickly." "If there is a manufacturer at the end of any enterprise . . . and he is a large minded man, that is the man whom I want to be under."[38] Henceforth Taylor increasingly identified with big business critics, particularly men like Louis Brandeis who shared both his enthusiasm for the modern bureaucratic factory and his disdain for the bureaucratic corporation.

Taylor's exposure to the financiers had one other result. It convinced him of his need for greater expertise in systematic accounting procedure. He had not been oblivious to accounting methods when he went to Madison; his Midvale records suggest that he had studied the cost systems used at Midvale and the Sellers Company and suggested various improvements.[39] But he had little familiarity with advanced accounting practice until his association with Whitney and the financiers. Indeed, the advent of R. D. Hayes in early 1892 was probably the most important single development in Taylor's accounting education. An experienced railroad man, Hayes was appalled at the state of the Manufacturing Investment Company's books when he became president.[40] Within a few months he introduced reforms that impressed Taylor.[41] In late 1892 or early 1893 he employed William D. Basley, a consultant who had worked for several railroads, to continue this work. By the time Taylor departed, Hayes and Basley had made substantial progress. The Hayes-Basley accounting system soon became the Taylor system.

During the summer of 1893, after his resignation as general manager, Taylor devoted much of his time to the Hayes-Basley methods.[42] In August,

> while I was in New York I stopped at our office and obtained a duplicate set of monthly exhibits made by the bookkeeper of the company. There is nothing at all unusual in the exhibits but the method of bookkeeping which enables our auditor and bookkeeper to make out a complete set of exhibits an[d] close and balance the books . . . in two hours (which I saw done the last time I was in New York) is quit[e] remarkable and I have regarded it as so valuable that I have been dev[o]ting about six weeks to mastering it so as to be able to apply it.[43]

The "valuable" features of the Hayes-Basley system became the "distinctive features" of Taylor's accounting system which "no other system has as yet attempted to accomplish."[44] They consisted of monthly financial statements; monthly cost reports, including comparative cost figures for each article manufactured; a daily financial balance; and a variety of safeguards to identify errors, to prevent chicanery by the clerical staff, and to insure rapid work. If Taylor did not at first identify the source of his ideas, it is only fair to note that he added refinements to what he copied, devised his own cost system (although he was aware of many published cost systems), and later acknowledged his debt to

Basley. By the fall he had mastered the Hayes-Basley methods and was ready to embark on a career as a consultant specializing in accounting practice, piecework, and increasingly, scientific management.

Lean Years, 1893–1896

The following years were undoubtedly the most difficult of Taylor's professional career. He had known the lot of a pioneer management consultant would not be easy, but he had not realized how perilous it might be or considered the possibility that three years later, at age forty, his future might still be as uncertain as it had been when he left Madison. Besides offering an ill-defined service to a skeptical public, he had to cope with the effects of the depression. In the mid-1890's few manufacturers were willing to undertake new and potentially expensive projects. Those who were interested often made novel demands on him. He had devised scientific management in an era of rising incomes. His aim had been increased production at lower unit costs, not lower costs per se. Now he was asked to facilitate contraction. The desperate conditions of the mid-1890's led him to place more emphasis on the differential piece rate and time study and to adopt attitudes toward workers that he would never outgrow. Still, there was a positive side to his experience. The storm of depression also nourished his prospects. Taylor's increased leisure enabled him to resume his metal-cutting experiments and to prepare papers on belting and the differential piece rate. These works, in turn, established his reputation as a practitioner of systematic management. By 1897 he stood on the threshold of his most productive period.

Taylor's first consulting job grew out of contacts he had made at Midvale. His inventions and his piecework system had attacted considerable local interest in the 1880's and a steady procession of visitors to the Nicetown plant.[45] In 1888 the Simonds Manufacturing Company of Fitchburg, Massachusetts, had acquired the rights to Taylor's forging patent. As he often did in later years, Taylor took stock in the company rather than cash for his invention.[46] He also promoted the company among his friends, urging them to buy shares. By the time he left Midvale, he was deeply involved in the Simonds operation.

Taylor was attracted to the Simonds Company because of its most promising product, the ball bearing. George F. Simonds, a pioneer metallurgist, had invented a rolling process "by which steel balls . . . are produced by straight reciprocating dies, rolling the material between them."[47] This technique enabled the company to make balls "of absolute sphericity . . . with a great saving in cost over existing methods for doing similar work."[48] In the early 1890's the company flourished, largely because of the bicycle boom. In 1892 Simonds built a factory in Chicago and opened offices in various cities. Apparently the Chicago plant produced saws, knives, and other hardware items; the Fitchburg factory continued to manufacture bearings.[49]

Despite its apparent success the company had serious problems. As early as July 1891 Taylor complained that "the management is poor . . . [but] the men are honest."[50] Two years later he bemoaned the fact that Simonds had "a practical monopoly" on the ball bearing business but was not exploiting it.[51] At approximately that time John J. Grant, the able superintendent, left Simonds and established a rival firm, the Cleveland Machine Screw Company, which quickly became the industry leader. It is not clear when George Simonds sought outside assistance, but Taylor had decided to go to Fitchburg by the time he resigned from the Manufacturing Investment Company. He wrote that he planned to apply the Hayes-Basley accounting system to the "returns, records, piece work system and the books" of the Simonds Company.[52]

Taylor remained at Fitchburg for nearly a year but never referred to his work, presumably an indication that he did not consider it particularly noteworthy or successful. Apparently, his only reform was the introduction of his accounting system, which should have required no more than a few months of his time. Whether Taylor voluntarily refrained from more ambitious measures or encountered resistance from the plant managers is unclear from his records. It was uncharacteristic of Taylor to forego any opportunity to implement his methods, especially his piecework system. On the other hand, his relations with the management must have been reasonably good at the time of his departure; he returned to direct a more thorough reorganization in 1897. It is conceivable that he remained at Fitchburg as long as he did simply because he had no other clients and, in effect, nowhere to go.[53]

In any case, the Simonds job was not devoid of achievement. In the process of applying the Hayes-Basley techniques, Taylor devised new procedures that became permanent parts of his accounting system. The most important of these was his "relative machine cost number," a method of distributing factory burden. As Taylor explained, he distributed indirect manufacturing costs

> by first making a careful study of the relative expense which should be borne by each machine . . . which works upon product that will be sold, and having obtained these relative cost numbers for each machine I find each month the wages per hour which each machine should charge in order to exactly apportion the shop expenses incurred during the month upon the product worked upon during the month.[54]

Copley wrote that Taylor got the "general idea" of the relative machine cost number from the Sellers Company and applied it in the Simonds machine and smith shops.[55] Taylor also introduced his mnemonic system (based on combinations of letters and numbers rather than numbers alone) for identifying and classifying accounts during this period.[56]

In the spring or early summer of 1894 he and Louise returned to Philadelphia and lived with Franklin and Emily for the next year. In September, Taylor began work at William Cramp and Sons, the largest American shipbuilding firm. This assignment, like the Simonds job, is shrouded in mystery; it is unlikely, however, that it proved any more satisfying for Taylor.[57] During the fall and winter he reorganized and consolidated the Cramp toolrooms, installed "special furnaces and a steam hammer" in the smith shop for "dressing and tempering" tools, purchased a Taylor grinding machine for the toolroom, and introduced his belting system.[58] He also continued his metal-cutting experiments. "I went back and ran a machine for the whole winter," he recalled. "I worked the same hours as the other workmen, and I tell you it was the easiest and happiest year I have had since I got out of my apprenticeship."[59]

Taylor's experiments again produced important results. He discovered that "a heavy stream of water thrown upon the shaving at the nose of the tool" permitted a one-third increase in the cutting speed of the tool.[60] He also learned that tools made of Mushet "self-hardening" tool steel, an alloy steel which included tungsten and manganese, worked effectively on more types and qualities of metals than had been known previously. Taylor soon became intrigued with the possibilities of alloy steels. He persuaded the Cramps and William Sellers to finance a series of tests of various self-hardening tool steels. These tests showed that tools made of Midvale self-hardening tool steel, an alloy steel that substituted chromium for manganese, were superior to those made of Mushet and other brands. Although his efforts to determine the best temperatures for treating the tools were inconclusive at the time, Taylor's discovery of the potential of chromium alloy steel was a critical step toward "high speed" tool steel, the invention which confirmed his reputation as a creative engineer.

By the spring of 1895, however, Taylor had exhausted the interest of the Cramp managers. They refused to permit a more extensive reorganization of the yard and seemed indifferent to his work in the smith and machine shops.[61] Apparently they were more concerned about expenses than potential results. Taylor reported that they criticized his efforts publicly, indicating that they were (in Taylor's words) "worse than useless."[62]

Taylor also narrowly missed an opportunity to introduce his methods in another large firm, the Deering Harvester Company of Chicago. George F. Steele had left the Manufacturing Investment Company shortly after Taylor and had become a vice-president of the Deering Company. An admirer of Taylor and scientific management, he strongly urged the Deerings to adopt Taylor's innovations, particularly the differential piece rate. In early 1894 Steele toured various eastern plants to study piecework plans; not unexpectedly, he found the Midvale operation most intriguing.[63] Soon he had won over James Deering, the company's operating head. But Steele had more difficulty with William Deering, James's father and the principal owner. The elder Deering was not opposed to the plan—Steele wrote optimistic letters to Taylor until 1897—but he was hesitant to proceed until they had "looked into all the angles" and were certain that "it will work at the Deering Company ."[64] Steele apparently was never able to satisfy the elder Deering.

In March 1895 the Taylors moved to Boston and lived there until December. Why they went to Boston is unclear. Taylor may have gone back to Simonds—he wrote in May that "most of my employers have given me work for the second and third time"—or he may have had some other client in the area.[65] A year later, just before he returned to the Simonds Company, he noted that he had worked for "one or two concerns" in New England.[66] Copley also reported that Taylor promoted at least two business combinations during this period, supposedly for large fees.[67] Whatever the nature of these activities, they apparently had no effect on Taylor's career or the development of scientific management.

In his free time, however, Taylor wrote "A Piece Rate System," a description of scientific management that did have a substantial impact on his future. Two years earlier, in 1893, he had presented his first formal report on scientific management to the ASME. A straightforward technical analysis of his belt maintenance system, "Notes on Belting" had attracted little attention; it could hardly serve as the basis for a successful consulting career. Taylor was determined not to repeat his error. He abandoned the circumspect, scholarly approach of "Notes on Belting." His introduction to "A Piece Rate System" was an outspoken indictment of the first factory system. Bemoaning the "old school of management," he enumerated the risks of delegating plant operations to superintendents and foremen. The primary danger, he argued, was not blatant mismanagement—that the manufacturer would recognize. It was the "more insidious and fatal failure on the part of the superintendents to insure anything even approaching the maximum

work from their men and machines." By contrast, the "modern manufacturer" eliminated this danger by surrounding "each department . . .
with the most carefully woven network of system and method."[68] Taylor
then turned abruptly to the labor features of scientific management. He
condemned day rates, piece rates, profit sharing, and the Towne and
Halsey incentive plans. The missing elements, he argued, were systematic "rate fixing" and an incentive wage that clearly and quickly
translated superior effort into higher earnings. Taylor did not dwell on
details. He briefly described the origins of time study and the differential piece rate, cited examples of their varied applications at Midvale,
emphasized the necessity of preliminary changes in the organization of
the factory, and, in an oblique attack on the labor reformers, argued
that his methods complemented traditional personnel policies and
eliminated any need for a structured or paternalistic approach. Taylor
ended on an optimistic note: because of the importance of manufacturing to the economic well-being of the firm, competition would force the
widespread adoption of time study and the differential piece rate.[69]

This time Taylor was not disappointed. His presentation to the June
1895 meeting of the ASME in Detroit was a resounding success. Even
the commentators, preoccupied with the differential rate, acknowledged that the paper was a seminal work, comparable to the essays of
Towne, Church, and Halsey. "A Piece Rate System" was Taylor's first
public relations coup, a stimulus to his consulting career, and a model
for his later writings. He soon obtained new clients and recouped much
of his personal wealth. By mid-1896 he could write that he had made
more money in the previous twelve months than in any other year.[70] The
interregnum of 1893 to 1895, marked by limited opportunities, modest
progress, and relative financial stringency, had ended. For the next five
years Taylor would be unusually busy and successful.

One indication of his improved situation was a project he initiated in
late 1895. Since his Midvale years Taylor had been eager to resume his
efforts to calculate optimum times for factory operations. His experiences had demonstrated that machine tool times, one area of
interest, were exceedingly difficult to determine, but that workers'
times posed few obstacles, providing a good time study man was available. His ultimate goal was to find and publish both types of data for
machine shop tasks and possibly other jobs. But the engineers' enthusiastic response to "A Piece Rate System" convinced him to proceed with
the time study experiments before he had completed his metal-cutting
studies. And in Sanford Thompson, his former colleague at the Manufacturing Investment Company, he had an ideal man to do the work.

Thompson had left the Manufacturing Investment Company in mid-1893 and had worked for another paper company and for several engineering firms. He had specialized in paper mill design at first, but gradually became interested in other types of construction, including reinforced concrete buildings.[71] When Taylor contacted him in late 1895, Thompson was intrigued with the proposal. A visit to Midvale "practically decided the matter."[72] In December 1895 Thompson agreed to work for Taylor for one and possibly more years. His salary was to be $1,200 per year.[73]

Thompson's assignment was to determine "what constitutes a day's work" in a variety of unmechanized manual labor occupations. He was to refine Taylor's and Miller's Midvale data and study various tasks—unskilled work like shoveling sand and loading pig iron, and skilled jobs such as plastering, bricklaying, and concrete work. (The choice of building trades occupations was a reflection of Thompson's background rather than Taylor's interests.) He would publish his results in a series of manuals that would enable employers to estimate costs and set wages quickly and accurately.

Thompson devoted the early part of 1896 to various preliminary steps. He made a systematic study of stopwatches, finally deciding to design his own. He also devised a special "watch book" to hold the watch and time study form, "so that the watches can be operated in the book and without attracting too much attention."[74] He spent many hours at the Boston Public Library reviewing previous work on "what constitutes a day's work and . . . what literature I can find on the subject of cost of labor."[75] He concluded that the existing material on "manpower" was virtually useless. To Taylor this was conclusive evidence that "we are almost pioneers."[76]

Thompson's next step was to compile and synthesize Taylor's Midvale time study data on manual labor jobs. This information was to be the subject of a book, as well as a model for subsequent studies.[77] After reviewing Taylor's notes, however, he concluded that the Midvale time studies had been inexact, unscientific, and ultimately worthless, at least for his purposes.[78] Taylor acknowledged that it had been "difficult to analyze the job into what constitutes really its essential elements and then put these together properly after making the analysis."[79] In some cases he had neglected to specify the various steps of the operation—"how many minutes in a day such a man . . . is actually shoveling and how much of the time he is resting, getting his tools out, and moving from place to place, etc."[80] In others he had been careless or inaccurate. As Taylor noted regarding one group of observations:

> Have written again to Mr. Coonahan [the Midvale time study man]
> to find out whether there is not another nigger concealed in the
> wood pile. The average of 94,000 pounds of coal unloaded per man
> per 10 hours throughout a period of four years seems to me too
> high, and I am not so sure that when we dig into the matter we will
> not find that this average includes some coal that has been dumped
> out . . . as well as what has been unloaded over the side. At any
> rate, I mean to chase this matter home and have our fundamental
> data . . . as nearly correct as possible.[81]

After unsuccessful efforts to improve the data, he and Thompson concluded that the Midvale records were unsalvageable, and they temporarily dropped the effort to set "scientific" rates for factory laborers.

In late February 1896 Thompson began time studies of various construction jobs. Through local contacts he was able to find builders who
would permit him to observe workmen at construction sites. After carefully dividing the jobs into basic "elements," he timed them using the
"watch book." To insure that the workers did not "soldier" or slow their
pace, Thompson used several approaches suggested by Taylor. Whenever possible he timed the men without telling them, but if this proved
impossible he explained what he was doing in a general way.[82] On some
occasions he also masqueraded as a writer for the *Paper Mill Journal*, a
trade paper he had written for in the past.[83]

By the end of the year, when his contract ended, Thompson had
become a time study "expert." He had developed the equipment that
Taylor's time study experts would use in the future, refined the Midvale
data, improved the methodology of time study, and gathered information on many new occupations. In the course of his work he had also
made a potentially significant discovery. As he reported to Taylor, "One
of the greatest difficulties I have found in arriving at averages is due to
the fact . . . that the 'personal equations' of different men vary
greatly."[84] This common sense statement, which should have sparked a
reconsideration of the entire time-study process, fell on deaf ears.
Nevertheless, Taylor was sufficiently impressed with Thompson's work
to renew his contract, increase his salary, and recognize him as the
most knowledgeable practitioner of this novel art. Thompson's 1896
studies, which eventually culminated in several books on concrete
construction work, also marked the beginning of the scientific management movement. From this time until the end of his life Taylor would
always be surrounded by followers like Thompson, men proficient in
one or more aspects of scientific management, indebted to him, and
dedicated to the perpetuation of his methods and leadership.

In the meantime, Taylor was preoccupied with his revived consulting practice. In August 1895, A. O. Fox of the Northern Electric Manufacturing Company hired him to systematize the company's accounting methods. A relatively small job, it was, nevertheless, an indication of Taylor's growing reputation and the effect of "A Piece Rate System."[85] Taylor also became more involved in "the combination of which I am a referee."[86] Presumably as a result, he and Louise lived in Chicago from December 1895 to late February 1896. Although he did not indicate the nature of his work there, it was, by his later testimony, highly remunerative. In any event, a third assignment, the reorganization of the Johnson Company's Johnstown, Pennsylvania, works, overshadowed the others. For the first time since 1893 Taylor was to have the power to initiate sweeping changes in the management of an industrial firm, to refine and apply scientific management.

The Johnson Company

The Johnson Company was a product of Tom Loftin Johnson's spectacular rise as a street railway magnate. In 1869 Johnson had joined the Louisville, Kentucky, streetcar firm owned by Alfred Victor DuPont of the Delaware DuPont family. He advanced quickly; by the late 1880's he owned or controlled, with DuPont, streetcar lines in a half dozen major cities. By the 1890's he had become a leader of the electric traction industry. One of his important technical developments was an improved rail for trolleys, which he and Arthur J. Moxham, inventor of a rolling technique, began to manufacture in 1889 for Johnson's lines. Johnson and Moxham called their firm the Johnson Company, and established their headquarters in Johnstown to be near their supplier of iron and rails, the Cambria Iron Company. Johnson continued to devote most of his attention to street railway promotions, while Moxham managed the Johnson Company.[87]

Under Moxham's direction the Johnson Company expanded rapidly. In the early 1890's, a boom period for the street railway industry, the company integrated forward and backward: Moxham set up sales offices in major cities to sell rails to traction firms not owned by Johnson and DuPont, and he established a rolling mill in Johnstown to manufacture rails from Cambria steel. By 1893 Moxham began to study the possibility of a new and larger rolling mill, together with a steel plant, at either Johnstown or some more advantageous point.[88]

In the meantime Johnson had undertaken the production of electric streetcar motors, as well as rails. In the late 1880's he had established a small motor repair company in Cleveland under the management of his brother, Albert L. Johnson. This company soon began to manufacture motors for Johnson's streetcar lines and then, like the Johnson Company, for the general market. A. L. Johnson claimed that his product "possessed a remarkable record"; in any event, the Steel Motor Company, as the firm was known after 1893, became one of the four major motor producers in the United States.[89] In 1894 it became a subsidiary of the Johnson Company.

By the mid-1890's the Johnson Company had become an important and prosperous firm. Moxham, a skillful organizer, was primarily responsible for its success. Johnson, on the other hand, was gradually forsaking business for politics; a Democratic congressman in the 1890's, he was soon to become one of the nation's leading progressives as mayor of Cleveland. DuPont, the third important figure in the Johnson Company, died in 1893, and his shares were divided among his brother Bidermann and three nephews—Coleman, Alfred I., and Pierre S. DuPont—who in later years would build E. I. DuPont de Nemours into the world's leading chemical company. Bidermann, Alfred, and Pierre, deeply involved in other activities, left the management of the Johnson Company to Moxham. Coleman became manager of the Johnstown works in 1894.

The company's success in the early 1890's, Johnson's preoccupation with politics, and the advent of the inexperienced DuPonts led to the decisions which brought Taylor to Johnstown and influenced his work there. Having concluded that the company should manufacture steel, Moxham in 1893 urged construction of a modern integrated steel mill at Lorain, Ohio, west of Cleveland on Lake Erie.[90] The panic of 1893 reinforced his conviction. In the short run, he argued, such a plant would help the company reduce costs and compete more effectively during the recession. In the long run it would free the firm from dependence on the steel industry. Perhaps because this move seemed a logical extension of Moxham's policy of vertical integration, Johnson and the DuPonts assented.[91] In 1895 the company transferred most of its operations and many of its employees to the new site. To utilize the buildings and machinery they had abandoned, they then moved the Steel Motor Company from Cleveland to Johnstown.[92] They hired new men, expanded the plant, and reorganized its operations.[93] To help with the latter task, Moxham hired Taylor, who began work at Johnstown in early March 1896.

Though initially wary of Johnson and Moxham because of their

reputations as financiers, Taylor soon became enthusiastic about his
superiors and his job. He found Moxham, whose office was in Lorain,
sympathetic but demanding—"a man who wants the most minute information regarding everything and wants it right away."[94] Coleman
DuPont and W. A. Harris, the manager of the electrical department,
were "a most willing and considerate set of men."[95] Harris, his immediate superior, was "practical," "energetic," and "active," "one of
the quickest men to improve the opportunities presented by the new
system."[96] By the early summer Taylor had become optimistic about
his prospects.

Another reason for his reassessment was Louise's reaction to Johnstown. Although there is no indication that she objected to Taylor's work
or resisted their frequent moves, she was clearly unhappy with their
transient life and prolonged absences from Philadelphia. Taylor wrote
that she expected "to have a miserable time" in the "small Pennsylvania
village."[97] But like him, she was pleasantly surprised. Soon she had

> fixed things so that we have had an uncommonly pleasant and
> agreeable stay. There is an incl[i]ned railway which starts about
> four minutes walk from the hotel and goes to the top of a neighbor-
> ing mountain about nine hundred feet away. She found that the
> choice site on this mountain had been reserved for a hotel and with
> a considerable amount of cheek and a great amount of tact secured
> the right from the Cambria Iron Company to build a small house
> where the hotel is to stand, so that we have a delightful little place
> . . . which is cool even on the hottest day and commands a magnifi-
> cent view of the country for miles around.[98]

Taylor also found diversions at Johnstown. He bicycled, played tennis,
and took up golf for the first time.

Taylor's principal task at the Johnson Company was to introduce his
accounting methods in the remaining Johnson facilities in Johnstown—
the electric motor factory, plus a foundry and switch works. The
specific measures Taylor introduced were those he had advocated since
1893. By October he could write that the managers

> have complete and elaborate returns each month of just what they
> had produced and the cost, not only of every piece made, but of
> every operation on every piece, and as this is a comparative state-
> ment they cannot fall behind their best previous cost in any opera-
> tion done in the works however small, without being called to their
> attention. The books are also completely closed and balanced at
> the end of each month.[99]

The reports were so complete "that if gang bosses or sub-foremen have employed one extra laborer during the month . . . it will be brought to [the manager's] attention."[100]

The new accounting procedures were closely related to other changes in the plant organization. One of these, Taylor's storekeeping system, was a new feature of scientific management. Although systematic purchasing and stores methods were prominent features of most production management plans, Taylor had disregarded them on his earlier jobs. Now he changed his approach. His first important reform, he wrote Moxham, would be "an accurate running balance of raw materials, merchandise, and stores throughout all of your establishments."[101] He may have stressed this point because of the chaotic stores methods that prevailed before his arrival. The company had, he recalled, "some hundred and fifty thousand dollars worth of valuable stores and supplies dumped down in a shed helter skelter, without even protection from the weather, and each workman dived into this pile for whatever he wanted without rendering any account to anyone of what he wanted."[102] As a result, the establishment of a stores system and inventory control methods proved to be a difficult, perhaps the most difficult, part of Taylor's work. The "issuing and charging of materials met with great opposition from all of the men."[103] This hostility was a major reason for an embarrassing delay in the preparation of the August cost reports. Though Taylor proceeded to "train" the men, it was "a very difficult task and left us very much mixed up."[104] By the early fall he had introduced a variety of forms for recording inventories of raw materials and semi-finished goods. The results were "so satisfactory and so very apparent" that the "opposition has almost entirely ceased"; yet he warned that any future compromises or shortcuts would sabotage the entire storekeeping and accounting system.[105]

Unfortunately this admonition was not heeded. Within a month after his departure in November 1896 Taylor received complaints that the cost system was not working properly. "The greatest problem," he replied, was that "the shop manager does not have the benefit of the elaborate balance records." To remedy this problem, "steps should be taken at the earliest minute . . . [to] get the system in thorough working order."[106] As late as January 1897 he lectured Harris on the necessity for strict adherence to his procedures.[107]

Taylor introduced the differential piece rate in the electric motor plant with somewhat greater success. Until 1896 the company had relied on the internal contract system: a "contractor" hired the men he wanted, paid them a day wage, supervised them, and hoped to make a profit on his "contract" by reducing costs. Taylor's first step was to replace the contractors with salaried foremen and the differential piece rate. Yet he was no more systematic in his approach than he had been at Appleton and Madison. He may have assigned the foremen to make time studies, but since he had not reorganized the machinery or installed his belt and machine maintenance systems, the times he allotted for machine operations must have been little more than guesses based on past operations.[108] Fortunately for Taylor, many of the workers were new and, in general, "docile and good natured." Even the contractors, whose earnings declined when they became salaried foremen, were a "very agreeable set of men to deal with."[109] By late September, Taylor reported that "rates and prices have been cut down throughout the shop."[110]

This was the one instance in his career when Taylor directly confronted the ancien régime of the American machinery industry. For three-quarters of a century the contractor's presence had reminded fellow workers that factory labor was not synonymous with wage labor, and that specialization was not inconsistent with technical creativity or a degree of autonomy usually found only in an independent enterprise. Yet by 1896 the contractors were under attack in many plants, in some cases because they had apparently exhausted the possibilities for cost reductions, in others because they were anachronisms in an era of increasingly centralized management. In most factories they were an "agreeable set of men" and surrendered their prerogatives without overt protest. It is unlikely, however, that any aspect of the transition to the new factory system proved of greater long-term importance. The economic consequences of the contractor's demise varied; the social effects did not. The labor problem in the precision machinery industries dated from the elimination of the contractor, the preeminent symbol of personal responsibility and decentralized control. Henceforth, labor relations in machinery factories began to resemble the pattern of the other mechanical industries. The salaried foreman and labor management conflict were two sides of the same coin.

As if aware of the potential consequences of his actions, Taylor emphasized the immediate economic value of his dramatic assault on the status quo. On October 22 he wrote that "in the classes of work to which it has been applied the cost has been fully cut in two. We have saved enough in armature winding alone to pay for all the costs of introducing the system and running it. Mr. Harris . . . has succeeded in getting the whole of this work done by women."[111] Taylor's rather incomplete account does not indicate which of the three changes—the elimination of the contractors, the hiring of low wage women workers, or the installation of the differential piece rate—he considered most important. (The women, incidentally, did not directly replace higher priced male workers; most of the plant employees were new and inexperienced.) In any event, the differential piece rate forced the workers—men and women alike—to attain high levels of production in a relatively short time. There was no immediate indication of labor unrest.

Again, however, Taylor's shop reforms were overshadowed by developments over which he had no control. At Johnstown, as at Madison, the owners' hopes that bold innovations would produce high profits soured quickly. Moxham and the DuPonts had built the Lorain plant on the assumption that the depression would soon pass, but business did not improve in 1895, and by January 1896 the company was forced to borrow $750,000 to meet its short-term obligations. In July, Moxham asked Taylor to curtail his expenses and turn over more of his activities to the company employees.[112] By October, Taylor reported that the plant was "almost shut down."[113] Thus, Taylor operated under severe financial constraints from the beginning of his work at Johnstown. His employers agreed that he performed admirably; indeed, by early 1897 the Steel Motors Works was the most profitable operation of the Johnson Company.[114] Yet the constant, if often indirect, pressure to avoid new costs and reduce existing expenses had a constricting effect on his activities. It undoubtedly led to his hasty and somewhat haphazard introduction of piecework. It also prevented him from implementing other important features of his system. It is likely that the company's weak financial position stopped Taylor from completing the development of scientific management at that time and from making the Johnson plant the first "scientifically" managed factory.

Taylor's reports to Moxham and DuPont indicate the additional steps he would have undertaken if resources had been available. In an outline he submitted to Moxham in late February, he proposed a planning department similar to the one he had established at Midvale. It would prepare written orders "covering the various items of work to be done, and each man throughout the establishment works from these written orders instead of from verbal orders."[115] In the following months Taylor introduced some features of a planning department—purchase and stores control procedures and a bulletin board, for example—but the company's financial plight led Moxham and DuPont to place these activities under the accounting department. Production management therefore became subordinate to record keeping, contrary to Taylor's recommendations. He made several other attempts to introduce systematic planning without an actual department, but these efforts failed, as he had probably anticipated.[116] He also tried to systematize the work of the accounting department employees, in part by recommending rigid work rules ("no talking above a whisper") and a reduction in the work day ("giving them all extra time for recreation rather than have them intersperse their recreation with their work, as they are now doing."), apparently with no greater success.[117]

Taylor adopted a similar approach to functional foremanship. His first proposal did not mention functional supervisors, but he soon suggested activities that required specialist managers.[118] In early November, when his work was virtually completed, he recommended the appointment of a speed boss—a man who would "devote his time to seeing that all machines work at their best all the time"—without much hope that this suggestion would be adopted, at least in the immediate future.[119] But his hesitation was also motivated by his own uncertainty about the role and significance of functional foremen. He had used them sparingly at Midvale and not at all in the intervening period; under more advantageous circumstances the Johnson Company assignment would have offered him the opportunity to develop this aspect of his system.

Finally, he recommended various mechanical improvements. His suggestions included his metal-cutting innovations, his belt maintenance methods, and the purchase of a tool grinder.[120] His fundamental point, however, was "the desirability of carefully experimenting with each machine and job to be done throughout the place, so as to determine the maximum capacity of each part of the plant and then insure each machine being operated at all times under the most favorable circumstances."[121] As he had at Midvale, Taylor saw these "experiments" as the key to the extension of his methods. A thorough knowledge of the machinery would affect each of the measures he proposed, as well as the stores and cost systems and the piece rates. Yet he knew that Moxham had not anticipated an extensive series of machine studies and, in any case, probably could not afford them. As a result, he resigned himself to an important, but limited, installation of scientific management.

By November, when Taylor left Johnstown, he was pleased with his efforts. With modest resources he had made substantial reductions in the cost of manufacture and impressed his employers. He had shown that he could achieve impressive results in a relatively short period of time, largely through the introduction of the differential piece rate. To attain these goals he had adopted a pragmatic approach to the major elements of his system—an approach that made scientific management in practice little different from other systematic management plans. But Taylor willingly paid this price for the opportunity to educate his clients to the desirability of a thorough installation of scientific management. Unfortunately, circumstances beyond his control prevented this strategy from succeeding in 1896 or afterward. The Johnson Company never fully recovered from the depression, and in 1899 Johnson, Moxham, and the DuPonts sold their interests to the new Federal Steel Company. In the ensuing reorganization Taylor's methods were discarded, apparently ending any influence he had on the operation of the Johnstown plant.[122]

Simonds, Phase II

In the meantime Taylor had returned to the Simonds Company and to an even more challenging assignment. The depression had reduced the demand for bicycles and forced drastic reductions in ball bearing prices. To complicate the situation, George Simonds had died in 1894, leaving the firm to his son Walter, who continued to live in Boston, an absentee and largely unenthusiastic owner. George Weymouth, who succeeded John J. Grant as superintendent, was also a poor replacement. By the fall of 1896 Simonds' production was only one-third that of the Grant firm, and the combination of low prices and low production threatened to bankrupt the company. Finally, in December 1896, the board of directors discharged Weymouth and employed Taylor "to get out all the balls which possibly could be produced."[123] Taylor's papers provide no hint of his role in these events; possibly he promised to increase production in exchange for the authority to introduce his management system. In any case, he moved quickly to demonstrate that his methods would produce the desired results. Expediency again became the principal determinant of his actions.

Taylor's course was predictable. Learning that the "rough" and "finish" grinding departments had been the most serious bottlenecks in the preceding months, he immediately switched the grinders from day work to the differential piece rate. Although he had to base the "high" rates on "rule of thumb" estimates, he assuaged the workers' concern about rate cuts by guaranteeing the high rates for three years unless some "radical improvement" occurred or "woman labor" was introduced. However, he refused to guarantee the "low" rates; indeed, he indicated that they would be progressively lowered "until each workman finds it for his interest to work fast and do the best quality of work only."[124] In areas where he had not yet set high and low rates, he ordered the foremen to raise or lower the conventional piece rate to create a similar effect. By March 1897 he had put most of the workers in the grinding departments on the differential rate. Production that month was three times the average monthly output for 1896.[125]

To insure that the workers did not sacrifice quality to earn the higher rate, Taylor introduced what he called "systematic supervision," essentially an elaborate system of inspection.

> The work of each one of the forty grinders was inspected for quality every fifteen minutes at least, so that no workman could produce a bad quality of work for more than this length of time without having the attention of the foreman called to this fact. . . . In addition to this inspection, each grinder's work was carefully kept by itself, and a sample lot of balls taken from each man's work each day and given the most minute inspection, and in addition to this inspection, the regular inspection which had been carried on in past years, was continued.[126]

In March, Taylor also began to reorganize the final inspection department, where the balls were reexamined prior to shipment. Here, however, he adopted a somewhat different approach. Instead of the differential rate, he introduced what he called "improved day work."

> An accurate daily record, both as to quantity and quality, was kept for each inspector. In a comparatively short time this enabled the foreman to stir the ambition of all the inspectors by increasing the wages of those who turned out a large quantity and good quality, at the same time lowering the pay of those who fell short, and discharging others who proved to be incorrigibly slow or careless. An accurate time study was made through the use of a stop watch and record blanks, to determine how fast each kind of inspection should be done. This showed that the girls spent a considerable part of their time in partial idleness, talking and half working, or in actually doing nothing.[127]

Taylor's papers and writings do not explain why he coupled his driving methods with "improved day work" rather than the differential rate.[128] Yet, as his statement indicates, the result was similar. The productive workers received a financial reward; the "slow or careless" were eliminated.

When time studies of the inspectors' work were completed, Taylor suggested a plan that he had first proposed to Coleman DuPont the previous fall. Observing that the inspectors, who were all women, wasted much time in conversation and other forms of "idleness" during their long workday (ten and a half hours per day and fifty-eight hours per week, the legal maximums for women in Massachusetts), he proposed to reduce the workday to ten hours and to require that they work steadily. He assured the employees that their wages would not be cut. Supposedly to underline his conciliatory approach, he then asked the inspectors to vote on the proposal. To his chagrin, "the girls were unanimous that 10½ hours was good enough for them and they wanted no innovation of any kind."[129]

With this exception Taylor's managerial reforms at the Simonds plant were generally successful, but hardly innovative. The differential piece rate was, of course, Taylor's creation, but without time study it was little more than a conventional piece rate plan with a minimum output requirement. The methods he introduced in the inspection department were no more refined. Taylor's defense was that these were temporary measures designed to protect the company's competitive position from further erosion. Though he was unquestionably sincere in his intention to install scientific management, his actions between December 1896 and June 1897 gave few clues to the nature of his ultimate goal.

Meanwhile, he was making important changes in another area. After "carefully inspecting the apparatus used throughout the works," he concluded that "very great improvements" could be made in the machinery.[130] His method of determining what "improvement" was feasible was reminiscent of his metal-cutting experiments. He hired "a first class experimenter," his friend and former colleague Henry L. Gantt. Gantt's studies soon extended "over several departments" and resulted in substantial "improvements in our manufacture and machines." In addition, Taylor purchased several new machines, since it was "for the interest of the works to employ the best methods of manufacture wherever they could be found."[131] By July 1897 he had spent $19,000 for new equipment and proposed to spend at least $13,000 more—all of which, he later acknowledged, came "right out of the earnings of the company."[132]

Thus Taylor adopted different, and, in some respects, contradictory approaches to the workers and the plant. His interest in immediate results and his belief that workers would respond to the promise of higher wages led him to adopt an expedient policy, emphasizing short-term gains, in his relations with them; his preoccupation with machinery, on the other hand, led him to undertake an expensive, long-term program of mechanical improvements at the same time. Both policies were probably consistent with the interests of the Simonds Company, but they raised doubts about Taylor's leadership and objectives in the minds of Simonds and the directors. Taylor's enemies soon capitalized on those misgivings.

On June 28 "every foreman and assistant foreman" and "all of the salesmen and the head man in the office resigned, effective July 1."[133]

Their purpose, Taylor believed, was to force the company "to shut down or else, as Weymouth hoped, discharge me and go back to the old system of management."[134] If his analysis was correct, they were unsuccessful. The board of directors backed Taylor, and Weymouth attempted to form his own company. This enterprise failed, apparently with Taylor's covert assistance.[135] Still, the victory over Weymouth was costly; Simonds and the directors henceforth viewed Taylor and his methods with even greater suspicion. By October their doubts, buttressed by unfavorable economic developments, had grown to the point that Simonds asked several of Taylor's clients if his methods had failed in their factories. Taylor was outraged.[136] It was at this time, nearly six months before his departure from Fitchburg, that he began negotiations with the Bethlehem Iron Company.

The conflict with Weymouth was nevertheless an important step in the rise of scientific management. The departure of Weymouth's friends forced Taylor to build a new organization, to recruit men sympathetic to his methods. It therefore hastened the appearance of a corps of disciples dedicated to Taylor's ideas and prepared to introduce his techniques in other firms. Gantt, Taylor's "first-class experimenter," became his chief assistant and eventual successor at Simonds. Sanford Thompson came to Fitchburg to supervise the inspection department. Taylor also employed James Gillespie and John E. Mullaney, two assistants who were to follow him to Bethlehem. Not surprisingly, he made substantial progress in the latter months of 1897.

On July 1, the day his subordinates resigned, Taylor submitted a detailed report of his activities and plans for the future. He proposed substantial changes in the organization of the plant, particularly in the rolling and grinding departments. He urged the extension of the differential piece rate system to "all standard operations throughout the place" and the adoption of his inspection methods in other departments. In addition, he suggested the introduction of "standard methods of repairing, cleaning, and caring for all our machinery, belting, etc." and more detailed cost sheets.[137] There is no way of determining how many of these proposals were implemented, but Taylor's later statements suggest that he was permitted to initiate most of the changes he recommended. In 1898 he wrote that the Simonds Company had the lowest costs and highest reputation in the industry. The only problem, he added, was that many workers still were not on piecework.[138]

Taylor did not specifically mention the final inspection department in his report, but his papers and recollections for the period after June deal almost exclusively with his work there. Whether this is because the inspection function and the inspectors became the focus of his efforts in late 1897 or because of some other factors is uncertain. Simonds and the directors may have restricted Taylor's work in other departments, forcing him to prove himself again by achieving greater economies in the inspection department. Or Thompsons' results may have over-shadowed those of Gantt and the other assistants. Or Taylor may have chosen to emphasize the inspection department in later years simply because of the non-technical character and dramatic appeal of his work there. In any case, Taylor left detailed accounts of his vigorous efforts to increase the inspectors' "efficiency." In June, probably before Thompson arrived, he completed his earlier work, substituting the dif-ferential piece rate for "improved day work." He reported that the "in-crease [in bearings inspected] per day from June on day work, to July on piece work" was "37 per cent."[139] Thompson later reported that the rates were "carefully and scientifically fixed."[140] The cumulative effect of Taylor's earlier changes and the differential piece rate was nearly to double output and to increase the workers' wages by a lesser amount.

During the following months Taylor and Thompson introduced three other important changes in the inspection department. First, they began what Taylor later called the "scientific selection" of the workers, the identification and replacement of the least able employees. Since the foremen had already discharged those "who proved to be incorrigibly slow or careless," the victims of this process must have been many hitherto acceptable workers who were unable to earn the high rate. In 1903 Taylor described this task as the "weeding out of the lazy and un-promising candidates."[141] In 1911 he recalled it in somewhat different terms: "For the ultimate good of the girls as well as the company . . . it became necessary to exclude all girls who lacked a low 'personal co-efficient' [quick perception and response]. And unfortunately this involved laying off many of the most intelligent, hardest working, and most trustworthy girls."[142] By his account the number of inspectors declined by more than 50 percent.[143]

Second, Thompson revived and implemented Taylor's plan to reduce the workday and eliminate "idleness." Despite the girls' earlier vote, Thompson concluded that the work was "very confining, and it was difficult . . . to maintain order . . . because they very naturally became tired before the day was done."[144] On August 1 he reduced the workday to nine and one-half hours and introduced a five minute break in the morning and in the afternoon. On September 1 he further reduced the workday to eight and one-half hours and extended the breaks to ten minutes each. At the same time, the girls were physically separated so they could not converse. Production in August and September was 33 percent higher than in July. The girls "worked steadily, instead of stopping frequently to rest or speak to their . . . neighbors," and "appeared less tired."[145]

Third, Taylor assigned a special worker to help the inspectors maintain their pace. In 1903 he described this person as an "assistant" to the foreman, in 1911 as a "teacher."[146] Each worker's output was recorded every hour, "and they were all informed whether they were keeping up with their tasks, or how far they had fallen short."[147] If the deficiency was serious, the "assistant" or "teacher" was dispatched "to find out what was wrong, to straighten her out, and to encourage and help her to catch up."[148] Coupled with the "scientific selection" of the workers, this tactic must have been a powerful stimulus to maintain production. A visit from the "assistant" or "teacher" was a sure warning that the individual would next be "selected" for discharge. Taylor and the early historians of scientific management later associated this innovation with the development of functional foremanship.[149] It is more probable, however, that Taylor's "assistant" or "teacher" became the "instructor" that Gantt later incorporated in his system in lieu of functional foremen.[150]

If Taylor's assessments are accurate, these changes substantially increased worker productivity in the inspection department. He claimed that each girl produced two and one-half times as much in September as in March and received 80 to 100 percent higher wages. There was also "a substantial improvement in the quality of the product" and "a material reduction in the cost of inspection" despite additional clerical and managerial expense. In addition, he argued, presumably with less certainty, "each girl was made to feel that she was the object of especial care and interest on the part of the management," and that "the most friendly relations existed between the management and the employees, which rendered labor troubles of any kind or a strike impossible."[151] His critics undoubtedly would have replied that the absence of trouble was more likely the result of an atmosphere of fear and intimidation than of any new cooperative impulse.

Yet neither Taylor's reorganization of the company generally nor his and Thompson's work in the inspection department fully satisfied the directors or saved the business. Despite his achievements Taylor never regained the owners' confidence. Remarkably, some of them continued to listen to Weymouth's charges against him long after the former superintendent had betrayed the company. Equally serious was the decline of the bicycle market. Ball prices continued to fall in 1897 and 1898; by the spring of 1898 Simonds received only 75¢ per thousand, as opposed to $3.00 per thousand in early 1897.[152] Faced with substantial losses, the prospect of even greater competition in the future, and the unwillingness of the Cleveland firm to merge, the Simonds directors decided to close the plant.[153] Taylor, who was working at Bethlehem by that time, protested vigorously, but to no avail.[154] In June, Simonds abandoned the ball bearing business. To Taylor it was a "most worrying thing . . . particularly since I induced so many other people to go in with me."[155] It was also another affirmation of the lessons he had learned about nonmanufacturers at the Manufacturing Investment Company. Fortunately by that time he was able to provide positions for Gantt and others he had lured to Simonds.

Taylor's work at Simonds underlined the fact that scientific management, as applied in the 1890's, often had a substantial impact on the workers, and that in many, perhaps the majority of cases, the effect was negative. Alternately perplexed and intrigued by the intricacies of machine operations, Taylor turned to the workers to achieve immediate results and to justify his presence until more fundamental changes were possible. Though it is impossible to measure the exact toll, or even the number of workers who were discharged, Taylor's papers and writings reveal a harsh, often ruthless approach that culminated in the winnowing of the Simonds inspection force. Such a policy was not inherent in scientific management, as events later demonstrated. But in the 1890's, when Taylor's goal was frequently to salvage endangered companies, the workers were more often the victims than the beneficiaries of scientific management.

In other respects Taylor's experiences at Simonds epitomized his career during the 1890's. Despite numerous obstacles he improved the performance of the factory and his managerial system; by his standards, his work was successful. Yet his success, so clear at the shop level, had little impact on the overall operation of the firm and left the economic benefits of his system in doubt. To a large degree this unsatisfactory paradox resulted from the depressed economy of the mid-1890's. By 1898 when he left Fitchburg for Bethlehem, however, the economic outlook, and presumably his prospects, had brightened. From this point his management system, and his fame, would grow more rapidly, though with no less controversy.

4

Years of Achievement, 1898–1901

In May 1898, when Taylor began to work at the Bethlehem Iron Company plant at South Bethlehem, Pennsylvania, he had more reason to be optimistic than at any time since 1890. He had recouped his fortune, obtained an important new client, and returned to eastern Pennsylvania. Most of all, he was able to apply his system in a climate of economic expansion. It is almost anticlimactic to report that he enjoyed a period of unprecedented achievement and influence at Bethlehem. Yet he was not uniformly successful. He also encountered problems reminiscent of the Simonds years, problems that resulted from his aggressive manner and biases—his growing intolerance of weak and irresponsible business leadership, for example—and from the stringent demands of his work. In the final analysis, however, neither Taylor's successes nor his difficulties determined the fate of scientific management at Bethlehem. Developments in Washington, Philadelphia, and Pittsburgh, more than anything he did in South Bethlehem, accounted for the rise and ultimately the fall of scientific management. Taylor had outlasted the depression; he had not yet gained control of his work or his destiny.

Bethlehem and the Arms Controversy

Taylor's role at Bethlehem was a result of the growth of American naval power and the peculiar dynamics of the domestic armaments industry. The "new" steel Navy of the 1880's had made the Bethlehem company one of the largest U.S. military contractors. By the 1890's it had become the nation's foremost producer of steel gun forgings and armor plate and a leader in the world armaments industry. When this position was endangered, the Bethlehem managers turned to scientific management. From the beginning Taylor was hostage to the uncertainties of an often capricious and unstable industry.

Bethlehem's position in the armaments industry was an outgrowth of its earlier response to the evolution of the U.S. steel industry. Under Joseph Wharton, the principal owner, Garrett B. Linderman, the general manager, and John Fritz, the plant superintendent, Bethlehem had been a leading manufacturer of rails for a quarter century. By the early 1880's, however, the company operated at an increasing disadvantage vis-à-vis the Pittsburgh-based rail producers because of its dependence on western ore and coal supplies. Fortunately new opportunities appeared with the rise of steel shipbuilding, the growth of expansionist sentiment in Congress, and the naval-building program of the 1880's. Supposedly, it was Fritz who concluded that the company could "sell a small amount" of armor plate for "hundreds of dollars per ton instead of a large amount in the shape of rails for tens of dollars per ton."[1] In 1886 Navy Secretary William C. Whitney, reflecting congressional sentiment for U.S. manufactured steel, advertised for bids on armor plate and ordnance from U.S. companies. In early 1887 Wharton submitted a successful bid. There are contradictory accounts of the affair, but it is clear that Whitney and Wharton cooperated closely on the project.[2]

Even before they had secured the order, Bethlehem representatives had negotiated with leading British and French manufacturers to buy modern machinery. Navy Lieutenant William Jacques, operating as an advisor to the company, purchased a complete forging plant from Joseph Whitworth and Sons of Manchester, England, and armor plate equipment from Schneider and Company of LeCreuset, France.[3] Since the Navy "expected the same method to be followed," the Bethlehem executives installed the Schneider system for forging armor plates under an enormous steam hammer rather than a rolling technique they preferred.[4] To supervise the new departments they hired Jacques and Russell Davenport of Midvale, two of the small number of American engineers with experience in the ordnance field. The first Bethlehem gun forgings were completed in the fall of 1888; armor plate deliveries did not begin until 1892, more than two years after the date specified in the original contract.

The Navy's advertisement for armor plate bids also interested the nation's leading steel manufacturer, Andrew Carnegie, who had briefly considered Whitney's initial proposal. In 1890 he was more receptive when Benjamin Tracy, Whitney's successor, reopened negotiations after Bethlehem failed to complete the armor plate contract on schedule.[5] In November the Carnegie Company agreed to manufacture armor plate for the Navy at the Bethlehem price and made its first deliveries in December 1891.[6] After 1892 both Bethlehem and Carnegie supplied the government with armor. The work was highly profitable, and relations between the two steel companies and the Navy Department were harmonious. By 1895 Bethlehem and Carnegie were "turning out the highest grade armor in the world."[7]

The Bethlehem armaments plant, appropriately, was one of the most impressive specialized steel mills in the world. Located next to the Bessemer works and rail mill along the Lehigh River, it consisted of a 1,155 foot open hearth and forging building, an 846 foot hammer shop, and a 1,250 foot machine shop, the largest in the world.[8] The equipment that Fritz installed was equally impressive. The open hearth furnaces were built with "extra-ordinary care."[9] The Whitworth machinery was "equal in design and execution to similar machinery built new for their own works," making the Bethlehem plant superior in many respects to the Manchester factory.[10] The hammer plant featured a 14,000 ton press, "the largest tool of its class in the world," and an enormous 125 ton, 90-foot-high steam hammer, also the world's largest.[11] The giant machine shop was the "most impressive" of all the Bethlehem structures. "It is traversed from end to end by railroad tracks, and is commanded by two 75 ton and one 30 ton pneumatic crane[s]. It contains lathes, planers, boring mills, slotters, shapers, of which a number are of exceptional size."[12] Engineers flocked to Bethlehem to be guided through the remarkable facility by H. F. J. Porter, Bethlehem's premier salesman.

Before the mid-1890's a proposal to reform the Bethlehem works would have astonished the Bethlehem managers. Though Linderman had died and Fritz had retired, neither the company's reputation nor its substantial profits had suffered under their successors, notably Linderman's son Robert, who became president in 1890. A succession of crises, however, soon raised doubts about the future of the armaments market and the Bethlehem complex. The first of these was a widely publicized scandal at Carnegie's Homestead plant in 1893. Employees in the armor plate department had carefully prepared plates for the government inspectors so the department's output as a whole appeared to be better than it was. When Navy Secretary Hilary Herbert learned of the fraud, he levied a substantial fine on the Carnegie company.[13] Insignificant by itself, the scandal had wider and more serious implications.

To congressmen, Navy officials, and engineers it suggested the possibility of widespread dishonesty by the manufacturers, since the inspectors had been easily duped and the department had been under the immediate control of Charles M. Schwab, Carnegie's trusted lieutenant.[14] To big business critics the incident confirmed suspicions of corporate arrogance, dishonesty, and mismanagement.

Spurred by the hostile reaction, Secretary Herbert in 1895 demanded a reduction in the price Carnegie and Bethlehem received for armor plate. When the manufacturers refused, Congress authorized an investigation of armor plate costs. To their consternation the lawmakers discovered that Bethlehem had sold armor to the Russian navy for $250 a ton at the same time it was selling armor to the U.S. Navy for $600 a ton. To make matters worse, when Herbert went to Europe in 1896 to study armor plate costs, he learned that agents from the American companies had convinced the European firms to make no damaging disclosures. Charges of an international arms conspiracy were added to the indictment against the manufacturers.[15]

For the next year and a half relations between the manufacturers and the government remained in this uncertain state. In 1897 Herbert recommended a price of $400 a ton for armor plate, but Congress reduced the figure to $300 and ordered a study of the feasibility of a government-owned plant. When Carnegie and Bethlehem refused to bid at $300 per ton, John W. Long, Herbert's successor, appointed a naval inquiry board, which met from August to December 1897. During this period the outlook for the manufacturers was hardly encouraging. At best, they could anticipate a substantial reduction in the contract price; at worst, competition from a publicly owned plant. Carnegie, who was much less dependent on government orders, offered to sell his armor plate works at cost.[16] In December, however, the Navy board estimated that a new plant would cost nearly $4,000,000, twice what the congressmen had expected and close to the manufacturers' estimates of their investment. The Navy board report dampened congressional enthusiasm for public ownership, and the war with Spain in April 1898 encouraged a compromise settlement. In May 1898 Congress set the price at $400 a ton; Carnegie and Bethlehem agreed to new contracts.[17]

A second, related conflict exacerbated tensions within the industry. Schwab became president of the Carnegie Company in 1897 and embarked on an aggressive campaign to increase Carnegie's share of the arms market. After the 1898 compromise with Long he demanded a larger percentage of the armor plate business as his "price" for not bidding against Bethlehem's gun-forging contracts. This ultimatum, in turn, produced a threat from Midvale. If Schwab bid on gun-forging contracts, Harrah warned, he would bid on armor plate; if Schwab backed down, so would he.[18] Meetings between Schwab, Harrah, and Linderman in the summer of 1898 failed to resolve the dispute. Finally, after extended discussions, Linderman and Schwab settled their differences. Bethlehem conceded Schwab a larger share of the armor plate business, then attempted to intimidate Midvale with low bids on gun forgings. Harrah, undaunted, retaliated by bidding on armor plate in 1900.[19] In the meantime Congress again reduced the price of armor plate to $300 a ton in 1899 and appropriated $4,000,000 for a government plant in 1900. Faced with this threat, the manufacturers accepted an armor plate price slightly above the 1898 compromise price and ended their rivalry.[20] By 1901 equilibrium had been restored and competition declined.

Throughout these complicated events Linderman appears to have been the least capable of the three company heads.[21] A small-town businessman who had inherited his wealth and position, he lacked the boldness and imagination of Schwab or Harrah. Thus, when the government demanded lower prices for armor plate, he sought ways to reduce production costs. When Schwab and Harrah raised the specter of an anti-Bethlehem cabal, he again took the defensive. Outmaneuvered by Schwab, he unsuccessfully challenged Harrah. By the spring of 1901, harassed and probably dispirited, he was ready to sell his interests to the imperious Schwab.

During the period of Bethlehem's rise as an armaments manufacturer, Davenport and Taylor had maintained their personal and professional relationship. In the early 1890's Davenport invited Taylor to visit the Bethlehem works on at least one occasion, but Taylor apparently was unable to make the trip.[22] Davenport also requested copies of Taylor's ASME papers and information on his consulting jobs.[23] But until the government demanded a lower price for armor plate, his letters suggest only the curiosity of a friend and fellow engineer.

In 1897 the situation changed. Faced with Herbert's demands and a hostile Congress, Linderman turned to his subordinates for advice. Davenport, noting costly bottlenecks in the forge and machine shops, recalled Taylor's Midvale achievements. H. F. J. Porter, who had heard Taylor read "A Piece Rate System" and had been deeply impressed, added his endorsement.[24] Linderman was initially cool to their suggestions, apparently fearful of confrontations between Taylor and the plant executives, who were either relatives or personal friends. But he was eager to reduce costs and agreed to consider Taylor's ideas. In November he authorized Davenport to contact Taylor "in connection with the proposed establishment of [a] piece work system in our machine shop."[25]

In the following months Taylor cautiously explained his system to the Bethlehem executives. In December he met both Linderman and Wharton; the latter, he reported, was shocked to learn that the men would earn higher wages. Only when Taylor explained that the men would also work harder, that his methods called for "really hustling piece work," was the elderly capitalist reassured.[26] Having successfully crossed this hurdle, Taylor expanded upon his original statements. On January 4 he warned Linderman that "before piece work can be successfully introduced," it would be necessary to take "entirely out of the [workers'] control" many "details connected with the running of the machines and management." Moreover, "a careful study of each type of machine should be made so as to ascertain its driving and feeding power . . . and a table should be made for each machine which indicates the best cutting speed, feed, etc. for doing work as well as the time required to do it." He also emphasized the need for "a good assistant" to "study the time problems of the shop" and fix piecework rates. Taylor cautioned that his work would generate controversy and that the directors must be convinced of the "desirability of piece work since otherwise any effort to introduce it would likely fail."[27] In mid-January he sent his most significant addenda. He explained to Linderman that "the whole method of putting orders into the shop and the inspection and payment for the work, and of making up your labor returns, must be overhauled and improved before Piece Work can be introduced." The entire process would require "nine months to two years," depending on the "tractability of your men" and the "energy of the foremen and assistants."[28]

Taylor's strategy worked brilliantly. After Wharton's initial protest the Bethlehem executives did not question the increasingly grandiose character of Taylor's "piece work" system. Despite his initial skepticism, Linderman demurred without complaint. On January 6, 1898, he wrote that he had discussed the plan with the directors and believed Taylor would "obtain the hearty cooperation of all the members of the Board."[29] The conflict with Congress was the principal reason for this endorsement, but Taylor's presentations had helped his case substantially. If he had revealed the exact nature of scientific management in December 1897, Linderman and Wharton probably would have rejected it at once. By January, however, he had won their confidence and could be more candid. Once again the value of "A Piece Rate System" and the approach he had adopted in it were apparent. In late January the Bethlehem board formally approved Taylor's proposal, and in May he arrived at the Bethlehem plant. Like Wharton and Linderman, the managers were cooperative. The superintendents and foreman, Taylor wrote, were very "favorable," "agreeable," and "progressive."[30] "But as you know," he added prophetically, "talk is cheap."[31]

Systematizing Bethlehem

Taylor's first year at Bethlehem, which coincided with the Schwab challenge and the renewal of the congressional conflict, was the most fruitful of his career. Linderman and the plant managers were cooperative, even friendly. The townspeople, Taylor recalled, were "much more agreeable than those in the other small towns in which we have been quartered," and the Taylors' home became a center of Bethlehem society during the winter of 1898–99.[32] In the plant Taylor boldly exploited his advantage. Supposedly preparing for the introduction of piecework, he attempted to install scientific management throughout the works. By early 1899 he could point to important technical and organizational achievements. "The beginning," he observed, "was as successful as I had expected."[33]

Taylor devoted the summer of 1898 to a study of the plant and the preparation of reports spelling out his recommendations for change. In part, this was a technique to familiarize himself with a factory so vast that, as he confessed, "it is very difficult to know where to start."[34] It was also a way to confront two unresolved issues: the scope of his activities and the status of the current managers. From the beginning Taylor thought in terms of the entire plant rather than the machine shop or the employees. His first report to Linderman emphasized the importance of "standards throughout the works."[35] He was equally aggressive in his dealings with the executives. On June 21 he reported to Linderman that "the worst blemish" was "the almost entire absence of a high order of cooperation" among the managers and departments. Aware that his presence was an affront to General Superintendent Owen F. Leibert and his assistant, Robert H. Sayre, he decided to challenge them immediately:

> Your general superintendent is called upon not only to look after
> the large general interest of the works, its future progress and
> development, but also manufacturing, and his office is situated so
> far away from the departments in which the greater part of your
> manufacturing takes place as to render frequent consultations be-
> tween him and the heads of the departments difficult.[36]

To correct this situation he proposed to divide the general superintendent's duties and appoint a "Superintendent of Manufacture":

> Under his supervision should be the piece work rate fixing, the wages of the workmen in the manufacturing departments, the direction of the laying out of the departments, the estimate of the cost of new work, and the making of promises for dates of delivery, together with the cost keeping. He and his assistants, clerks, etc., should be located in the centre of the manufacturing departments, and he should have no duties which would take him away from these departments.[37]

After a survey of various candidates he announced, probably to no one's surprise, that Davenport was the only executive qualified for the new post.[38]

As Taylor expected, Leibert and Sayre opposed his proposal, particularly the transfer of their power to Davenport. The latter was, in their opinion, "entirely unfitted" for the post, "a disorganizer instead of an organizer."[39] Under other circumstances their judgment might have proven fatal to Taylor's plan, but in 1898 their influence was limited. Linderman and the directors agreed to Taylor's proposal, and in July Davenport became superintendent of manufacture.

Shortly thereafter Taylor conducted a similar purge in Machine Shop No. 2. Despite the machine shop's renown there was a constant backlog of work, and output per man was low. Taylor argued that the problem was identical to the larger problem he had just confronted. Harry Leibert, machine shop superintendent and brother of the general superintendent, had too much responsibility and, like his brother, neglected his managerial tasks.

> Mr. Leibert is held responsible not only for the performance of one set of duties which require him to be a skilled mechanic (namely, turning out the best quality of work), but also for another set of duties which require him to be a first class clerk (namely making and keeping accurate promises for delivery), and also for a third set of duties which can only be properly accomplished by a mathematician with one or more clerks to assist him (namely, getting the largest possible output from the machines).[40]

Taylor proposed to remove Leibert's managerial responsibilities (his second and third "sets of duties"), leaving him only the power to suggest "the best method of turning out good and cheap work."[41] Linderman again deferred to Taylor's judgment. Leibert retired rather than accept demotion, and E. P. Earle, his assistant, and in Taylor's opinion a "first rate" man, became the new superintendent.

Taylor then recommended a variety of organizational changes. He called for the appointment of functional foremen and for "minor physical changes" affecting the "smaller engineering elements" in the machine shops. The latter were, in fact, his metal-cutting innovations and belt maintenance methods. He proposed the construction of a new building to house the planning department, the extension of functional foremanship to other departments, and a new cost system. While requiring a "considerable expenditure of money," these changes would prepare the way for the introduction of "the best type of piece work."[42] Linderman agreed to most or all of these suggestions; Taylor's later reports mention specific approval for soda water to cool machine tools, functional foremanship, the planning department, Taylor's cost system, and the respeeding of the machinery.[43]

Working under the beneficent aegis of Davenport, Taylor introduced scientific management in Machine Shop No. 2 in early 1899. Beginning in February he assigned two assistants, Joseph Welden and James Kellogg, to respeed the machine tools. Taylor taught them "the art of making, grinding, and dressing tools," so they would not be dependent on the regular smithshop employees.[44] When the machine shop supervisors, perhaps reflecting Leibert's influence, objected to this work, Earle came to the assistants' aid. Due to his "tact and good management . . . in inducing several of [the] foremen to cooperate," Kellogg and Welden continued their activities without interference.[45] Taylor also assigned another assistant, E. B. Lewis, to reorganize the toolroom and stores system.[46] Unfortunately, Taylor's papers do not explain why he omitted these important reforms from his initial recommendations or what the nature of the final arrangements was.

Taylor also introduced functional foremanship in the machine shop. After regrouping the machinery, he gave the supervisors specialized assignments:

> One Foreman will . . . show his men how to prepare the work for the machines and to run the machines; another man will see that the work is done in the proper order of precedence; another that proper tools are provided for the work; another that the machines are pulling the heaviest possible cut and running at the highest speed practicable; another that the machine is kept in proper condition and the belts kept tight, and capable of pulling their maximum cut, while still another will study the shortest time in which work can be done and fix piece work rates.[47]

In early June, Taylor added a limited form of production planning. This was confined to one group of lathes selected for the "simple duplicate work they handled."[48] Working under Gantt's supervision, Welden made slide rules indicating the proper speed, feed, depth of cut, pulling power, and time required for each machine operation. Kellogg and Welden then devised instruction cards and assigned the functional foremen to "see that they are lived up to."[49] By mid-summer this part of the machine shop operated under a reasonably complete system of scientific management except, of course, for a piecework plan.[50]

Over the next two years Taylor's shop reforms of early 1899 gradually evolved into the system of production planning and functional supervision that he described in "Shop Management" (1903). Welden, Kellogg, Lewis, and others completed the reorganization of the machine tools, toolroom, storeroom, and accounting systems. Taylor refined his time and instruction cards, as well as his mnemonic system for classifying materials and machines. By 1901 he had recruited a full complement of planning department officials—production, route, balance of stores, instruction card, time study, order of work, recording, and cost accounting clerks—to direct the activities of the machinists and to assist the forty to fifty functional foremen.[51] Gang bosses were responsible for all preparatory operations, and speed bosses for all steps "from the time [the forging] is in the machine . . . until the job is completed and the machine stopped." The department superintendents or "general foremen" acted as "disciplinarians."[52] The cumulative effects of these changes were so great that Gantt later characterized the Taylor system at Bethlehem as overly elaborate and "autocratic."[53]

By 1901 Machine Shop No. 2 was the world's most modern factory and potentially a prototype for manufacturers and engineers in other industries. Yet for various reasons it never received the recognition or scrutiny it deserved. Most notably, Taylor's technical triumphs overshadowed the significance of his other achievements. He had resumed his metal-cutting studies in late 1898 and by early 1899 had confirmed his reputation as an inventor of the first rank. By contrast, the gradual transformation of the machine shop commanded little attention. Taylor's relations with the old guard managers also tended to obscure his work in Machine Shop No. 2. In 1899 Liebert and Sayre launched a determined campaign to regain control of the plant. The ensuing struggle inevitably diverted attention from the work of Welden, Kellogg, Lewis, and the others. Lastly, Taylor's post-1901 promotional strategy led him to neglect the machine shop in his autobiographical writings and speeches. A major reason for this strategy, ironically, was his failure to undertake the final step of the machine shop reorganization, the introduction of piecework.

Innovation and Conflict, 1898–1900

With Linderman's approval Taylor began to improve the "smaller engineering elements" of the machine shops in the fall of 1898. His initial effort was to standardize the cutting tools used in the plant. Five years before, at the Cramp Shipyard, he had studied the relationship between different alloy steels and tool performance and had concluded that Midvale "self hardening" chromium alloy steel was superior to other makes. At Bethlehem he resumed these tests in an attempt to determine whether a better steel had appeared in the intervening years. Performing the lathe work himself, he decided by mid-October that the Midvale steel was still preferable to other brands and should be used for all Bethlehem machine work. At that point, however, he suffered what proved to be a significant setback. Maunsel White, the Bethlehem metallurgist, recalled:

> In order that all of the men in the works most interested in this subject should be of the same opinion regarding the choice of a standard Mr. Taylor arranged to have an experiment made in the presence of a number of the superintendents and foremen of the works. In this experiment the tools made from Midvale Air-Hardening Tool Steel instead of proving to be better than the other makes of steel were shown to be considerably worse than any of the rest.[54]

Taylor was embarrassed and perplexed. To ascertain what he had over-looked, he obtained Davenport's approval for a "carefully tried experiment . . . to determine the effect of heating Midvale Self-Hardening Tool Steel at different temperatures."[55]

With White's assistance Taylor reheated four Midvale tools that had performed poorly in the earlier tests. He raised the temperature of each tool progressively above the recommended level until he reached the melting point. The effects of these treatments, apparent in tests between October 31 and November 4, were extraordinary. With each increase in temperature tool performance improved. The third and fourth tools, which were heated 300° to 400° higher than recommended, could be operated at speeds twice as fast as conventional tools. Taylor and White thus "invented" high speed tool steel, perhaps the single most important machine tool innovation of Taylor's lifetime.[56]

Taylor devoted much of his time during the winter of 1898–99 to high speed steel. He, White, and other associates conducted more tests and devised equipment to treat and cool the steel, to measure temperatures, and to adjust machines to the higher speeds permitted by high speed steel tools.[57] Taylor also pursued his metal-cutting studies with a new urgency. In the summer of 1899 he persuaded Linderman to employ Carl G. Barth, a draftsman and mathematician Wilfred Lewis had known at the Sellers Company, to carry on the research at an accelerated pace.

Linderman permitted these activities because of the obvious and immediate impact of high speed steel on Bethlehem's machine shop operations. The tool steel tests were expensive—Taylor later estimated their cost at $100,000 by 1900, not including patent fees and costs—and could be justified only in terms of larger savings in production expenses. The surviving records do not indicate any attempt to measure those reductions, but Taylor claimed that the savings more than compensated the company for his experiments, and Linderman apparently believed him.[58] Taylor and Gantt, disagreed on whether high speed steel eliminated the "bottleneck" in Machine Shop No. 2.[59] Both men, however, agreed that it advanced the effort to standardize machine shop operations by making uniform tools possible for the first time.

Engineers and businessmen soon discovered that high speed steel created problems, as well as opportunities. To take full advantage of the new tools, it was necessary to redesign the machines in which they were used. It was also desirable to install speed-changing devices and electric motors.[60] In short, high speed steel lost much of its value if introduced in isolation. This fact limited its dissemination in the early twentieth century to large and progressive firms that could afford expensive alterations in their machine shop operations.[61]

The discovery of high speed tool steel had a substantial impact on Taylor's career. It increased his stature among engineers, spurred additional inventions, and advanced his metal-cutting investigation. Two other effects were even more important in the long term. The money he received from the sale of the high speed steel patents was the largest single increment to a fortune that provided the financial base for the diffusion of scientific management. As he wrote, he "intended to exploit" the discovery himself, but "finally concluded that the Bethlehem Steel Company could do it much better." The $50,000 that Bethlehem paid Taylor and White for the U.S. patents and the substantial sums they received from foreign sales seemed to confirm the wisdom of this decision.[62]

Equally important, the interest that high speed steel generated among engineers and manufacturers projected Taylor into the role of propagandist for his work, anticipating his "second" career. To recoup some of the company's investment, Linderman and Davenport sold "shop rights" to interested manufacturers. Taylor directed this operation,

which involved a lecture and demonstration at the Bethlehem plant.[63]
He wrote that he had a "daily string of visitors" to Machine Shop
No. 2.[64] By 1900 more than one hundred such "visitors" had witnessed
the demonstration, and a substantial number had bought the rights. In
late July 1900 Taylor conducted a special session for journalists—
including a photographer from the *American Machinist*—which was
enthusiastically reported.[65] At the Paris Exhibition in August, Bethlehem sponsored a high speed steel exhibit, which also attracted widespread attention. Dwight Merrick, a young engineer Taylor had
employed to assist him with the metal-cutting experiments, was in
charge of the Paris display, but Taylor also went to Europe to negotiate
with several large firms that were interested in purchasing rights to the
invention.[66]

In his formal presentations Taylor always used the same format. It
included a history of his and White's efforts, an account of their remarkable results, a practical demonstration, and, if the customer desired, a
contest between Taylor-White and conventional tools. He pointedly
corrected any suggestion that the discovery had been an accident rather
than the result of systematic experimentation.[67] Taylor was equally
insistent that no one but he, White, and presumably Merrick was qualified to explain the process. When the secretary of the Franklin Institute
inquired whether other Bethlehem engineers could discuss the discovery, Taylor answered with an emphatic no. "Of course," he added,
"they can read what is written about it in the patent but this would not
allow them to explain . . . what has been done and answer the questions
which would undoubtedly be asked."[68]

In the meantime Taylor continued his metal-cutting investigations, at
least when the experimental lathe was not being used to impress potential customers. In late 1898 or early 1899 he employed S. L. Griswold
Knox, a mathematician at Lehigh University, to help Gantt devise an
improved procedure for calculating the appropriate speed, feed, power,
and machine times for machine tool operations. By the spring of 1899
they had invented an "especially made slide rule accompanied by
diagrams" to perform these tasks quickly and accurately.[69] Joseph
Welden began to make slide rules for the machines. Barth took over this
work in June 1899 and soon refined and extended the innovations of
Knox, Gantt, and the others. By the end of the year he had prepared
slide rules for thirteen of the largest lathes in Machine Shop No. 2.
Taylor was ecstatic. At last he had a way to determine proper machine
tool methods. Control of the metal-cutting machinery, the most elusive
element in the machine shop enviroment, was within his grasp.[70]

High speed steel and Taylor's other technical innovations were also vital ingredients in the politics of the reorganization process. On the one hand, they enhanced Taylor's reputation and enabled him—at least in 1899—to initiate his organizational reforms with a minimum of opposition. On the other hand, the technical discoveries underlined the open-endedness of the company's commitment to Taylor. An outsider might reasonably question whether metal-cutting studies were a necessary prerequisite to the introduction of piecework. More important from Linderman's perspective was the expense of the metal-cutting experiments. Bethlehem presumably would profit in the long term, but it was the present that was so troublesome. And what if Taylor's subsequent experiments did not result in profitable inventions? Beset with such concerns, Linderman began to waver in his support for scientific management. While publicly endorsing Taylor's efforts, he became more attentive to Leibert and Sayre, his demoted aides. The other Bethlehem managers quickly sensed his hesitancy. Taylor bitterly complained that it was virtually impossible to recruit assistants from the Bethlehem staff.[71]

Even in early 1899, when Taylor was publicly unassailable, Leibert and Sayre found ways to frustrate his plans. Their principal weapon was their control of the engineering department, which was charged with major construction and repair projects. Through it they could delay the implementation of reforms that required changes in the plant layout. Furthermore, by holding back Taylor's projects, which required substantial expenditures, they could pose as the true friends of economy. In this situation Taylor was effectively limited to two responses. He could appeal to Linderman, or he could utilize the limited resources at his disposal to outflank his enemies.

Taylor's appeals to Linderman brought mixed results. When the issue was a proposal that Linderman had already approved, Taylor was usually successful. For example, when Leibert and Sayre refused to help with the installation of the "smaller engineering elements" in Machine Shop No. 2, Taylor sent Linderman a strongly worded attack on the engineering department. Presumably as a result, he reported at the end of May 1899 that Leibert and Sayre had "at last . . . set about speeding up the shop and introducing soda water in earnest."[72] Conversely, when the issue was a new—and costly—commitment, Linderman was more likely to side with his subordinates. In such cases Taylor's conflict with Leibert and Sayre often evolved into a confrontation with Linderman. The first such dispute arose over Taylor's staff. In February 1899, when he had five or six men working for him, he requested fifteen or twenty more.[73] By May, Linderman had approved only one additional assistant. When Taylor requested salary increases for White, Earle,

Kellogg, Welden, Sidney Newbold, another assistant employed in the metal-cutting experiments, and others, he again received little satisfaction.[74] By October his patience had worn thin.

> You have not in your employ anything like the number of trained and skilled men (of the type of Kellogg and Welden) which are needed to properly systematize and run your works. . . . No adequate effort has been, or is now being made, to get new men, and some of the most important of the old men, to whose training the writer has given a great amount of time and attention have been taken away by other Works who offered them more salary.[75]

Complaining of poor wages and widespread dissatisfaction among the supervisory workers, Taylor issued a lightly veiled threat to resign.[76] Although Linderman's exact response is unknown, he must have made some concessions. Taylor was temporarily mollified, if not satisfied; in this case, at least, his strategy had succeeded.

Perhaps as a result of Linderman's concessions, Taylor made a final concerted effort in late 1899 to win (or retain) the support of the plant executives. In a long speech to the assembled managers he tried to explain his objectives. The highlight of the talk was a list of "fundamental principles underlying good management":

> Each man in an establishment, high or low, should be subject to the following conditions: 1. the result or object which is to obtain should be clearly defined and within the scope of his ability, 2. he should be given the opportunity to accomplish this result including the necessary authority and undivided responsibility, 3. in case of success he should feel certain of receiving full credit and adequate reward, 4. in case of failure he should receive full blame and appropriate punishment.[77]

This was Taylor's first suggestion that management could be reduced to a body of principles. Unfortunately, it did not have the same positive effect that a somewhat different set of "principles" would have on countless audiences in later years.

While Taylor overlooked no opportunity to buttress his position and hold Linderman to his commitments, he also sought to show that he could succeed without the managers' cooperation. He urged his assistants to do what they could in Machine Shop No. 2 and other departments. By 1900 the results, as noted earlier, were highly satisfactory. Yet Taylor's principal effort to outflank his opponents occurred outside the metal-working departments; indeed, it was only tangentially related to the reorganization effort. It was, however, a predictable move. Frustrated and impatient, Taylor turned almost instinctively to the one area of opportunity that remained—the unskilled laborers who performed the back-breaking manual labor jobs that abounded in the plant. Was there any difference, he might have asked, between the restrictions imposed by adverse economic circumstances and those imposed by shortsighted men like Linderman? As resistance to scientific management mounted between 1899 and 1901, Taylor increasingly looked to the laborers to demonstrate the efficacy of his methods. Unlike the machine shop reorganization or the metal-cutting experiments, he did not find this task particularly interesting or intellectually challenging. It was an expedient, a way to combat his enemies.

Taylor and the Bethlehem Workers, 1899–1901

When he went to Bethlehem, Taylor had every intention of introducing the differential piece rate at any early date. Apparently his plan was to bring Thompson to Bethlehem for a few weeks to train other men.[78] He did not do so in 1898 or early 1899 for two reasons, one practical and one emotional. The first was the progress of his metal-cutting experiments, which promised to make the calculation of accurate machine times a reality. It would be foolish to undertake time studies that would have to be redone in a few months. The second consideration was the character of the work. Taylor's principal task at Bethlehem was to reorganize a large and complicated machine shop, not a paper mill, motor assembly plant, or grinding department. The distinction was crucial to a man who had devoted much of his time and creative talents to improving machine tools and machine shop processes. Technical obstacles notwithstanding, Taylor was at first reluctant to adopt the expedient tactics that he had used in other industries. After mid-1899 it was too late; his conflicts with Linderman delayed and ultimately prevented the introduction of the differential piece rate in the machine shops. In the meantime, Taylor introduced an incentive wage for the laborers that bore little resemblance to the system he had described in "A Piece Rate System" and had intended for the machinists.

Taylor decided to introduce piecework at Bethlehem in early 1899, the period when he began to complain to Linderman of Leibert's and Sayre's obstructionist tactics. The association was not coincidental. As Taylor encountered resistance in the metal-working shops, he looked to the plant yard, where the work was "so crude and elementary," as he later recalled, that "an intelligent gorilla" would be as useful as the East European immigrants who toiled there.[79] The laborers were the poorest paid and least efficient of all the Bethlehem employees. Supposedly they did only one-third to one-fourth as much as comparable laborers at other plants.[80] Under these circumstances Taylor believed it would be relatively easy to demonstrate the value of scientific management at minimal cost. Since the work did not warrant Thompson's services, he brought James Gillespie from the Simonds Company. Gillespie began time studies of laborers in the open hearth department in early February.[81]

At first Taylor assigned this activity a low priority. His conflict with Leibert and Sayre was still in its formative stages, and his concern for Gillespie's future was an important secondary reason for initiating time studies in early 1899. As a result he was easily diverted from his original plan when unforeseen events created a slightly different opportunity. In February the price of pig iron rose sharply, and Bethlehem sold 10,000 tons which had been produced several years earlier and stored on land adjacent to the plant.[82] When Davenport dispatched a group of laborers to load the iron on railroad cars, Taylor persuaded him to put them on piecework. Together with Hartley C. Wolle, a veteran Bethlehem supervisor, Gillespie began the introduction of piecework on March 11.[83]

Employing time study techniques Gillespie had learned at Simonds, they first attempted to ascertain the maximum output of the nineteen or twenty "Hungarians" who composed the gang. On March 13 Gillespie and Wolle selected ten of the "very best men" and ordered them to load a car "at their maximum speed." Working at that rate, each man loaded the equivalent of seventy-five tons per day, nearly six times the previous average of thirteen tons. The men, however, were exhausted after filling only one car. Additional observations confirmed the conclusion that seventy-five tons per day was the theoretical limit. "From this amount," Gillespie and Wolle reported, "we deducted 40 percent for rests and necessary delays and set the amount to be loaded by a first class man at 45 tons per day." Why they selected 40 percent as an appropriate deduction "for rests and necessary delays" is unclear; presumably it was a "rule of thumb" decision.[84]

Gillespie and Wolle took their findings to Taylor on March 15. After consulting Davenport and other officials, he set a piece rate of 3.75¢ per ton, a rate that would enable a "first class" pig iron handler to earn $1.68 a day, the average wage of the 3,100 employees (including supervisory workers) at Bethlehem in 1899.[85] The day rate for laborers was $1.15, so a man who loaded forty-five tons would receive a 46 percent wage increase. In view of Linderman's concern about costs this was, at least on the surface, a bold move. Did Taylor emphasize that few men would actually earn the "first class" wage? Did he point out that men who merely doubled their former output (twenty-six rather than thirteen tons) would earn 91¢ per day, or 21 percent less than the going rate? Either point presumably would have assuaged Linderman's anxiety. In any case, Taylor did not set a second, lower rate, the distinctive feature of the differential piece rate. This probably seemed unnecessary since the pig iron loader whose output was not at least two and a half times the former average would earn less than $1.15. Taylor believed that the promise of parity with the other Bethlehem workers would encourage the laborers to exert themselves. He did not actually expect them to earn $1.68; in fact, he anticipated that most of them would earn less than their customary $1.15. Essentially he planned to "drive" the pig iron loaders, much as he had driven workers during the depression years.

Gillespie and Wolle assigned the ten "best men" to piecework starting the next day, March 16. After initial objections the laborers consented. But when Gillespie and Wolle arrived in the morning, they found the men working with the rest of the gang. The laborers had refused to follow orders, and neither the foreman nor his supervisor wanted "to take the responsibility of discharging so many men." When Gillespie and Wolle told the laborers that "having promised to load by the piece . . . they could not work on any other terms," the men "quit work." Exasperated, Gillespie and Wolle summarily discharged them and began to consider other, presumably less capable, men. However, on

> their way to the time office [the ten laborers] were met by Mr. Robert Sayre, Jr. Ass't Gen'l Supt., who having inquired what the trouble was, told the men to wait at the Scale House until he had looked into the matter. He stated . . . that he feared a strike would follow the discharge of these men and that he wished to consult the General Superintendent, Mr. Owen Leibert (Mr. Davenport being absent) before taking any further action.[86]

Taking his cue from Sayre, Leibert ordered the men to rejoin the gang "until the return of Mr. Davenport when the matter could finally be settled." This was surely an unprecedented move. At Bethlehem the foremen ordinarily hired and fired. The wholesale discharge of machinists or other skilled workers might have warranted the attention of the plant superintendent, but the discharge of laborers was a different matter. They were transients, easily replaced and powerless. Sayre's professed concern about a strike was hardly credible. A strike was unlikely and, if it did occur, would be no more than a temporary inconvenience, a matter for the foremen to settle. Clearly, Sayre intended his action as a rebuke to Taylor and his nefarious management system. There is no account of the meeting between Leibert and Davenport, but, having made their point, Leibert and Sayre did not press the issue. After the meeting Sayre told Gillespie and Wolle to fire the men if they refused "to work by the piece." On March 17 Gillespie and Wolle "again asked each man individually if he was willing to load by the ton, and as each and every man refused they were given their discharge and paid off the same morning."[87]

The incident nevertheless had the desired effect. What had begun as a simple demonstration of the promise of scientific management had become a complex and uncertain undertaking. Sayre's intervention emboldened the laborers, legitimized their instinctive resistance to "driving" methods, and, it could be argued, covertly sanctioned continued opposition. The laborers had little in common with Leibert and Sayre, but for the moment their fates were intertwined. As a result, there developed "a strong prejudice on the part of the [other employees] against [the] piece work system."[88]

For the next month and a half this "prejudice," coupled with threats by the discharged workers, made it difficult for Gillespie and Wolle to find candidates for the laborers' jobs. Taylor's assistants did not attempt to introduce piecework again until March 30; when they did, the "majority of men" selected "either did not report for duty at all or worked only one day."[89] To circumvent the "Hungarians'" influence, Gillespie and Wolle attempted to recruit Pennsylvania Dutch or Irish workers, with no better success. In the prevailing climate of suspicion and hostility the promise of a higher wage was insufficient. In April, Gillespie and Wolle finally capitulated. Besides the higher wage they promised to treat the pieceworkers in "a liberal way," giving them "work of a higher description" when they were tired or hurt. This was an unprecedented concession. As news of it spread, opposition declined, and laborers began to volunteer for piecework. By the middle of May, Gillespie and Wolle "had little difficulty in obtaining men for the work."[90]

They did have difficulty finding "first class" men, however—an indication of the ominous meaning of that term. On March 30, for example, they recruited seven men from another gang. Of the five who reported for work, only Henry Noll (whom Taylor was later to make famous as "Schmidt") proved to be a "first class" worker. A small, vigorous man, Noll was apparently unaffected by the antagonism of his fellow workers or the rigors of his vocation.[91] Other laborers joined Noll during April and May, but he was the only one who remained on the job until the end. Gillespie and Wolle reported that they had hired forty men by the end of May, but found only three "first class" men and ten others who "can make a fair day's wages." Most of the rest, they added, "break down after two or three days."[92]

Despite the paucity of volunteers and "first class" men, Taylor began to accumulate the type of data he had sought. From March 30 to May 31 the cost of pig iron loading under piecework averaged 4.8¢ per ton, as opposed to more than 8¢ per ton under day work. Gillespie and Wolle set rates "covering all the conditions for loading iron" and improved the lot of the able workers. Noll, for example, averaged between $1.35 and $1.70 per day. Workers who were unable to maintain the pace received less taxing assignments that were better paying than their old yard labor jobs. Those who refused piecework or in the opinions of Gillespie and Wolle did not make a genuine effort lost their jobs altogether.[93] Thus, while the project proved more difficult and time consuming than Taylor had anticipated, the results were gratifying. At a time when relations between Taylor and the old guard managers were increasingly factious, the pig iron loading episode provided a welcome vindication of scientific management. In later years Taylor always mentioned it in his recollections of his Bethlehem experiences.

Yet, in retrospect, the most striking feature of the incident was not its demonstration of the efficacy of scientific management, as Taylor claimed, but the casual, unsystematic nature of the rate-setting procedure. Gillespie, a relatively inexperienced man, and Wolle, a novice, timed the men for several days and concluded that seventy-five tons minus 40 percent for "rests and necessary delays" was the task of the "first class" worker. Taylor then arbitrarily set a rate that would enable the "first class" pig iron handler to earn the average wage of all the Bethlehem workers. Although the differential piece rate was not introduced, the rate Taylor set for the pig iron handlers was in effect the "high rate," and the yard labor rate was the "low rate," since Gillespie and Wolle discharged or transferred workers who did not make at least that much. Taylor probably adopted this approach because he considered the work relatively unimportant, and because it preserved the principle of a high premium rate and a low penalty rate and thus, like the conventional differential rate, "scientifically" selected or eliminated workers.

Taylor later claimed that pig iron loading also provided an answer to his quest for a scientific relationship between the workers' physical exertions and their output. In early April 1899 Taylor asked Gillespie and Wolle to consider the problem, using their pig iron data. In response they prepared a table, based on the records of the three "first class" men, "showing the amount of energy expended under different conditions of height and distance reduced to foot pounds." They concluded, however, that the major variable was "the ability and endurance of the man to lift a certain number of pigs, irrespective of the walk or height," and that Taylor's theory "was not applicable to work of this particular character."[94] Gillespie and "three or four others," Taylor recalled, "wanted me to give that up, but I was sure the thing was there."[95] Seven months later Taylor asked Carl G. Barth to conduct new time studies. Barth returned "in a great state of excitement," having discovered a "law of heavy laboring": "that for every load that [a] man carries on his arms he must be free from load a certain percentage of the day and under load only a certain percentage. That is to say, a man carrying a [ninety] pound pig can only be under load 42% of the day. He has to rest 58 percent of the day."[96] This "law," in fact, had no more substance than the other "lessons" of pig iron handling that Taylor cited in his writings. Except for the percentages of rest and work, it was little more than Gillespie and Wolle's common sense observation that some "rest" was necessary. And the proportions were only "rule of thumb" estimates. As Charles D. Wrege and Amedeo G. Perroni have noted, they were averages based on a number of dissimilar observations.[97]

Though the pig iron episode ended in early June 1899, its apparent success spurred Taylor to reorganize other groups of unskilled workers. This activity produced more evidence of Taylor's ability to reduce unit labor costs, but little improvement in his position. One reason for this disappointing result was a variety of problems that delayed the work and thus the positive consequences that Taylor sought. Another, more serious, was the fact that his achievements had less and less impact on Linderman. By 1901 the new equilibrium in Washington and the continuing conflict in the plant were more important to the Bethlehem president than the labor-cost statistics that Taylor generated in ever more prodigious quantities.

In May 1899 Gillespie and Wolle resumed the work that Gillespie had started in the open hearth department the previous February. By July they had set a rate that enabled the "best 10 men out of a gang of 40" who unloaded ore to average more than $2.00 per day.[98] The reason for the two month delay was apparently the problem of finding "first class men" to take the places of the original ore loaders. A high wage of $2.00 meant that the successful laborer received an increase of 70 percent or more. Taylor may have been more generous than usual, but he surely demanded that a "first class" worker triple his output. Even if he expected the other thirty men to earn only $1.60 or $1.70 per day, a substantial number of new employees must have been required.

In the following months other problems also slowed the project.

Gillespie and Wolle left in July for better paying jobs, and their successor, Atherton B. Wadleigh, a Lehigh graduate and a Taylor acquaintance, "had not before handled this class of labor" and had to be "taught the art of determining how much work a first class man can do in a day."[99] Taylor also insisted that the time studies be done carefully and thoroughly. His caution was understandable; instead of a handful of men he now was dealing with several hundred (by his count as many as 600). Moreover, he expected the rates set by Wadleigh to be permanent—"to last," as he suggested in one statement, "perhaps for twenty years."[100]

Another reason for the delay may have been the opposition of Leibert, Sayre, or even Linderman to reductions in the yard labor force. Like Gillespie and Wolle, Wadleigh laid off men who could not earn the de facto "low rate."[101] Taylor later recalled a confrontation with his adversaries over this practice:

> I got into a big row with the owners [*sic*] of the company on that labor question. They did not wish men, as they said, to depopulate South Bethlehem. They owned all the houses in South Bethlehem and the company stores, when they saw we were getting rid of labor and cutting the labor force down to about one-fourth, they did not want it. They came to me and said so frankly, "We don't want that done." I said "You are going to have it, whether you want it or not, as long as I am here. You employed me with the distinct understanding that is what I was going to do. You agreed to it, and got me here for that purpose."[102]

There is no evidence that Taylor "depopulated" South Bethlehem.[103] But it is conceivable that Linderman and other plant officials urged restraint in this area while demanding cost reductions in others. In any event, as Taylor noted, "it was . . . of great importance not to fall down on any line in the labor business. I therefore had every one of those data come to me personally to fix."[104]

Relatively little information about the actual rate setting process has survived. Wadleigh presumably recorded the workers' times (including "rest" periods) and then combined his observations to find an optimum time for a particular type of work. Taylor did not indicate how he determined the rates, or whether he again used the average wage of all employees at the plant as a goal for the "first class" man. He did summon Sanford Thompson to Bethlehem in the summer of 1900 "to instruct us in the art of working up timed observations."[105] There is no evidence that he or Thompson attempted to shift to the two rate system; they probably reasoned that the "first class" group was so small that a specific penalty rate for the others would destroy morale and precipitate new conflicts. Wadleigh apparently studied shovel sizes, but the other aspects of the "science of shoveling" remain a mystery.

Taylor's retrospective accounts provide the only documentation for other activities—the calculation of optimum shovel loads, the construction of a toolroom to store the shovels, the creation of a labor office to plan the laborers' work, and the establishment of a detailed record system which indicated to each man whether he had earned the de facto "high rate."[106] Taylor proudly proclaimed that he had eliminated covert opposition among the laborers; yet he also admitted on several occasions that individuals inexplicably "forgot" how to shovel.[107] In 1912 he recalled that a "teacher" had helped men who failed to earn the high rate.[108] But the teacher, like the "science of shoveling," was most likely a product of later wishful thinking. If the experiences of the pig iron handlers were indicative, the Bethlehem "teacher" simply applied the "appropriate remedy," which in most cases was dismissal. Taylor's statements that the workers were contented and friendly toward the management must also be discounted, if only because he had no way of determining their sentiments.[109] His assertions that the laborers were (or became) sober responsible citizens—"Many if not most of them were saving money, and they all lived better than they had before"—cannot be confirmed or denied on the basis of existing data.[110] The Bethlehem management had long emphasized these qualities.[111] Perhaps it was only irony that Henry Noll, whom Taylor admired for his self-discipline, later lost his job and home because of excessive drinking.[112]

If the reorganization of the yard laborers was less innovative and important than Taylor later claimed, the results were nevertheless impressive. During Taylor's final year at Bethlehem (April 1900–April 1901) yard labor costs were 3.3¢ per ton of material handled as opposed to 7.2¢ per ton under day work. On the averrage, the men handled three times as much material and earned 60 percent higher wages than formerly, figures that again imply a large turnover in the labor force.[113] Noll had made only $1.72 per day in early June 1899, while the laborer who received a 60 percent increase in 1900–1901 presumably earned $1.84. Since there was no indication of resistance (except perhaps by managers who owned South Bethlehem real estate and by workers who "forgot" their jobs), the workers apparently accepted their fates with resignation. Once more, it appears, Taylor had demonstrated the effectiveness of the ad hoc "driving" methods he had developed in the 1890's.

Still, after nearly three years at Bethlehem, Taylor had not demonstrated his ability to elicit greater output from the workers who really counted. Moreover, he showed no inclination to initiate time studies in the machine shops. According to Gantt he had no immediate plan to install the differential piece rate as late as March 1901.[114] Taylor never explained this delay, but it was most likely the result of his strained relationship with Linderman, which forced him to spend much of his time defending himself and his work when, presumably, he should have been devoting his attention to the machinists. Whatever the exact reason, the delay meant that the differential piece rate was never introduced and that few machinists or other machine workers were involved in the reorganization of the Bethlehem labor force. Equally important it meant that the effort to extend scientific management to the workers in the metal-working shops occurred under Gantt's aegis rather than Taylor's.

Despite the introduction of high speed steel, production planning, and functional foremanship, Gantt was dissatisfied with the performance of Machine Shop No. 2. The workmen, he wrote, "would run their machines at the feed and speed called for, but . . . it seemed impossible to prevent them from losing time between operations." When approached, each man "could give a more or less plausible excuse why his machine was not running." In short, "no matter how efficiently the machines were run . . . the men found good excuses for taking more than the prescribed time on every job, and for wasting enough time to hold down the output of the shop very materially."[115] Gantt studied this problem for several months before concluding, as Linderman might have suggested, that piecework was the solution. In early 1901 he discussed his idea with Taylor, who agreed that some action was desirable. In March, Taylor approved Gantt's proposal for a temporary bonus plan to remain in effect until the differential piece rate could be introduced. Neither Taylor nor Gantt ever mentioned time studies, but Barth's slide rules and Wadleigh's experiences presumably insured that these studies were more accurate than those Taylor had used to set rates at Midvale. By mid-May the operators of twenty lathes engaged in roughing operations were working under the bonus, and the productivity of the shop had increased substantially.[116]

Gantt's bonus plan was a variation of the differential piece rate, similar to the scheme Taylor had introduced in the yard. In a 1901 ASME paper Gantt described it as a less stringent and imperfect form of Taylor's incentive wage.[117] "Task work with a bonus" provided a "high" rate for workers who completed the job assigned by the planning office and a "low" rate for those who failed, for whatever reason. The "high" rate was comparable to Taylor's premium rate and was earned for output two to four times above the previous norm. The "low" rate was simply the worker's day wage. Gantt's contribution was the more humane treatment of the workers who failed to earn the high rate.

Whereas Taylor, Gillespie, and Wadleigh penalized workers who would not or could not earn the high rate, Gantt, like Halsey, did nothing.

As a result, Gantt conceded, the incentive did not operate automatically. His assistant in Machine Shop No. 2, C. H. Buckley, described the methods they used to encourage the workers:

> When he [the worker] receives his instruction card he glances at the time allowed for each operation and the total time to finish the piece. He then begins a mental calculation based on his work experience with similar work, the result of which is, *'Impossible'*. A very stupid observer can readily see this stamped on his countenance.
>
> If this is the man's first introduction to the system, we rarely try to convince him of the accuracy of the instruction card, but the next morning will approach him and get him to perform a few of the operations with the stop watch in plain sight. In a short time he sees that nothing unreasonable has been asked, and will nearly always start from that moment working with a good will; when once he earns a bonus we experience no further trouble.[118]

Acknowledging that his approach was imperfect, Gantt permitted the workers to improve the system if they could. "For the moral effect," he allowed machinists to disregard the instruction cards and attempt the assigned tasks by other methods.[119] If they succeeded, the planning office revised the instruction cards. At the suggestion of one of the Bethlehem supervisors, Gantt also introduced a bonus for the functional foremen based on the number of their subordinates who earned the bonus.[120] "The next and most obvious step," he added, "is to make it to the interest of the *men to learn more than their cards can teach them.*" Though "no entirely satisfactory method . . . suggested itself," he considered rewards for workers who proposed new ideas or developed new techniques.[121] Increasingly, Gantt's wage system became something more than the stopgap measure it had been in 1901.

In Machine Shop No. 2 the task and bonus plan was an immediate success. Machine times were cut, in some cases almost as much as Taylor's innovations had cut the pre-1898 times. According to Gantt, the machinists accepted the task and bonus with enthusiasm.[122] Although only a handful of men were involved, Taylor and the Bethlehem managers must have been impressed. Under more propitious circumstances it is likely that the task and bonus would have been extended to other departments, perhaps to the entire works, fulfilling Linderman's original expectations and Taylor's promise.

In the meantime, however, Taylor's standing at Bethlehem had continued to decline. The cost of his work and the conflict with Leibert and Sayre were all contributing factors, but external developments were decisive. The 1900 truce between the steel manufacturers and the government temporarily relieved the pressure for internal economy, and Schwab's overtures to Linderman and Wharton suggested a permanent solution to their anxieties. Sensing that events which he could not hope to control were irrevocably undermining his position, Taylor became angry and irritable. By March 1901 he had decided on a showdown: either he would obtain the authority to proceed unhindered or he would resign. He met Wharton and another director in Bethlehem in late March and apparently presented his demands. He subsequently stated his position to Linderman on April 4. His only interest, he explained, was in matters "immediately affecting" the installation of scientific management, but in those areas he insisted "that the various officers of the Company be instructed to carry out all orders which may be given by me in relation to those subjects."[123] Taylor then left for a golfing vacation while Wharton and Linderman considered his fate. It is unlikely he was surprised when, on April 17, Linderman terminated his contract effective May 1.

Gantt, Barth, and the other assistants soon found their positions equally untenable. After Taylor's departure Gantt proposed to introduce instruction cards in Machine Shop No. 3 and in the smith shop as a prelude to bonus work. Apparently trying to continue Taylor's activities and yet distinguish his work from his mentor's, Gantt wrote that "the system . . . is distinctly my invention. . . . Nobody now in this works has given the subject a fraction of the thought that I have."[124] But Linderman paid no attention. As Taylor's lieutenant Gantt was no longer welcome. Barth fared no better. Both men and most of the other assistants left Bethlehem in the summer and fall of 1901.

One month after Taylor's exit Wharton and Linderman sold Bethlehem to Schwab, who subsequently developed it into the country's second largest steel producer.[125] Taylor's departure, however, was at least as important. It marked the end of his consulting practice and, in most respects, the creative phase of his work. But it also signaled the beginning of a new career, radically different in character from his earlier work. Frederick W. Taylor, the inventor, engineer, and developer of scientific management, became Taylor the publicist, educator, and social reformer.

Synthesis, 1901

In May 1901 Taylor's personal attack on the first factory system came to an end. In later years he subsidized metal-cutting and time study research and assisted his followers in other ways, but he never resumed his consulting practice or embraced techniques he had not tried at

Bethlehem. As far as he was concerned, scientific management was complete and, within relatively narrow limits, fixed. To Taylor it encompassed five broad categories of managerial reforms.

First were the preliminary measures, mostly refinements of systematic management procedures, that logically preceded Taylor's more distinctive innovations. These included his purchase and stores methods, developed at the Johnson Company in 1896; tool standardization and toolroom reorganization, which he began in the 1880's; and machine layout and design, improved belting, and belt maintenance methods, likewise results of the Midvale years. Taylor's accounting methods, which he developed in 1893, also fall into this category because of their similarity to other contemporary accounting plans and their importance to Taylor's career in the 1890's.

Second was a production control system based on a specific planning department. Though production control measures were common to most systematic management plans, Taylor's approach, with its separate office, corps of clerks, bulletin boards, detailed instruction cards, and numerous forms, was far more thorough and complex than most others. Of his key innovations, the planning department is unquestionably the least well documented. A product of his work at Midvale, Johnstown, and Fitchburg, its exact evolution is uncertain.

The third category, functional foremanship, was a unique feature of Taylor's approach to systematic management which evolved after 1882. Though functional supervision was a novel answer to the deficiencies of conventional foremanship, Taylor did little to perfect his innovation. The speed boss, for example, was strictly a machine shop functionary, while the "disciplinarian" was, by the standards of contemporary personnel management, an anachronism.

Fourth, stopwatch time study, was another distinctive aspect of scientific management that Taylor invented by 1883 and developed sporatically in the following years. Despite Thompson's research, the experiences of Gillespie and Wolle suggest that Taylor's time study methodology was no more "scientific" in 1901 than it had been in 1889.

Finally, there were the incentive wage plans, the differential piece rate, introduced in 1884, and the task and bonus system, devised in 1901. Taylor later attempted to distinguish his and Gantt's wage plans from Halsey's and others that did not rely on time study or a single "high" rate, but the similarities are more striking. Both Taylor and Halsey believed that men worked largely or wholly for pecuniary rewards and would work harder for more money; both eschewed more complex "paternalistic" approaches to worker satisfaction, such as welfare work. Both, in short, operated within the framework of systematic management. In practice, Taylor's expedient approach, his frequent disregard for time study, and his use of the incentive wage as a "driving" technique also resembled the tactics of businessmen who—despite lip service to the goal of solving society's ills—introduced the incentive wage to increase labor productivity.

In spite of occasional acknowledgements of intellectual debts, Taylor always believed—and argued—that scientific management was a product of his personal experiences in the 1880's and 1890's. An inventor and an engineer rather than a philosopher or an intellectual historian, he never fully understood the extent to which he and his work were products of the *fin de siècle* technical and political environment. Thus he failed to distinguish between systematic and scientific management or to realize how his antipathy toward big business led him to neglect the larger organizational and financial aspects of business administration. In later years he always prefaced discussions of his innovations with accounts of his experiences at Midvale, Simonds, and Bethlehem rather than analyses of the late-nineteenth-century management movement. Taylor's parochial outlook helped account for the controversy associated with his post-retirement career, controversy that became most heated when he characterized scientific management as a "partial solution to the labor problem."

5

Taylor and American Industry, 1901–1911

When he left Bethlehem, Taylor recalled many years later, he "stopped working for money," he "retired."[1] In fact, Taylor "retired" only in the sense that he ceased to work for other men. His departure from Bethlehem marked the beginning of a more complex but equally demanding career. Though his dominant interest continued to be the operation of American industry, his approach became more varied. Now he dealt with the heads of firms on a more equal basis, as an investor, inventor, and authority on shop management. His experiences enhanced his understanding of the contemporary economy, improved his public relations skills, and led him to reexamine the role of the consultant. Above all, they enabled him to become the best-known spokesman for systematic management and the leader of a dedicated group committed single-mindedly to the introduction of a new factory system.

An Enterprising Rentier

Taylor's "retirement" was possible because of the fortune he had made in the 1890's and enlarged in the following years. His investment income was the basis for his varied activities, the sine qua non for his new career. Yet Taylor was not, perhaps could not be, a mere rentier. He had always taken a personal interest in his investments. After 1901 he became more aggressive than ever. Common stocks promised higher returns than bonds, providing he purchased the shares of well-managed, profitable corporations. Eager for the maximum return to finance his retirement projects, Taylor typically opted for equities and vigilance, if not direct involvement. He became an activist investor, an enterprising rentier. For the first time since 1893 his involvement in American industry transcended shop management.

Although the exact amount of his fortune is unknown, it is clear that Taylor had become a wealthy man by 1900. In the following years his annual income was often close to $50,000, and his estate amounted to approximately $700,000 in 1915.[2] He had never been poor; his investments in the Manufacturing Investment Company and Simonds Rolling Machine would not have been possible on his Midvale salary. Yet he later claimed that he had earned all his money except for a $10,000 bequest from his mother's estate, which he received in 1905.[3] His son believes that Taylor rejected his share of his father's estate, which amounted to approximately $900,000 at the time of Franklin's death in 1910.[4] In any case, Taylor's family ties did have an important effect on his finances. His close association with the Clarks, particularly Clarence M. Clark, gave him access to up-to-date financial information and opportunities for promising investments that a less fortunate, but equally enterprising, individual would not have enjoyed.

Initially, Taylor's earnings derived from two related sources, his consulting fees and his inventions. His standard fee for introducing scientific management was $35 per day plus expenses, a substantial amount for the 1890's. In 1899, probably his peak year, he earned more than $9,000 from fees alone.[5] In addition, he supposedly received large sums for acting as referee for several industrial pools in the mid-1890's.[6] The Taylors lived simply and saved much of the money he received from these sources. They augmented their savings with the proceeds from patent sales and licensing agreements. High speed steel, Taylor's best-known and most successful discovery, earned him at least $40,000 by mid-1901 and probably much more before the Taylor-White patents were canceled in 1909.[7] Other inventions such as his grinding machine were less important and less profitable. Altogether he had probably made $60,000 from his patents by the time he left Bethlehem.[8]

The bulk of Taylor's fortune, however, resulted from the appreciation of securities he had purchased during the 1890's. As his resources grew, Taylor developed a twofold investment strategy. He continued to put substantial sums into enterprises that interested him and that he hoped to influence. In 1903, for example, he invested more than $20,000 in the Tabor Manufacturing Company, which his friend Wilfred Lewis had recently joined. As an apparent quid pro quo Lewis agreed to introduce scientific management.[9] More common was a second type of investment, intended simply to make money. Clarence M. Clark often apprised Taylor of promising opportunities, and Taylor, in turn, advised other friends. Maunsel White, Sanford Thompson, and George F. Steele eagerly sought his counsel, more perhaps because of his ties with the Clarks than his financial acumen. Clark and Taylor, and in many cases other relatives or friends, frequently invested as a syndicate. Most of their efforts were amply rewarded.

The securities Taylor selected in the 1890's were usually those of growing firms in new industries. He later recalled that he had invested his money in speculative ventures with the hope of windfall gains.[10] Yet his reliance on Clark, his careful management of his portfolio, and his refusal to borrow for stock and bond purchases hardly suggests a gambler's approach. His favorite securities were mining and street railway company common stocks. Taylor's shrewdest purchase was Flat Top Coal Land Association common stock, which he had bought in large quantities at prices ranging from $15 to $65 and sold several years later for $165 a share. His profit was more than $150,000 and probably closer to $250,000.[11] Still, he was not uniformly successful. Catskill Cement Company common stock, in which he invested nearly $30,000 declined in value when the company failed to pay dividends.

The best illustration of Taylor's second type of investment and the methods he devised to protect his capital and indirectly his retirement activities was his extensive role in the "Copper Skyrocket" of "Colonel" William C. Greene.[12] A wily Arizona miner and rancher, Greene created a mining empire in Cananea, Mexico, in the 1890's and became a flamboyant Wall Street personality. His mines' potential and his apparent recklessness soon attracted rivals, most notably the industry giant, the Amalgamated Copper Company. A dramatic Wall Street battle ensued with the fast-moving, fast-talking Greene pitted against the Copper Trust.[13] Taylor, who had little respect for promoters and absentee owners but even less regard for big business corporations, developed and retained the "greatest confidence in old man Greene."[14] Convinced that Greene's mines in Cananea, Mexico, "are the largest, richest, and cheapest to operate of any that are known anywhere," Taylor began to purchase Greene Consolidated Copper Company common stock in mid-1900.[15] By late 1901 he owned 2,300 shares and anticipated additional purchases. For years he believed that the stock he had bought at prices between $12 and $40 per share would reach $100 or $150 per share.

In October 1901, when a bear raid by Amalgamated Copper interests depressed the value of his Greene Consolidated holdings, Taylor interviewed the Colonel at length and received an optimistic report on the Cananea property and the company's facilities for smelting and refining ore. Apparently he did not realize that he had merely heard Greene's standard pitch to potential investors. But neither was he so naive as to accept the Colonel's statements at face value. Taylor reported to a confidant that he had "spent a great deal of time looking this up and have a friend down at the mines with his own copper chemist to go over the mines thoroughly to satisfy himself that they were as represented."[16] He did not reveal the identity of his friend, but the results of the inspection seemed to confirm the Colonel's positive assessment. "The only cloud in the sky at present," Taylor concluded, "is the question of supplying the money necessary to finish the plant."[17]

Having confirmed the wisdom of his original decision, Taylor sought to eliminate that single cloud. Before the price decline he had invested with Clark; now he solicited funds from a variety of former business associates. As he explained to Steele:

> Just before the copper scare enough stock was subscribed for at between $40.00 and $50.00 to furnish ample funds for completely finishing the plant, but owing to the copper scare a lot of timid holders backed out and refused to take up their allotments. . . . Just at present a number of us are getting up a syndicate to furnish the required money to completely finish the plant. . . . We know that [the stock] can be had at $20.00 and possibly lower, but we consider the purchase a phenomenal good one at $20.00 providing we buy enough to supply ample funds to completely finish the whole thing.[18]

By the end of the year Taylor's friends had purchased nearly 5,000 shares of Greene Consolidated.

To this point there was nothing unusual about Taylor's actions. Like any scrupulous investor, he had demanded more detailed information about the company when his capital seemed in jeopardy. Until the end of 1901 this step, coupled with some independent checking, seemed adequate. Indeed, Taylor's scrutiny made him even more enthusiastic about the company. But Taylor had misjudged Greene's Wall Street enemies and, perhaps more importantly, the Cananea management. Customary methods of safeguarding investments were inadequate in the frenzied climate of the "Copper Skyrocket."

Several months after Taylor's conclusion that the "only cloud" was a shortage of capital, the skies over Cananea became considerably grayer. The Amalgamated Copper campaign, reports of managerial incompetence at Cananea, and delays in getting the new concentrator and convertor plants into operation sent the price of Greene shares plummeting. Worried stockholders apparently forced Greene to install Anson W. Burchard as general manager at Cananea in an effort to reverse the situation there.[19] Burchard proved himself a capable administrator, but no friend of the Colonel, and left in less than a year.[20] To complicate the situation further, copper prices declined precipitously in early 1902, diminishing the company's profit margin.

Taylor was profoundly shocked by this sudden turn of events. The decline in Greene Consolidated stock prices was bad enough; the breakdown of his effort to monitor Greene's operations raised fundamental questions about the investment and about his ability to safeguard it. His uncertainty was apparent in a letter to other members of his "syndicate."

> I spent a good deal of time during the past three weeks in thinking over and trying to study into the affairs of the Greene Consolidated Copper Company. The showing at the mines during the month of January, as nearly as I can find out, was the poorest that has been made for the last four months. . . . I went over to New York twice last week for the purpose of bringing the matter to a head and making up my mind whether it would not be very much wiser for us all to sell out immediately at least a portion of our holdings. The last time I was there however I was shown the daily smelter returns for the month of February, and these are very much better than they have ever been before. The treasurer of the company told me that he was having no difficulty whatever in financing the balance of the construction. Both he and Greene however have lied to me so many times about all sorts of matters that I can place no reliance on what they say. I had fully made up my mind to sell out at least a portion of their holdings. . . . At present I have personally made up my mind not to sell until later in the spring, if I do at all. It would seem as though the stock ought to go higher when the returns for the month of February are published. It would also seem as though there ought to be a further rise as soon as the convertor plant is started. This they expect will start about April first. I have no idea however when it will really start. The only fact which I feel certain of about the property is that the mines themselves are exceedingly large and rich. Beyond that I hardly feel sure of anything.[21]

Perhaps it was the anticipated rise in Greene Consolidated prices, the emergence of Burchard, or simply a reluctance to admit defeat, but Taylor decided by early March not to sell his shares or to advise his friends to abandon the Colonel. Whatever his reason, he was in no mood to permit a recurrence of the disasters of January and February. Clearly a new intelligence strategy was in order.

In characteristic fashion Taylor soon identified the deficiencies of his previous effort and devised a more satisfactory approach. First, he resolved to maintain a closer and more critical watch over Greene's New York operations. While confident of Greene's entrepreneurial abilities, he recognized the need to separate fact from fancy in the Colonel's statements. As he noted to a confidant, Greene "lies consistently to any man in the East. The extent of his lies is in every case only limited by what he thinks the other man will swallow."[22] Taylor prepared to harass Greene officials until he obtained the truth. Second and more important, he decided to install his own operative in Cananea. No longer would he rely on superficial inspections by acquaintances; the new man would be a full-time spy.

Taylor implemented his new plan in the spring of 1902. For his part he made frequent trips to New York. "To get at the truth to any extent," he reported, "it takes me at least a whole day and sometimes two days."[23] His technique was anything but subtle. "After persistent cross-questioning of Greene and Berolzheimer [the treasurer] and after getting them to contradict themselves over and over again," he noted, "they came out with the flat truth about the affairs of the company outside of Cananea."[24] To keep abreast of conditions in Cananea and obtain the all-important cost figures, Taylor depended on his Bethlehem time study expert, Atherton B. Wadleigh. Taylor had brought Wadleigh to Greene's attention in early 1902, probably in conjunction with the reorganization that brought Burchard to the fore. Greene employed Wadleigh to introduce time study and an incentive wage at the mines and smelters. Whether Taylor considered Wadleigh a spy at that time is unclear from their correspondence; probably he did not. His goal most likely was to secure a promising position for a devoted follower and to improve the Cananea management. If so, he revealed a better understanding of the Cananea situation than Greene or the local managers. Had Wadleigh performed the function originally assigned to him, it is conceivable that the famous "Cananea incident," the strike and riot by Mexican workmen in June 1906, might have been averted.[25] In any event, Wadleigh was "dependable and trustworthy" and could be relied upon for a variety of services.[26]

Wadleigh arrived at Cananea in March to find that the local authorities were less interested in improving the labor situation than Greene and Taylor. He reported optimistically that he had been "treated with the greatest consideration" and that "as long as Mr. Greene is . . . for it everyone else is sure to be."[27] Yet his expected assignment did not materialize. His one contact with the workers was of a very different character. In May 1902 he was in Denver on company business when a strike of construction workers halted progress on the plant. When the Greene managers were unable to find local men to replace the strikers, they wired Wadleigh to send men from Colorado. Despite opposition from the Denver unions, Wadleigh recruited forty-nine men who took the strikers' places and ended the dispute.[28] His superiors were pleased, but still did not authorize time studies or an incentive wage. They assigned Wadleigh to an office job and disregarded the workers. Perhaps it was fitting that Wadleigh's last important service for Greene Consolidated was to command the men who guarded the Colonel's house during the 1906 riot, a direct result of the chaotic and discriminatory wage system.[29]

Almost from the day of his arrival Wadleigh sent Taylor detailed assessments of the Cananea operation and management. On March 10, for example, he reported that "all the work is being done in good style and . . . there is an enormous quantity of fine ore in sight. . . . I tell you, Mr. Taylor, I think that this is a wonderful property and . . . I am inclined to think that it is very well managed."[30] Burchard, he wrote, was "a first class man" who "has done much in straightening things out"; James Kirk, a superintendent, was "hard working," "efficient," and yet "unassuming."[31] On the other hand, J. T. Morrow, Burchard's successor, "utterly failed to make good."[32] Equally important for Taylor's purposes, Wadleigh sent data on costs and earnings. By the summer of 1902 he had become Taylor's secret agent.

Wadleigh's role obviously required caution and discretion. Taylor repeatedly warned him against any action that might compromise his position. In October, for example, he devised a special safeguard.

> If the expenses . . . amount to more than $295,000 . . . then write me a letter stating that they amount to so many dollars more than stated. If they amount to less than $294,000, write me a letter stating that they amount to so many dollars less than stated. In case such a letter as this were opened or were to fall into the wrong hands, no one would be any the wiser.[33]

Taylor was also careful to protect his operative in the East. Most of the syndicate members probably never knew why their information improved so rapidly after March 1902. Yet on occasion Taylor could not resist the temptation to gloat: "My present figures," he wrote one of his fellow investors, "are the only ones [in] which I have ever had much confidence, and my reason now for feeling any greater confidence than in the past comes from the fact that my information does not come through either Greene or Berolzheimer."[34]

By circumventing Greene, Taylor soon confirmed what he had suspected: the enterprise was sound, and its future promising. In late 1902 Taylor bought an additional 900 shares of Greene Consolidated and urged his friends to increase their holdings. Confident that the price would go at least to $100 per share, he concluded that "the stock is a very much better investment now than it ever has been in the past."[35] Surely, it seemed, he had triumphed in his contest with the wily and disingenuous Greene.

Taylor may have bested the Colonel, but he failed to consider the other critical factor in the equation, Greene's Wall Street enemies. This proved to be an all-important error. As a consequence, Taylor was perplexed when Greene Consolidated fell to $10 a share in late 1903, distressed when it failed to return to its former price, much less $100 per share, and positively astounded when Amalgamated Copper interests deposed the Colonel in early 1907. Neither Taylor's nor Wadleigh's activities provided an explanation for these events. Even after Greene's fall, the takeover of Greene Consolidated by Amalgamated Copper, and a financial settlement favorable to the Greene stockholders, Taylor remained confused. As late as January 1908 he talked of organizing a counterattack against the new management.[36]

In the end Taylor was sadder but presumably wiser for his experiences. When customary methods had failed to safeguard his investment, he had innovated. Yet like most nineteenth-century investors he had assumed that the company's profits depended on the quality of its resources and its management; his task he had believed, was simply to penetrate the wall of secrecy erected by Greene and his subordinates. Having successfully confronted Greene, he discovered, to his surprise, that his victory was meaningless. Like the Colonel, he had underestimated the new role of corporate power in the American economy. Though his error was not costly, it affected his outlook and activities. By reinforcing his long-standing suspicions of big business and Wall Street it made him more receptive to the appeals of the anti-big-business critics who had appeared since the turn of the century. Within a year after the Colonel's fall Taylor began work on *The Principles of Scientific Management*, an essay that marked his emergence as a "progressive."

Return to Philadelphia

There was never any question that Taylor would undertake his "retirement" in Philadelphia. He had never been happy in other settings, and Louise's discomfort, from all indications, had been much greater. By 1901 family ties and the mystique of Proper Philadelphia exerted a near-irresistable pull. A final, possibly decisive consideration was Louise's health. Taylor wrote in the summer of 1900 that she suffered from a "lack of nervous energy" and reported in early 1901 that she was "recovering from another painful illness.[37] Though she apparently improved after their departure from Bethlehem, these problems either initiated or foreshadowed the severe emotional disturbances that would later mar her life. Her illnesses, together with the "regular strain due to introducing new methods," had "overworked" Taylor's nerves and were responsible for his own "very poor health."[38]

In the fall of 1901 the Taylors returned to Philadelphia, ostensibly to begin anew the life they had left in 1890. They rented Red Gate, a large home on School Lane near Cedron, where Clarence and Mary Taylor Clark and their children now lived, rejoined the Unitarian Society, and reestablished contacts with old friends and relatives. Sunday afternoons were spent with Franklin and Emily Taylor. The Clarks, and less often the Edward Taylors, were regular guests at Red Gate (like Franklin, Edward had become a nonpracticing professional man; Frederick and Edward, however, were never close after their Exeter Days). In late 1901 the Taylors acquired a family, the three orphaned children of William and Anna Aiken, relatives of Louise's who died in a well-publicized murder-suicide. Apparently the adoptions were Taylor's idea; at least he seems to have shown far more interest in the children than Louise. He insisted that Elizabeth, Kempton, and Robert—aged ten, eight, and six, respectively—all use the middle names Potter Aiken, their mother's and father's family names.[39] (An older boy, Conrad Aiken, was not adopted and became a well-known poet and literary critic.) To outsiders it must have seemed that the Taylors had had children of their own during their years away from Philadelphia.

In other respects the Taylors' return marked a break with their pre-1901 lives. In late 1901 they purchased an eleven-acre estate in Chestnut Hill, an exclusive area northwest of Germantown.[40] Located on a ridge overlooking the Wissihickon Valley and Fairmount Park, "Boxly" included a large house, which became the servants' quarters, and a magnificent, though neglected, garden, which provided the major technical and scientific challenge of Taylor's later years. Taylor immediately commissioned a new house and began to reorganize the garden. The house, Georgian in style and elaborately furnished, contrasted strikingly with the substantial but conservative homes of their Germantown friends and relatives. Louise was largely responsible for the grandeur of the Boxly mansion, but Taylor also indulged himself.[41] The garden and grounds, which ultimately cost far more than the house, were his province. It is unlikely that any other garden in Philadelphia, perhaps in the United States, received such intensive or expensive care from its owner.

Boxly became the focal point of Taylor's creative energies after 1901. When he wrote in 1910 that "investigation, or rather invention, is a mental dissipation . . . a very great amusement, rather than a labor," he referred to his gardening experiments, not to his metal-cutting studies or scientific management. Gardening, he added, was "an innocent outlet to my tendency to dissipation in the speculative field in which no one is hurt except myself. Any money I choose to put in it, or any time, is at my own expense, and even if no results follow no company is hurt."[42] Beginning in 1902 he completely reorganized the garden, devising novel methods for transporting the ancient boxwood shrubs, which were its outstanding feature. In the following years he refined these techniques and used them to transplant a variety of trees and shrubs. He also experimented with greenhouse techniques, and began a series of extensive tests to determine the best types of grass for golf greens. Robert Bender, who had been a gardener for the Sayres in Bethlehem, became the head of Taylor's garden staff. Bender had a half-dozen assistants, and Taylor periodically employed ten to thirty other men, in addition to a civil engineer and several nurserymen.[43] The garden and grounds were undoubtedly Taylor's largest annual expense.

Taylor's other hobby was likewise an outlet for his "dissipations." Since 1896 he had become an avid and highly successful golfer. His distinctive swing won him considerable notoriety and several amateur tournaments. He also devised several new pieces of equipment: a two-handled putter that was later banned, a special pitching wedge, and a long whiplike driver that enabled him to outhit taller and stronger men.[44] Taylor tried to play daily, and the family's regular summer and winter vacations were invariably spent at resorts with adjoining golf links.

In contrast, Taylor had little direct contact with the technical work that had previously absorbed his attention. Three factors accounted for this change: his wealth, which freed him from the necessity of personally performing his machine shop experiments; his expanding corps of disciples, who oversaw the investigations he had directed in earlier years; and, above all, his conception of himself as the coordinator and promoter of scientific management. Taylor's new outlook was apparent in his approach to the two types of research that he continued to subsidize. In November 1901, the same month he moved back to Philadelphia, he arranged to resume his metal-cutting experiments at the Sellers Company. But unlike the 1880's when he had supervised the work, and 1894 and 1895, when he had done most of it himself, Taylor now hired Barth to conduct the experiments. He kept in touch with his assistant, eagerly read his reports, and ultimately wrote a massive summary of the studies, "On the Art of Cutting Metals" (1906), but he seldom went to the plant or participated in the work. His role was important, but was confined to organizing the activities of a subordinate.[45] Taylor's relationship with Sanford Thompson and his time study investigations was similar. He had never been directly involved in Thompson's work, so his post-1901 approach, at least on the surface, was not new. Yet there was a change of emphasis. Before 1901 Taylor had depended on Thompson because he did not have time to do the work himself. After his retirement he relied on Thompson because he did not want to be involved.

Taylor soon discovered that his new role had certain disadvantages. Whereas the pleasures of his "dissipations" had offset to some degree the anxieties of patent controversies and negotiations with potential clients, now he had only the problems. Between 1901 and 1910 Taylor spent much of his time promoting his earlier inventions or, more often, resolving disputes over their use. Since the early 1890's he had been engaged in a running battle with the manufacturer of his grinding machine, a conflict that was costly and frustrating and ended only when the Tabor Company took over production of the machines.[46] Taylor's most distasteful experience, however, involved his most successful invention, high speed steel. In 1906 Bethlehem instituted a suit against the Niles-Bement-Pond Company for infringement of the Taylor-White patents. Taylor and White, who had also left Bethlehem, refused to cooperate until they received ample compensation, a demand that was not met until late 1907, when Bethlehem granted them the rights to saws and milling cutters made under the patents. As Taylor indicated, he did not "propose to bother [himself] . . . and possibly injure [his] . . . health in worrying over the affairs of the Bethlehem Steel Co." without adequate payment.[47] Even then, the job was difficult. In February 1908 Taylor reported he had worked to his "extreme limit for four days" making a deposition.[48] "It was one of the most trying ordeals I have had for many years, testifying from morning til night as to facts which were eight or nine years old, and prepar[ing] myself for cross examination."[49] Taylor naturally was outraged when in early 1909 the trial judge struck down the patents, in part because Taylor and White had refused to testify until they were assured remuneration.[50]

To make matters worse, the concessions they received from Bethlehem also became sources of conflict. In 1908 Taylor, White, Sidney Newbold, and Wilfred Lewis, as president of Tabor, had formed a corporation to manage the Bethlehem patent rights and to produce saws and milling cutters under them.[51] However, the arrangement was not profitable, and by 1910 Taylor suspected that Lewis and his Tabor associates were sacrificing his, White's, and Newbold's interests to those of the company.[52]

Taylor's relationship with Sanford Thompson was more satisfactory, though it too involved him in a series of minor controversies after 1901. Thompson had completed the bulk of his empirical work at approximately the time Taylor left Bethlehem, and he had attempted without success to find a publisher for his studies.[53] The exception was his data on concrete construction, a new technology, which John Wiley and Company published as *A Treatise on Concrete Plain and Reinforced* (1905) and *Concrete Costs* (1912). Taylor and Thompson personally arranged for the printing of *Concrete Plain and Reinforced*, which involved them in numerous disputes with the printer, the Plimpton Press of Norwood, Massachusetts. At one point they almost switched to the Williams and Wilkins Company of Baltimore.[54] Yet their ideas, if not their argumentative manner, appealed to the managers of both companies. The Plimpton Press and Williams and Wilkins both introduced Taylor's management methods, illustrating how even Taylor's technical work blended into his larger preoccupation with scientific management.

Promoting Revolution

While Taylor's investments, hobbies, and technical activities absorbed much of his time and resources between 1901 and 1910, they were of distinctly secondary importance compared to his other retirement interest, the promotion of scientific management. For more than a decade Taylor and other engineers had spread the message of systematic management through professional society appearances, trade journals, and consulting assignments. Though they had had a substantial impact, Taylor was dissatisfied. He was harried, overworked, and, despite "A Piece Rate System" and his Bethlehem work, it seemed, unappreciated. Fortunately, his new affluence permitted him to reassess his situation. By the time he returned to Philadelphia, he had decided to try a new approach. If scientific management were to succeed, he would have to convert more businessmen, but equally important, he would have to insure the expert's independence from bureaucratic controls and managerial interference. In the following years he rejected the accommodating attitude of other consultants and sought to promote scientific management on his, not his clients', terms.

Although Taylor left no specific plan for implementing this strategy, it is clear that he envisioned a revised version of his own climb to professional eminence between 1895 and 1901. The crucial step in his rise had been the publication of "A Piece Rate System"; hence the starting point for his new effort would be an expanded and updated description of scientific management.

During 1902 and early 1903, when he was able to free himself from the demands of Greene Consolidated, Boxly, and golf, Taylor worked on a book-length guide to the factory revolution, which he called simply "Shop Management." He wrote very little about this activity, but his occasional comments and the observations of others suggest that there was nothing haphazard about his undertaking. Kempton Taylor recalled that "he could revise, cut down and piece together his manuscript with the single aim of making his meaning clear."[55] His purpose, as Kempton inadvertently noted, was not to incorporate new information or refine his data. It was to prepare the most persuasive statement possible, to make "his meaning clear."[56]

The result was a series of four separate but interrelated essays reflecting Taylor's concerns of 1901 and 1902. First and foremost, "Shop Management" was a report on scientific management, a description of Taylor's innovations and a plea for their implementation. Taylor employed the same outline he had used for "A Piece Rate System." One can almost visualize him cutting "A Piece Rate System" into sections, rewriting each section, inserting new material, and putting the pieces back together in the original order. The work that emerged began with a comment on the factory revolution, described the major features of scientific management, and ended with a discussion of labor unrest and personnel policy. Where Taylor had nothing new to add—on personnel management, for example—he simply quoted from "A Piece Rate System." One consequence of this approach was a remarkably disjointed presentation, especially for a work whose central message was the virtue of system and careful organization. Taylor treated time study in four separate places, the expert's independence in two places, and other features of scientific management in seemingly random and haphazard fashion. He changed topics abruptly, with little or no transition. Another result of this approach was an extensive examination of the labor features of scientific management. The reaction to "A Piece Rate System" had demonstrated that discussions of the labor problem appealed even to engineers. Now Taylor sought to exploit that interest in order to publicize his system in its entirety. However, he was careful to indicate that his answer to the labor problem was time study and the incentive wage, not simply the latter. He devoted nearly 20 percent of the manuscript to "rate fixing," but only a few paragraphs to the differential piece rate and the task and bonus.[57]

Second, "Shop Management" was a statement of Taylor's professional concerns. The most arresting feature of the work was its beginning. In "A Piece Rate System" Taylor had been optimistic, noting the progress of the factory revolution and predicting that competition would force its spread. By 1902 he was less positive.

> We . . . who are primarily interested in the shop are apt to forget that success, instead of hinging upon shop management depends in many cases mainly upon other elements. . . .
> And even in those cases in which the efficiency of shop management might play an important part it must be remembered that for success no company need be better organized than its competitors.
> . . . it is an interesting fact that in several of the largest and most important classes of industries in this country shop practice is still twenty to thirty years behind what might be called modern management. . . .
> In these industries, however, although they are keenly competitive, the poor type of shop management does not interfere with dividends, since they are in this respect all equally bad. . . .
> It would appear, therefore, that as an index to the quality of shop management the earning of dividends is but a poor guide.[58]

Conceding that the "day of trusts is here" and that there was little reason to expect more rational behavior in the future, Taylor shifted the basis of his appeal. While his methods would increase profits, their greatest value, he suggested, might be social rather than economic. By ending labor unrest, systematic shop management would obviate one of the leading sources of conflict between groups and classes. By implication the promise of scientific management was the redemption of American society.

Taylor was more forthright in discussing the expert's relationship with his client. Taylor's experiences in the 1890's had convinced him that scientific management was impossible to introduce in the context of the customary employer-employee relationship. If as a Simonds stockholder and a Bethlehem insider he had encountered insurmountable difficulties, what chance would a mere employee have? The conflict with Linderman had been the last straw. After 1901 Taylor insisted that the expert must be free from bureaucratic controls. In "Shop Management" he asserted that "the first changes . . . should be such as to allay the suspicions of the men."[59] This was a judicious approach to a difficult topic. By "men" Taylor meant the employees generally, including the managers, whose potential for interference made the workers' threats of strikes and efforts to restrict production pale by comparison. But if the expert was free of managerial control, what assurance did the client have that he would perform competently? In 1902 Taylor had no

answer to this fundamental question. He emphasized the importance
of careful screening and a clear understanding of the expert's obligations, but he had not yet devised a way to guarantee competence and
professionalism.

Taylor was outspoken on another matter of professional concern. In
"A Piece Rate System" he had briefly criticized Halsey's premium because it relied on customary times rather than scientific rate fixing. In
"Shop Management" he attacked it in uncompromising terms. Charac-
terizing the premium as the Towne-Halsey plan, by implication a sequel
to Towne's discredited "gain-sharing" plan, Taylor condemned it as an
unsatisfactory "drifting" approach.[60] Taylor's motive for these intem-
perate and hypocritical statements (in view of his own predilection for
the "drifting" approach when it was expedient) is not apparent from
either his published or unpublished papers. His desire to stress the importance of time study was probably one consideration. Personal
animosity may have been another. In "A Piece Rate System" he had
pointedly emphasized that the differential piece rate dated from the
early 1880's, before Halsey had devised the premium, but Halsey had
not acknowledged his claim. Now Taylor would have his revenge.
Finally, he was well aware that he and Halsey were competitors for a
limited number of clients. If he could demonstrate that the premium
was inferior to the differential piece rate and/or the task and bonus, he
might gain the advantage.

Third, "Shop Management" was an affirmation of the engineers'
approach to management. In one paragraph inserted between discussions of standardized tools and time cards, Taylor urged executives
above the shop level to confine their attention to problems the plant
managers could not handle. Adherence to this "exception principle"
would give them more opportunity "to consider the broader lines of
policy and to study the character and fitness of the important men" and,
not least, would eliminate interference in the shop.[61] In short, Taylor's
"exception principle" was a plea for the delegation of authority from the
shop manager's perspective. It was his only contribution to the principles of administration aside from factory management; it was, indeed,
his only statement on business administration generally before 1909.

Taylor more clearly revealed his sympathies in his discussions of
labor issues. Despite his preoccupation with workers, he had little
sympathy for the labor reformers or personnel work. His long quota-
tions from "A Piece Rate System," summarizing the nineteenth-century
approach to employer-employee relations, were an indirect slap at
them. He was more explicit in a comment on John H. Patterson and the
labor problem at National Cash Register:

Mr. Patterson . . . has presented to the world a grand object lesson
of the combination of many philanthropic schemes with, in many
respects, a practical and efficient management. He stands out a
pioneer in this work. . . . Yet I feel that the recent strike in his
works demonstrates all the more forcibly my contention that the
establishment of the semi-philanthropic schemes should follow
instead of preceding the solution of the wages question."[62]

Taylor's views on labor unions were equally predictable. Unions, he
wrote, were acceptable as long as they did not demand excessive wages,
conduct boycotts, employ "force or intimidation," coerce nonunion
workers, or encourage the limitation of production.[63] Had he lived
through the World War I period, Taylor might have conceded the value
of company unions. In 1902, however, he believed that systematic production management obviated the need for special personnel measures
of any type.

Finally, "Shop Management" was a memoir of Taylor's activities
during the 1880's and 1890's. "Notes on Belting" and "A Piece Rate
System," like most professional papers, had included little personal or
anecdotal material; "Shop Management" was different. To illustrate his
points or support his claims, Taylor relied heavily on incidents from his
career—Thompson's time study experiments, the reorganization of the
Simonds inspectors, pig iron loading at Bethlehem, and Wadleigh's
work with the Bethlehem laborers. He did not explain why he adopted
this approach or why he selected those particular incidents. Judging
from the many factual errors that marred his accounts, potential
dramatic appeal must have outweighed any consideration of historical
authenticity.[64] In that respect Taylor proved a shrewd judge of his
audience. In his readers' minds his work became irrevocably associated
with "Schmidt," the Simonds inspectors, and the Bethlehem laborers.

Taylor read his paper to the June 1903 meeting of the ASME at
Saratoga Springs, New York. Although several commentators criticized
him for insufficient attention to the union menace, and Halsey vigorously defended the premium, most of the discussants were lavish in
their praise. Henry R. Towne called "Shop Management" "the most
valuable contribution to the subject which has yet been made." Harrington Emerson, soon to be Taylor's disciple, lauded it as the "most
important contribution ever presented to the Society and one of the
most important ever published in the United States." Oberlin Smith, a
New Jersey machinery manufacturer and systematic management
pioneer, was probably the most perceptive analyst, however. He noted
that Taylor "had taken in all that is good that he could get from anywhere."[65] The published version of "Shop Management" evoked similar

enthusiasm. By 1904 Taylor's paper had had precisely the effect he had intended.

Besides "A Piece Rate System," the other critical factor in Taylor's rise had been the introduction of scientific management at the Johnson Company, Simonds, and Bethlehem. Despite his own difficulties, Taylor assumed that a painstaking plant-by-plant installation of his methods was essential for their diffusion and planned accordingly. He would improve the expert's position, not abandon it. But who would play the role of expert? Since he was determined to "retire," the obvious alternative was to rely on men he had recruited and trained in the 1890's. In theory there was a substantial pool to draw upon, perhaps twenty to twenty-five individuals who had earned his trust. But most of these men had found other positions during or after the Bethlehem debacle. In practice Taylor had to depend on a handful of his Bethlehem associates and newcomers he recruited after 1901. A majority of the men who became prominent "disciples" did not meet Taylor until 1899 or after. In other respects, however, they resembled their predecessors. They had university engineering degrees or backgrounds as machine shop apprentices. They also shared the assumptions and biases of the contemporary systematic management movement. In particular they believed that factories could operate with machine-like regularity and that obstacles to this end could be removed by adjustments in plant layout, machinery, and managerial communications.

The veteran of the group was Henry L. Gantt, a Stevens graduate of 1884 and Taylor's long-time associate. Independent, opinionated, and irascible, Gantt was a caricature of Taylor. He was also a creative technician and a competent manager. At Bethlehem he had worked apart from the other assistants, developing his own ideas and approach. In late 1901 he began his own consulting business and soon had a corps of assistants and a flourishing practice.[66] Increasingly Gantt specialized in production control techniques, particularly the charts, which became his most enduring contribution, and in incentive wage plans.[67] The latter led him to embrace a technocratic social philosophy that even Taylor, hardly a sophisticate in such matters, would never have countenanced.[68] Yet Gantt remained personally devoted to Taylor and his ideas. As late as 1911 he complained of the many "fakirs" whose selective and haphazard approaches theatened to discredit scientific management.[69]

Carl G. Barth, who soon surpassed Gantt in Taylor's estimation, received an engineering education in his native Norway and became a draftsman at William Sellers and Company in 1881. Joining Taylor in 1899, he became known and feared for his mathematical ability and irrepressible candor. Unlike Gantt, he was a poor organizer and manager; Harlow S. Person, a later disciple, described him as "neither an executive nor a practical engineer, but . . . a research man."[70] His lack of business acumen and tactless personal manner could exasperate even Taylor. When Barth was employed by the Pullman Company to reorganize its massive Chicago plant, Taylor was unusually frank:

> There is one piece of advice which I wish to reiterate over and over again, and it is this—Never tell them that what they are doing is rotten, or that they are wrong in any way, but simply say 'this is our way and we do it this way because we think it is the best.' Dont say one single thing to criticize their way of doing it. Next—Do not ever blow your own horn with them. This will only result in their discountenancing what you have to say . . . anything in the nature of boasting only reacts adversely on you instead of in your favor. I am sure that you can do an immense amount of good if you will only stand solid and make them think that you are really the real stuff instead of telling them that you are the real stuff.[71]

Barth conducted Taylor's metal-cutting experiments at the Sellers Company from 1901 to 1903 and began to introduce scientific management at the Tabor Company and the Link-Belt Engineering Company, a Philadelphia machinery firm, in late 1903. He did not develop a group of assistants (except for his son Christian) and remained dependent on Taylor for most of his clients.

Dwight V. Merrick was a Germantown resident and a family friend of the Taylors. He served an apprenticeship at the Southwark Foundry and Machine Company and worked at the Sellers Company before going to Bethlehem. He went to Link-Belt as Barth's assistant in 1903 and soon began to make time studies, which became his specialty.[72] Taylor recognized his expertise in that area and even encouraged him to write a book on machine shop time study, but apparently had little confidence in Merrick's ability to handle larger assignments.[73] Taylor's other Bethlehem associates played little or no role in his retirement activities. Wadleigh, who presumably would have been a more logical candidate for further time study work, remained in the Southwest after Greene's fall and had no further contact with Taylor. James Gillespie and Joseph Welden disappeared from view after their departure from Bethlehem.[74] Sidney Newbold worked at the Tabor Company after 1901, selling high speed steel tools, as well as molding machines. Maunsel White, scion of a wealthy New Orleans mercantile family, retired to his native Louisiana after leaving Bethlehem. Russell Davenport also left Bethlehem after Schwab's takeover. He went to William Cramp and Sons as vice-president and was about to be named president at the time of his death in 1904. Taylor grieved at the loss of a friend, but also at the loss of an opportunity to introduce scientific management at the massive shipyard under more propitious circumstances than those of 1895.

Taylor soon attracted an extraordinary group of young recruits to supplement the services of Gantt, Barth, and Merrick. Of these, Horace K. Hathaway, who served an apprenticeship at Midvale in the 1890's, was at first the most notable. Hathaway became Barth's assistant at Link-Belt in 1904, but soon moved to Tabor, where he became vice-president in 1906 at the age of twenty-nine. His importance grew as Tabor became a training center for Taylor's "apprentices," and he became Taylor's alter ego after 1911. Nevertheless, his taciturn manner, slavish adherence to Taylor's strictures, and modest success as a businessman limited his influence outside the Taylor circle.[75]

The others, while similar in background, had more diverse interests. Charles Day, for example, was an 1899 University of Pennsylvania engineering graduate who worked at Link-Belt and then founded a prosperous civil engineering and construction firm. He supposedly applied scientific management to the operation of "street railways and light and power plants."[76] Robert Thurston Kent, son of an early leader of the engineering profession, graduated from Stevens in 1902 and took a job as an engineer at Link-Belt. By 1904 he had become an ardent and highly useful convert. A talented writer, Kent soon embarked on a career in technical journalism. His *Industrial Engineering and the Engineering Digest* became the unofficial organ of scientific management between 1910 and 1914.

But the most versatile and ultimately the most important of the recruits was Morris L. Cooke, a Lehigh University graduate of 1893 who brought his abundant public relations skills to the scientific management movement at a crucial time. A wealthy Germantown native, Cooke had known Taylor socially, possibly through the Unitarian Society, for several years. In 1903, while working for a Philadelphia publishing firm, he expressed an interest in introducing scientific management in the printing and publishing industry.[77] During the following years the two men became better acquainted and, when Taylor was elected president of the ASME in December 1905, he hired Cooke as his assistant. Cooke's job was to reorganize the society's accounting, budgeting, and publishing procedures, which under Frederick R. Hutton, the long-time secretary, had fallen into disarray.[78] Cooke worked at the ASME for a year and a half with considerable success. But the indirect effects of his efforts were at least as important. His ASME activities strengthened his ties with Taylor, made him a well-known, if controversial, engineer, and encouraged the notion that scientific management was applicable to a variety of nonindustrial situations.[79]

Most important, Cooke profoundly influenced Taylor's promotional activities. The publication of "Shop Management" and "On the Art of Cutting Metals" assured Taylor a larger and more enthusiastic audience, but Cooke inspired additional steps that enabled Taylor to take maximum advantage of his popularity. Cooke's impact was apparent almost immediately. His 1906 suggestion that the disciples act as a consulting team—much like functional foremen replaced the all-around supervisor—inspired a successful collective effort at the Plimpton Press and a less satisfactory one at the Williams and Wilkins Company.[80] During the same period he helped Taylor develop the lecture presentation that soon became the principal method of "selling" scientific management. With the completion of Boxly in 1904 and the Tabor and Link-Belt reorganizations in 1906 and 1907, Cooke realized that Taylor had the ingredients for a unique presentation. At his urging, Taylor began to invite prospective clients to his home for a "discussion" of scientific management followed by a tour of Tabor or Link-Belt. Boxly convinced them of his success; the lecture introduced scientific management in the most compelling fashion; and the plant tour provided firsthand evidence of the system's effectiveness.

Taylor prepared his lecture with the same painstaking attention he devoted to his written works. Drawing on his speech-making experiences and "Shop Management," he devised a talk that judiciously mixed entertainment, education, and business. Taylor relied on dramatic incidents from his career to convey the substance and potential of scientific management. The stories of his Midvale "fight," the Simonds inspectors, and "Schmidt" were his favorites. He then turned to a less appealing, but no less important, subject, the manufacturer's role and obligations. To achieve the kind of results he had talked about, Taylor argued, the owners would have to grant the consultant complete freedom to revise production methods, reorganize machines and functions, and reassign or even fire employees for two years or more. An open-ended commitment, he insisted, was a prerequisite for success.

Cooke worked closely with Taylor to make this message as palatable as possible. In early October 1907, for example, he argued that Taylor was "making a vital mistake" by insisting that "the Taylor system meant all of it or none of it and particularly that the person introducing it must be clothed with absolute authority in matters of management." Potential clients would "stall on absolutism." "I think that absolutely nothing will be lost in softening the presentation to those who are not ready for [scientific management] . . . and they will be made . . . efficient missionaries."[81] Several weeks later he wrote that Taylor's lecture "was certainly very much more convincing than heretofore and . . . less likely to put a man on the defensive."[82]

By all accounts Taylor's lecture, which often lasted more than two hours, was the high point of the Boxly visit. Yet even Cooke's yeoman efforts could not disguise its ominous message. Barth recalled that at the conclusion of the lecture there was frequently "a pronounced movement toward the door."[83] However much they might endorse Taylor's attack on the status quo and applaud his vision of a machinelike factory, most manufacturers were unwilling to trust their fate to an outsider. If Taylor's and Cooke's comments about the number of Boxly "pilgrims" are even reasonably accurate, no more than 10 percent of the businessmen who listened to the lecture subsequently employed one of Taylor's select corps of scientific management practitioners.

For the undaunted minority Taylor provided two invaluable services. First, he selected an appropriate expert or group of experts to reorganize the client's factory. He wrote Gantt, for example, that the Cheney brothers, Connecticut silk manufacturers, were "about the finest set of men who have ever been here." "I urged them strongly to get next to you."[84] He wrote Barth that the Packard Motor Company "would be a splendid one for you to land."[85] On another occasion he asked Barth to contact the McElwain Company, which was interested in accounting reforms, despite the managers' preference for Gantt, because Gantt "knows too little about the accounting system."[86] He urged Barth and Gantt to contact the Stanley Company jointly, and, at Cooke's urging, suggested that Cooke, Hathaway, and Gantt work together at the Plimpton Press to achieve "the largest returns for the money paid out by Plimpton."[87]

If the client and expert could agree on terms—by no means a certainty; Cheney and Plimpton Press proceeded, but Packard, McElwain, and Stanley did not—Taylor performed a second service. He supplied advice and moral support to both the employer and the disciple, acted as conciliator in the event of disputes, and, above all, guaranteed the expert's competence and professionalism. The latter activity, a natural outgrowth of his involvement in the disciples' early consulting jobs, was the indispensable element Taylor had overlooked in "Shop Management." It became increasingly important as the ranks of the experts and clients grew. No matter how thorough their conversion, businessmen were uneasy with Taylor's stipulations. Anxiously they turned to him for reassurance or intervention. Between 1907 and 1915 Taylor probably devoted as much time to the complaints of distraught clients as he did to his writings and lectures. Usually his task was to assure a worried manufacturer that the expert knew what he was doing and would overcome momentary obstacles. Occasionally it was to criticize or admonish the expert for some questionable activity.

Two incidents illustrate the latter function. In 1908 Gantt began to reorganize the bleaching and dying department of Joseph Bancroft and Sons Company, a Delaware textile manufacturer. As his work proceeded, it appeared that the Bancrofts were as interested in certain machines he had developed for the Sayles Bleachery, a competitor, as they were in scientific management. When Gantt agreed to supply the Bancrofts with his Sayles inventions, Taylor was appalled. "This will certainly not appeal to other people if they hear about it," he cautioned.[88] In 1910 Barth became involved in a similar predicament. While working for the Erie Forge Company, a subsidiary of the Disston Company, a saw manufacturer and Tabor competitor, Barth sought information about the high speed steel saws that Tabor made and Disston coveted. Barth apparently acted sincerely to advance his client's interest, but Taylor was astounded at his naïveté. "I submit that your duty and your obligations toward the Tabor Company are vastly greater than your obligations toward any of your clients," he replied.[89] In both cases Taylor's efforts "to establish . . . the proper ethics between us all" had the desired effect; Gantt and Barth soon left their controversial employers.

Managing Success: Gantt and Emerson

Maintaining the "proper ethics between us" proved to be increasingly difficult as the popularity of scientific management grew. Before 1903 Taylor had had competitors, experts in cost accounting, production management, and incentive wage systems. But with the publication of "Shop Management" a new species appeared, the expert who took his cue from Taylor and offered a variety of services or even a comprehensive plant reorganization. Taylor might have viewed imitation as a compliment except for two considerations: the welfare of the disciples, whose careers and livelihoods depended on his leadership, and his imitators' opportunistic approach. Like Taylor, they sensed the possibilities inherent in the "labor problem." Unlike him, they did not balk (or devise elaborate stratagems, à la Bethlehem) when prospective clients talked exclusively of ending restrictions on production or otherwise increasing worker productivity. And because of their flexibility they did not demand or make the commitments that were the hallmarks of Taylor's relationship with his clients. To Taylor they were pseudo experts, "fakirs" who left the first factory system intact while precipitating strikes in their rush to introduce time study.

Of the many challenges that Taylor confronted after 1903, by far the most trying and difficult involved disciples who for one reason or another violated the tenets of the promotional strategy. Men like Merrick, cast in subordinate roles due to inexperience or limited ability, often became restive. But their aim was to rise to the first rank, and they remained faithful to Taylor's standards. More serious problems arose when men of the first rank chafed at the intellectual and ethical constraints Taylor imposed on them. Gantt and especially Harrington Emerson and Frank B. Gilbreth, flamboyant businessmen who became identified with Taylor after the publication of "Shop Management," were the prime sources of contention. Unlike the other disciples, they were middle-aged men who had had varied careers before 1903 and did not easily or willingly accept secondary positions. But personal animosity and jealousy were at best secondary factors; Taylor appreciated the force of ambition as well as any man. The real differences developed when, in Taylor's opinion, they compromised their responsibilities to him and to their clients. Flexibility and opportunism had their place, but only so long as they did not jeopardize the integrity of the larger enterprise.

The first such challenge came, predictably, from Gantt. Taylor had long recognized Gantt's creativity and independence and, in the case of the task and bonus system, had readily accepted Gantt's improvisation. He presumably had read Gantt's reports to the Bethlehem managers and knew of his assistant's efforts to succeed him. If he disapproved of Gantt's recruitment of a corps of assistants after 1901, he gave no sign of his displeasure. And he viewed the Bancroft incident as only a momentary lapse. As late as 1910 he wrote that Gantt, Barth, Hathaway, and Cooke were his principal followers.[90] Nevertheless, Taylor became increasingly distressed at Gantt's efforts to publicize the task and bonus. In his work Gantt was sufficiently conventional to warrant Taylor's approval, but in his writings he devoted more and more attention to his innovations, particularly the task and bonus, and less to Taylor's. By 1908, when he published "Training Workmen in Habits of Industry" in the ASME *Transactions*, he seemed to be advocating a separate and distinctive type of management centered on the worker rather than the manager. Taylor supposedly urged him not to publish the paper and became noticeably less friendly when he did.[91]

There was considerable irony in this dispute between the best-known spokesmen for scientific management. Both men were engaged in extensive efforts to publicize their ideas. Both emphasized the labor features of scientific management in order to create popular interest. Yet they fell out, presumably because Gantt stated his position in more extreme terms and seemed to suggest that much of Taylor's system— and standards—could be jettisoned. Taylor knew that Gantt was more orthodox in practice than he appeared in his writings and thus restrained his criticism, but his response to Gantt's initiatives helps explain why he was neither subdued nor circumspect in his reactions to the activities of Emerson and Gilbreth.

Emerson was a promoter, speculator, publicist, and self-taught engineer, a Renaissance man among adventurers. The son of a nomadic clergyman, he spent his youth in a half-dozen European countries. His first career, as professor of modern languages at the fledgling University of Nebraska from 1876 to 1882, foreshadowed his many subsequent careers. At Nebraska, Emerson was an innovator, an exponent of the new secularism and flexibility that would undermine academic traditionalism in the late nineteenth century. His outspoken attacks on convention soon antagonized the college's hidebound administrators and led to his dismissal for insubordination and scandalous behavior—public beer drinking with colleagues and students.[92] In the following years Emerson became an industrial manager, entrepreneur, publicist, and promoter of Harrington Emerson. Brilliant but erratic, he never tired of schemes to advance himself. Complaining about his seemingly pedestrian existence in 1903, he wrote, quite seriously, that "I ought to be preparing articles for publication, attending conventions, appearing in the swell clubs, traveling on the exclusive trains, interviewing the Goulds, Griscoms, Hills, . . . etc."[93] Yet somehow his plans never materialized. His repeated financial debacles cost his father's savings, alienated other members of his family, and involved him in numerous legal disputes.[94] Only when he became a promoter of scientific management—"efficiency engineering" as he called it—did his fortunes improve.

Emerson's knowledge of systematic management supposedly dated from his youth. He wrote that he had had "functional teachers" in German schools, witnessed scientific management in the operations of the German army during the Franco-Prussian war, and studied music with a teacher who used systematic methods. He claimed to have systematized the University of Nebraska, making the "professors [correspond] to foremen, [the] students to machinists and laborers."[95] Presumably these experiences had little immediate impact, for Emerson devoted himself to other endeavors until the turn of the century. In the 1890's he became involved in efforts to manufacture electric boats, to lay a Pacific telegraph cable, and to establish Alaskan mail routes during the gold rush.[96] He also attempted, without success, to obtain backing for schemes to build an electric boat that would sail around the world, to erect a shipyard in Tacoma, Washington, to salvage a wrecked steamship, and to create a submarine fleet for the Russian navy.[97]

In early 1900 one of Emerson's associates appointed him temporary manager of the Appert Glass Company in Port Allegany, Pennsylvania. He acknowledged that it was "rather novel to be called on to direct and manage an enormous factory making something about which I know nothing," but was "glad to find that I am entirely competent to fill [the job]."[98] He later claimed that the assignment, which lasted approximately six months, permitted him to demonstrate his "ability to manage a large factory."[99] He told Taylor that "by a crude use of the time unit system, by careful analysis of the time and cost of every operation," he had saved the company $150,000.[100] Though the Appert job was his first "immediate contact with American labor," he encountered no problems, averting a strike in May 1900 by making "wise concessions."[101] Nevertheless, the experience was not entirely satisfying. Despite his economies, the company's financial situation did not improve appreciably. At the time of his departure he wrote that it was "discouraging to be connected with an unsuccessful enterprise."[102]

From late 1900 to mid-1903 Emerson became involved in other ventures reminiscent of his earlier experiences. He inspected mining properties in British Columbia and Alaska and presented a "coal proposition" to "five distinct and different parties" without success.[103] On a return trip from England (he always traveled first class in order to meet "swell" people) he became acquainted with F. C. Payson, a machinery manufacturer who offered him an important, though apparently temporary, job in his Portland, Maine, factory.[104] He also became entangled in a law suit that prevented him from "taking up other profitable work." And he attempted to convince the managers of the Grand Trunk Railroad to make him their land development agent in western Canada.[105] In the meantime he attended the December 1902 ASME meeting in New York and heard Gantt present his first paper on the task and bonus system. Afterward he met Taylor, and the two men had a "long and kindly talk."[106]

The turning point in Emerson's career came in 1903 when Payson introduced him to several Union Pacific Railroad executives. The Union Pacific subsequently employed him as a consultant. "Every employee," he wrote, "is strictly instructed to heed my requests . . . and then I sail around and find all the fault I can and propose various improvements." At first he had "serious misgivings" when he was taken into the railroad repair shops "to see twenty or thirty locomotives in every possible stage of dissolution and . . . called on for technical advice." Yet, "everything has gone well." The Union Pacific shops were "very complete in modern design and equipment . . . [but] there was nobody to introduce the new methods that should go with the shop." Drawing on his experiences and his familiarity with Taylor's writings, he proposed "a board of tests and methods whose business will be to listen to suggestions and put them into effect."[107] Emerson hoped that such suggestions would "open up for me many other railroad shops throughout the country so that I shall keep steadily busy at high rates of remuneration."[108] For once Emerson's hopes materialized. He was soon employed to undertake a similar study for the Atchison, Topeka and Santa Fe Railroad. His survey, in turn, led to one of the more extensive and successful applications of scientific management.

As Emerson was about to start his work for the Santa Fe, he read an advance copy of "Shop Management." He immediately recognized its relevance to his work and notified Taylor that "Shop Management" was "the most important paper ever prepared for presentation to the Society."[109] When he repeated his compliment publicly at the ASME meeting, Taylor was pleased.[110] The two men corresponded occasionally during the following years. But their divergent personalities and attitudes toward managerial reform made a close relationship unlikely. More than any other development, Emerson's rise suggested the problems Taylor would face in attempting to promote and control scientific management.

From the beginning Emerson viewed his Santa Fe work as the possible basis for a lucrative consulting business and planned accordingly. In 1903 he wrote that "I ought to have canvassers to go around and drum up business with the great magnates. . . . I ought to have good offices, several dozen specialists as assistants, canvassers. Then I ought to . . . give a place two days at $100 a day and then send my underlings at $30 a day to accumulate material. It is toward this that I am working."[111] By 1906 he had attracted several important clients. In January he made his initial contacts with the American Locomotive Company, which had already employed Gantt for a brief period. In July he returned to New York for more talks with American Locomotive officials and with Charles Schwab, who had become interested in Emerson's methods as a result of work he had done for a Franklin, Pennsylvania, machinery plant. Both negotiations were successful. Emerson was employed to reorganize the American Locomotive Company shops and "to visit the great Bethlehem plant."[112]

In 1907 Emerson established the Emerson Company to further his work as a systematizer. Since he and his associates (his brother Samuel and several former Santa Fe assistants) were occupied at American Locomotive, the Emerson Company was at first something "to fall back onto."[113] But after the spring of 1908, when he lost his American Locomotive Company position, he implemented his plan largely as he had outlined it five years before. By utilizing his substantial talents as a publicist and associating with "swell' people, he finally obtained the recognition and income that had always eluded him.

Emerson's approach to managerial reform differed radically from Taylor's. As he had indicated in his 1903 statements, he devoted his energies to promotions and solicitations, leaving the actual work to assistants. Superficially this arrangement resembled the relationship between Taylor and his followers, but Emerson's assistants—despite frequent raids on Tabor, Link-Belt, and other Taylor firms—were seldom a match for Merrick, much less Hathaway or Barth. Samuel Emerson had no relevant training or experience when he started at Santa Fe in 1904; he asserted that "common sense goes much farther than technical knowledge."[114] On more than one occasion he acknowledged privately that he "was entirely ignorant as to the workings of such a plant when I arrived there, and had to be cautious about opening my mouth, lest I put my foot in it. By saying nothing I was credited with deep knowledge."[115] Fortunately, Taylor never learned of his presumably silent inspection of the Bethlehem shops.

Emerson was able to use untrained and inexperienced assistants because of another fundamental difference with Taylor. As he readily admitted, he had no system, prerequisites, or necessary sequence of operations. He did as much or as little as the client would finance. Though in practice he usually introduced time study and an incentive wage to improve the workers' "efficiency," he had no particular area of specialization. C. Bertrand Thompson succinctly contrasted the Taylor and Emerson approaches when he wrote that "the Taylor System begins where the Emerson System ends."[116]

As Taylor became familiar with Emerson's promotional techniques and procedural "short cuts," he became increasingly disillusioned with his admirer. After 1908, when the Emerson Company flourished, he became outspoken in his criticism. He had Emerson in mind when he wrote that "there are . . . a very great number of incompetent men" in the systematizing business.[117] More candid was his judgment that Emerson was "very earnest and hard working but . . . on the whole more interested in making money, than in doing anything else at present."[118]

Gilbreth

Taylor's relationship with Gilbreth followed a remarkably similar pattern.[119] Like Emerson, Gilbreth was a talented technician, a flamboyant personality, and an aggressive, occasionally unscrupulous promoter. Like Emerson, he understood the truth of Taylor's perception that audiences responded most enthusiastically to discussions of the labor problem. And like Emerson, he made that insight the basis of a career that dismayed and finally antagonized Taylor and his conventional followers. It was one thing to exploit public interest to promote scientific management; it was quite another to disregard the standards Taylor had made the basis for the expert's role in the diffusion of scientific management.

Gilbreth had a successful career as a builder long before his contact with Taylor.[120] Starting as a bricklayer, he became a prosperous contractor in the 1890's. From that time until 1911 he made his mark in two areas—as an innovative advertiser and promoter and as a creative technician. His goal was to spread the Gilbreth name as widely and as rapidly as possible. And despite an often hectic schedule, he constantly tinkered with construction equipment. Like Taylor, he soon realized that a businessman could not view technological innovation in a vacuum; to realize the potential of improved machinery, it was often necessary to improve management as well. Yet the nature of the construction industry dictated a different approach to organizational change. Though Gilbreth developed a comprehensive "Field System," his principal innovation, motion study, applied to the individual worker. From the beginning his foremost concern—a legitimate concern given his background—was the worker and his activities.

Appropriately, the original link between Gilbreth and the Taylor movement was Sanford Thompson. As early as 1898 Gilbreth permitted Thompson to make time studies of his men. Thompson appreciated this favor, since he considered Gilbreth "one of the brightest men . . . one of the most accurate estimators" in the construction business.[121] Later, Gilbreth read Thompson's work on bricklaying and suggested several improvements. Yet Thompson was uncomfortable with Gilbreth. He reported that Gilbreth was "a great bluffer" who was rumored to have a "way of doctoring his accounts" to make "things appear to cost sometimes double their actual cost."[122]

Like Thompson, Taylor was drawn to Gilbreth by his desire for cost data and by Gilbreth's professed interest in scientific management. The two men met at an engineering society meeting in New York in December 1907. Taylor reported afterward that he had spent several hours with Gilbreth and obtained valuable information. If, he concluded, Gilbreth was indeed a leader in the construction field, as Thompson had suggested, "it certainly appears to me of great importance for us to get next to him."[123]

In January 1908 Taylor spent a half day with Gilbreth reviewing the latter's concrete and bricklaying methods. He reported afterward that Gilbreth would permit Thompson to "take whatever stop watch observations you want . . . as he is particularly interested in our management at present." Taylor was also convinced from reading a manuscript Gilbreth had prepared on bricklaying that he was "a thorough master of this art" and that the book would be the "finest . . . which has yet appeared."[124] He suggested that Gilbreth and Thompson combine their efforts to produce a single book on bricklaying.

Neither Thompson nor Gilbreth found Taylor's proposal satisfactory for reasons that foreshadowed more serious conflicts in the future. Thompson objected that he would be tainted professionally by association with Gilbreth and that Gilbreth would "probably do almost anything" to transform the "Taylor System" into the "Gilbreth System." "I am not yet ready to trust the man to an extent where it might be to his advantage to throw one over."[125] Gilbreth was equally concerned that he receive appropriate credit for his work.[126]

Thompson, nevertheless, was willing to continue his limited relationship with Gilbreth. Taylor and Gilbreth may have discussed the introduction of time study and an incentive wage on Gilbreth's jobs at their January meeting; in any event, Thompson and Gilbreth considered it soon thereafter.[127] By early February, Gilbreth agreed to introduce the labor features of scientific management on his next construction project, a factory building at Gardner, Massachusetts. Thompson and Hathaway were to help him. Gilbreth wrote that he was eager to supplement his "motion study schemes" with time study and an incentive wage.[128] He confessed that he had contracted "Tayloritis."[129]

Gilbreth began the introduction of scientific management in April 1908 with Thompson making the time studies and Hathaway installing a modified planning department. From the beginning, however, there were problems. On some occasions Gilbreth seemed to be delaying the work, on others to be acting precipitously.[130] A new method he had devised for handling bricks was introduced improperly, causing additional delays and hard feelings. Finally in May the union masons and bricklayers struck in opposition to the introduction of the incentive wage, and Gilbreth was forced to restore the day rate. Thompson, nevertheless, found the Gardner experience extremely useful. His work, though incomplete, "proved that tasks on intricate work . . . can be accurately fixed from our tables." "The only question . . . at present" is whether "the 'strike' if allowed simply to blow over will affect the chances of introducing the system on another job."[131] Taylor apparently shared Thompson's generally optimistic assessment of the situation.[132] Gilbreth was even more positive: "I have not dismissed the Taylor System; I will not dismiss it, and I intend to devote the rest of my life to installing the Taylor System."[133]

In November, Gilbreth proposed to introduce Taylor's methods on another construction job, a factory in Chelsea, Massachusetts. He convinced the local building trades union leaders to permit the introduction of an incentive wage, thus eliminating the danger of another strike. Thompson was willing to try again and made the necessary arrangements.[134] Yet this time Gilbreth himself sabotaged the project by attempting to shift some of the costs to Taylor and his followers.[135] By late November, Taylor and Thompson were thoroughly disillusioned. "It appears," Taylor wrote, "as if Gilbreth had the idea in his head that we were somehow going to get a great profit out of his introducing our scheme of scientific management on his job, and that it is therefore up to us for some reason or other to pay all the bills and for him to get the benefit. This, of course, I take exception to."[136]

Despite these problems, Gilbreth continued to be a vigorous and effective exponent of Taylor's ideas in the following years. He gave lectures on scientific management at "Frederick W. Taylor Hall" in Providence (a room in his sister's music school), wrote books and articles for lay audiences, made convincing presentations at government hearings, and conducted a summer school for college professors. Because of his past experiences with unionized workmen, he was particularly valuable in countering the criticisms of organized labor. Though he still talked about introducing Taylor's methods on his construction jobs, he no longer made serious overtures to Thompson or the other disciples.[137] He acknowledged that he was not a practitioner of scientific management and suffered slights by Hathaway and even Merrick in silence.[138]

Yet he also continued to develop motion study as an adjunct to scientific management. In 1909 he wrote Taylor that he was "installing small bits that are reducing costs and increasing speed."[139] The favorable public response to *Motion Study* (1911), a description of his activities, encouraged him to continue his efforts.[140] And while he tolerated the condescending attitudes of the Taylor disciples on other matters, he became incensed when Taylor implied that motion study was merely a refinement of Sanford Thompson's time study methods.[141] In mid-1911

Gilbreth announced that he had developed a rate-setting technique that would make stopwatch time study obsolete and began to send Taylor photographs of workmen. At first he considered his pictures "an assistant to the instruction card to show the workman what is to be done."[142] By March 1912, however, he had devised a method of photographing the worker, together with a stopwatch "with precision to the thousandth of a second."[143] He described this "micro-motion technique" as a way of "recording time and motion studies that eliminates the human element."[144] He reported diplomatically that his new approach would not "wholly do away with the present stopwatch method," but Taylor could not have been oblivious to his implication.[145] To make matters worse, Gilbreth announced that he had changed his mind and was embarking on a new career as a scientific management expert. He had obtained two major clients, the New England Butt Company of Providence, Rhode Island, and the Herrmann Aukam Company of South River, New Jersey, and Lebanon, Pennsylvania.

Undoubtedly recalling his experiences with Emerson, Taylor reacted coolly to Gilbreth's announcements. Micromotion study, he wrote, "should . . . prove a most valuable method for studying movements which cannot be analyzed in any other way."[146] He added that he knew "nothing about photography and therefore am entirely the wrong man to follow [it] . . . up properly."[147] He was even less enthusiastic about Gilbreth's entry into the consulting field. Gilbreth, he noted to Hathaway, "had no business whatever to undertake the systematizing of a large company."[148] These reactions, the results of nearly four years of discord, were unfortunate, for Gilbreth's work might have alerted Taylor to the deficiencies of his approach to the labor problem. Though Gilbreth subscribed to the engineers' assumptions about worker motivation and the irrelevance of special personnel measures, he might at least have helped Taylor perceive the unscientific character of time study.

For nearly two years Taylor's fears seemed unwarranted. Gilbreth employed Hathaway and Merrick to advise him at New England Butt, and Hathaway acknowledged his satisfaction with Gilbreth's activities. Reluctantly Hathaway concluded that there was "no reason why he should not ultimately be able to do good work in the systematizing line if he plays the game according to the rules."[149] To Taylor it must have appeared that Gilbreth had resumed, in modified form, his earlier plan to introduce aspects of scientific management with the aid of other certified experts. While never reconciled to Gilbreth's consulting activities, he advised his followers to be more tolerant and even indicated enthusiasm for Gilbreth's attempts to apply micromotion study to hospital operating room procedures.[150]

Taylor's attitude changed abruptly in early 1914 as a result of a dispute between Gilbreth and the Herrmann Aukam management. In early March, Milton Herrmann, the head of the company, and his factory manager called on Taylor for "a general kind of grouch." They accused Gilbreth of a variety of derelictions: he devoted too little time to the job, entrusted the day-to-day work to incompetents, charged too much, and had resigned before completing the assignment.[151] Complaints, even complaints of this gravity, were nothing new to Taylor. Yet because of his previous experiences with Gilbreth he found them more disturbing than usual. When Herrmann asked him to supply a substitute expert, he did not immediately refuse and promised a full investigation. A week later Taylor dined with the Gilbreths in Providence. For once Gilbreth was unpersuasive.

> I had a long talk with Gilbreth about his work with the [Herrmann Aukam] handkerchief people. He said that they were simply a lot of tricky jews, etc. etc. I do not take any stock whatever in Gilbreth's talk. My feeling is that he has very distinctly 'taken them into camp.' Certainly, for the triffling work that he has done, $35,000 seems a tremendous gouge. I think there is no question that he has simply dropped these people so as to get the men who are working with him there to go to Germany, where he has a much larger contract.[152]

Though Taylor had not selected Gilbreth for the job, he felt morally responsible for his behavior because of Gilbreth's public identification with scientific management. He soon arranged for Hathaway to take over the Herrmann Aukam assignment and, buttressed by Hathaway's negative reports of Gilbreth's activities, became increasingly critical of him. By August 1914 he had consigned Gilbreth, like Emerson, to the "fakir" category of "incompetent men."[153]

Taylor's break with Gilbreth, like his unhappiness with Gantt, his hostility toward Emerson, and his disapproval of other lesser figures, was as predictable as the "movement toward the door" that often followed the Boxly lectures. He had been attracted to Gilbreth because of the latter's technical expertise, only to find that Gilbreth associated scientific management with innovative labor measures and personal advancement rather than with the highly disciplined, often hazardous, "systematizing" process. Taylor's disillusionment turned to outright hostility when he became familiar with Gilbreth's flexible approach to money matters. Belatedly, Taylor realized that Gilbreth, for all his ability and enthusiasm, was no different from the other "fakirs." "Competent" experts, he discovered, were as rare as compliant manufacturers.

Despite his many problems with "incompetent" imitators and associates, Taylor had reason to consider his new career—his effort to overcome the obstacles that had beset and frustrated him in the 1890's— a tentative success by 1911. He had become a prominent engineer, possibly the preeminent engineer of his generation. He had developed a better understanding of the economy and of the potential contributions of scientific management to the nation's economic and social health. He had, of course, publicized his managerial innovations and attracted a small coterie of devoted and "competent" followers. Still, he viewed these achievements as means to an end. They were significant only if they accelerated the transition to the new factory system. The ultimate test of his new career was not the number of Boxly pilgrims, Hathaways or Gilbreths he attracted, but the number of manufacturers who introduced his managerial techniques, and more important still, the impact of those techniques on the day-to-day activities of their plants. In these areas, too, Taylor had reason for qualified optimism about his work and his future.

6

Scientific Management in Practice, 1901–1915

During the last decade and a half of Taylor's life, Barth, Gantt, and other "competent" disciples introduced scientific management in a substantial number of American factories, perhaps as many as 180.[1] In some instances they worked alone; in others, Taylor played a major role in their activities. In general, their experiences were as diverse as Taylor's had been before 1901. Yet with few exceptions they were faithful to what might be termed the "Bethlehem model"—they attacked the problems of unsystematic machine functions and plant organization before they attempted to reorganize the labor force. Their fidelity often complicated their relations with clients, who despite promises to Taylor could not resist the temptation to introduce "improvements." It also meant that they devoted most of their time to the operations of managers and machines. Contrary to the impression Taylor gave his audiences, scientific management in practice had relatively little direct impact on the character of work or the activities of production workers.

Taylor's Clients

The industrial firms with the longest exposure to scientific management were Taylor's employers between the 1880's and the turn of the century. This group had varying experiences, both at the time of Taylor's work and afterward. The Johnson Company scrapped many of Taylor's reforms when it became part of the Federal Steel (later U.S. Steel) Company, and the Manufacturing Investment and Simonds companies,

137

also reorganized in the 1890's, probably took similar steps. Midvale and Bethlehem, on the other hand, were more fortunate. Their challenges were to accommodate Taylor's work to expanded, highly profitable operations.

When Taylor left Midvale, he created a void that was never filled. Sellers had ceased to have any influence, and Harrah, though impressed with Taylor and his ideas, was basically an outsider. Since the factory performed satisfactorily in the following years, he did not insist on strict adherence to Taylor's methods. In addition, since department heads were responsible for reducing production costs, it seemed only fair to allow them a certain latitude in performing their duties. Consequently, while the company grew and prospered, scientific management became less and less recognizable.

The occasional reports of former employees or observers confirm this melancholy conclusion. Hathaway, who had worked at Midvale until 1902, recalled that Taylor's methods had been gradually "sloughed off."[2] Horace L. Arnold had reached a similar verdict at the turn of the century. Despite the advantages of scientific management, notably labor cost reductions and the docility of the workmen, the absence of any individual committed to the maintenance and improvement of the system led to its gradual decline.[3] As late as 1909 Taylor argued that there was "hardly any company in which the general principles of modern scientific management are more thoroughly applied."[4] Yet in 1913 he reluctantly acknowledged that "they simply drifted along allowing the head of each Department to do pretty nearly as he saw fit. . . . The only thing which remains . . . is a certain spirit between the foremen and the men."[5]

A closer examination of the Midvale experience indicates marked differences in the extent to which various features of scientific management were "sloughed off." A variety of commentators, both proponents and opponents of the Taylor system, attested to the effectiveness of the Midvale metal-cutting and tool maintenance techniques. George F. Steele, for example, reported after touring the plant in 1894 that "Midvale has a most decided lead in their machine tool methods."[6] A union organizer complained shortly afterward that workers were fined for "any improper condition of tool."[7] Harrah himself testified in 1900 that "we give the workers . . . their tools and teach them how they can get the best results from the use of those tools, and we have three men to clean the tools for them and to sharpen the cutters and the other tools."[8] On the other hand, the Midvale managers seemed oblivious to other aspects of "the art of cutting metals." Taylor reported in 1912 that they were still using the tables on machine feeds and speeds that he and Gantt had developed in the 1880's.[9]

Similar variations appeared in the Midvale approach to the labor features of scientific management. Like Taylor, the later Midvale managers were strict disciplinarians. To insure that the employees obeyed orders, they continued the practice of fining workers who bungled instructions or otherwise erred. By 1900 the fining system had achieved infamy in Philadelphia labor circles.[10] But Taylor's successors were not equally zealous in maintaining the complementary measures he had introduced. In particular, they neglected time study and the differential piece rate, violating Taylor's premise that positive, as well as negative, sanctions were essential. Taylor's time studies had had many deficiencies, as Sanford Thompson's research had shown, but the problems became much worse. Steele reported in 1894 that the "estimating" department had been reduced from eight men to one and that new piece rates were based entirely on data from earlier jobs. The workers objected that "the estimating department had fallen behind and did not give them their piece work rates fast enough, and that they had to work on day rates too much."[11] Worst of all, from Taylor's perspective, the managers—one critic charged Harrah himself—arbitrarily cut piece rates that seemed too high.[12]

The most perceptive critique of these practices appears in a letter by Hathaway recalling his career at Midvale between 1896 and 1902. By the turn of the century, he noted, rate setting

> was in the hands of Tim Coonahan, who had one assistant, and later a boy, none of them especially qualified for scientific rate setting, but they were expected to set rates for the entire plant. It is perfectly obvious that it would be impossible for three men to do this properly, and as a result there was no real time study being taken, and such as was taken, was not at all elementary. There was a great deal of guessing, and it is my impression that the bulk of the rates were made for new work by selecting some job, and the time that the old job had taken was arbitrarily modified for the new.[13]

When piece rates were set for work under his control, Hathaway "found it necessary to have them always sent to me instead of direct to the men, and after checking them up with a sort of crude elementary time study, frequently had them either increased 100 percent, or cut in half before assigning the job to a workman."[14] Finally, "I saw several instances where the time allowed for turning projectiles and tires continued the same for years, and was then arbitrarily cut in half. . . . There was, of course, considerable feeling engendered by such an action."[15]

The Midvale managers were equally complacent in administering the differential piece rate. According to Taylor they substituted a conventional piece rate on certain jobs in 1893 only to restore the two-rate system when production dropped.[16] As the plant grew in the late 1890's and after, they apparently made little effort to extend the differential rate to new departments or jobs.[17] In the absence of any central direction each department head determined the method of wage payment used in his area. By 1915 at least four incentive plans were in operation, including the Halsey premium. The plant superintendent maintained that Taylor would not recognize any of them.[18]

In short, it appears that Taylor's methods had only a limited, and in many respects temporary, effect on the operation of the Midvale shops. Ironically, their impact was probably greatest in those areas of factory management, such as the operation of machines and tools, that Taylor seldom recalled in his writings and least significant in areas, like the control of the workers, that he cited repeatedly. Possibly this was due to coincidence or inadvertence, but it is more likely that the Midvale managers, like many of their contemporaries, believed that machines, rather than men, were the real keys to improved shop performance, no matter how much they talked about workers, their motivation, and their activities. Certainly the behavior of the Midvale executives tended to confirm the accusations of union leaders and social critics that industrialists bemoaned the "labor problem" in public, but gave it short shrift in their plants.

The fate of scientific management at Bethlehem Steel was remarkably similar, despite the radically different circumstances of Taylor's departure. The similarity was due largely to Schwab, who succeeded Linderman and Wharton shortly after Taylor's dismissal. Like Harrah, Schwab was tough-minded, unsentimental, and pragmatic. He had had no direct contact with Taylor and probably would have viewed the animosity that developed between Taylor and Linderman as silly and irrelevant. From his perspective any system of management that produced results— which he defined as lower unit production costs—was desirable. Thus the purge of Taylor and his disciples and the conflict over the Taylor-White patents (as well as Schwab's public disavowals of the Taylor system) had no more bearing on the actual operation of the Bethlehem plant than Harrah's friendship with Taylor and public endorsement of scientific management had on the Midvale factory.

Schwab's attitude made the elimination of Taylor's methods from the Bethlehem shops as difficult as their introduction had been. Supposedly he ordered the termination of Taylor's techniques in late 1901 or early 1902 because they were too expensive and disruptive. The department heads obeyed his order, only to find that output fell in the following months. As a result, Archibald Johnson, the new superintendent of Machine Shop No. 2, and possibly other department heads covertly reintroduced the system.

for several years the use of our slide rules and time study, etc., was carried on in the Bethlehem Works without Schwab's knowledge. The slide rules were operated in a room back of the kitchen, which Schwab never visited, and all of the slide rule, time study men, planners, etc., were carried on the payrolls as mechanics; that is, machinists who were supposed to be working in the shops.[19]

In 1903 or 1904, however, a fire destroyed the slide rules and time study data, and output declined again. Only after Schwab replaced Johnson did he learn that his order had not been obeyed. Thereafter he permitted department heads who were familiar with Taylor's methods to practice them openly and engaged Harrington Emerson to make additional improvements. By 1905 or 1906 Bethlehem had evolved to the Midvale position of the mid-1890's: the executives tolerated, even encouraged, scientific management, but left the initiative to the department managers.

The result was a situation similar to Midvale. A few features of scientific management remained intact, others were modified, and others disappeared. In 1910 a government inspector reported that the department heads "who are familiar with all the detail of the Taylor system and who have given it a trial . . . consider it altogether too elaborate." They believed "as a matter of economy" that "much detail" had to be eliminated. This meant reducing the number of clerks and functional foremen, notably "speed bosses and runners" and instruction card clerks.[20] W. D. Hemmerly, who worked in the Link-Belt planning department, noted the results after a visit to the plant: the "orders are sent . . . to the foremen after they are made out, and the matter of arrangement of work is left to the foremen."[21] C. B. Thompson toured the plant in 1912 and concluded the Taylor system "was barely recognizable."[22]

All observers agreed that time study and the incentive wage had been retained. Some saw the persistence of time study and the bonus as the best evidence of Taylor's impact on the plant; others viewed them as perversions of scientific management, expressions of Schwab's "driving" philosophy.[23] Such confusion was probably inevitable given Schwab's pragmatic approach and Emerson's tinkering. While no detailed account of Samuel Emerson's work at Bethlehem has survived, the Schwab bonus plan, which appeared during this period, resembled the Emerson efficiency wage plan.[24] By 1910 the labor features of scientific management reflected the diverse approaches of Taylor, Schwab, and Emerson. It is not surprising that observers had difficulty identifying and categorizing the curious amalgam that resulted.

Thus the experiences of Midvale and Bethlehem permit only limited generalizations about the long-term impact of Taylor's work. In neither factory was the initial installation complete, and in neither was there a concerted effort to maintain what had been accomplished. Moreover, in neither was there a systematic effort to evaluate the strengths and weaknesses of Taylor's methods or to measure their economic results, despite the impression that they had had a positive effect. In general, after Taylor's departure managers at both firms reverted to the "rule of thumb" techniques that had prevailed before the introduction of scientific management. As a consequence, it is possible to argue that scientific management was either retained or discarded, that it had a substantial or a negligible effect at Midvale and Bethlehem. In the end Taylor's failure to win the allegiance of men like Harrah and Schwab obscured and to some degree negated his success with others like Archibald Johnson and Henry Noll.

Synthesis: Link-Belt and Tabor

Although Taylor remained an important, perhaps decisive, factor in the diffusion of scientific management after 1901, he seldom visited the plants where it was being installed or had any direct contact with the employees. The actual impact of his methods therefore depended on the disciples' activities rather than his. As a result there were variations and differences in emphasis growing out of the disciples' personal styles and perspective. The degree to which these variations changed the character of scientific management was widely debated among contemporary observers.[25] In retrospect, however, the deviations appear less important than the underlying similarities in the work of the various disciples, "competent" or otherwise.

Like Taylor, the disciples obtained their first clients through personal contacts. Most of the firms that introduced scientific management before 1906, when Taylor initiated his sophisticated promotional effort, were located in the Philadelphia area and were operated by acquaintances of Taylor or Gantt. This meant that Taylor's influence on the day-to-day introduction of his techniques was somewhat greater than it would be in later years when the disciples' clients were scattered throughout the Northeast. His role was especially pronounced in the reorganizations of the Link-Belt Engineering Company and the Tabor Manufacturing Company between 1903 and 1907.

The installation of scientific management at the Link-Belt Company was a direct outgrowth of Taylor's work at Midvale and Bethlehem. In the late 1880's Taylor's metal-cutting experiments attracted the attention of Link-Belt president James Mapes Dodge, a member of the Unitarian Society and a Taylor acquaintance of long standing. Dodge was sufficiently impressed to employ one of Taylor's assistants, Lewis Wright, as his superintendent.[26] Wright brought "a number of exceedingly clever things" to Link-Belt, "so that the earlier work of Mr. Taylor was engrafted on the Link-Belt management."[27] The nature of these "things" is not clear from the surviving records, but Wright (who died in the late 1890's) made few lasting changes; when Barth began to reorganize the Link-Belt factory in 1903, he noted that by Taylor's standards it was "very poorly run."[28] Even Dodge acknowledged that his shop was "not especially different" from the factory where he served his apprenticeship in the early 1870's.[29]

Besides his interest in improved machine techniques Dodge was concerned with the state of society, especially with the "labor problem." He developed a reputation as a benevolent employer whose men were well paid and contented. Still, he was an engineer and shared the values and assumptions of Taylor and the new generation of professional engineers. Self-interest and self-help, he believed, were the only legitimate answers to labor unrest. Before the introduction of scientific management he guaranteed piece rates against rate cutting and apparently used the premium on some jobs. He was hostile to unions, but made no overt effort to suppress them. When the workers organized in the 1890's, he told them he would insist they strike if ordered to do so by the national leaders. "If you would break faith with the union, can you be trusted to keep it with me?"[30] This attitude so disarmed the union militants that the organization collapsed.

Dodge became aware of Taylor's work again in 1898 when he learned of the discovery of high speed steel. He witnessed one of Taylor's demonstrations at Bethlehem and decided to introduce the Taylor-White process at Link-Belt, a decision that reflected his personal interest in mechanical innovation more than any expectation of financial gain.[31] Link-Belt used cast iron rather than steel for most of its products, and the installation of high speed steel tools required additional experimentation. Belatedly, Dodge's engineers realized that the problem was bigger than they originally imagined. To their dismay the increase in cutting speeds created numerous difficulties elsewhere. The plant manager reported that "breakdowns were so frequent that the increases in expenses more than outweighed the advantage of added output."[32]

In response Dodge introduced a series of ad hoc shop reforms, probably modeled after Taylor's work at Midvale and Bethlehem. "We were strengthening our tools, putting in electrical driving, and doing everything we could to make [high speed steel] useful in our shop."[33] He also appointed a "speed foreman" to supervise the use of high speed steel and introduced the premium for machine tool operators to insure their cooperation.[34] But these steps proved inadequate. Carl Barth recalled that "they had gotten some machines running too slow, while others were running at ridiculously high speed."[35] By 1903 Dodge decided that outside assistance was necessary. After consulting Taylor, he hired Barth to make the necessary adjustments.

Barth proceeded slowly and deliberately at Link-Belt. "The first work I did was scientifically to investigate their machinery and speed it according to our methods."[36] In the following months he introduced Taylor's tool maintenance techniques and supervised the production of various "handling facilities."[37] By 1905 he was satisfied that sufficient progress had been made to add other features. He selected functional foremen and put them in charge of two lathes. He also made a special effort to prepare the lathe operators. "The two men who were used in the introduction of the system were taken into the superintendent's office and talked to by me personally in the presence of the three functional foremen appointed to run them . . . I set forth the whole principle on which we proposed to treat them in the future."[38] The men agreed to cooperate and were given bonuses. Soon others volunteered to work under the new methods.

Barth and several assistants soon introduced additional innovations. Barth appointed a man to help him make slide rules and others to begin time studies. He and his associates set up an elaborate planning department, reorganized the storeroom and toolroom, and revised the Link-Belt accounting system. Gradually they shifted the workers from the premium to the task and bonus system and then to the differential piece rate. By 1908 their work was largely complete.[39]

The results were persuasive evidence of the Taylor system's potential. Dodge testified in 1910 that output per man had doubled, that costs had decreased 20 percent, and that the average wage had risen 25 to 30 percent.[40] In the Chicago plant, where Dodge's associates had introduced Taylor's methods in 1906 and 1907, the financial results were even more favorable.[41] Moreover, both plants operated smoothly, without many of the difficulties common to traditional factories. The managers met delivery schedules, reduced inventories, and seemingly eliminated labor unrest (which had been a serious problem in the Chicago plant before 1906). One visitor to the Philadelphia plant reported that "there is no apparent rush. Each man has his work and apparently does it. . . . There was no false motion."[42]

Taylor's defenders often cited Link-Belt to support their claim that workmen under scientific management were happy and contented. By 1912, 91 percent of the men worked under the differential piece rate, and most apparently were satisfied with their lot.[43] After interviewing many Link-Belt employees, Robert Thurston Kent concluded that scientific management had eliminated the labor problem at the Philadelphia plant. Since the workers' primary goal was higher pay, they did not object to the managerial controls, the steady pace, or the time studies that were prerequisites for earning the "high" rate. "'I'm after the coin,'" one man told him. "'If I could get more over at Midvale than I can here, I'd quit and go over to Midvale, even if I had had to work harder than I do here.'"[44] Others reportedly complained if they could not work under the differential rate because a particular job was new and had not been timed. Men who did not share this viewpoint left of their own volition. "If they cannot maintain the standard set, they make a very low rate per piece. . . . It is seldom necessary to discharge a man for inefficiency."[45] Given his biases and unrepresentative sample, Kent likely exaggerated the effects of scientific management. Dodge's firm but sympathetic approach had won the employees' loyalty and cooperation before the advent of scientific management and undoubtedly continued to have an impact. L. P. Alford probably best summarized the Link-Belt experience when he wrote that "a deliberate attempt" had been made to "so arrange shop conditions that the men would find their work not only profitable but pleasant."[46]

By 1908 Link-Belt had become a model plant, one of two establishments where the Taylor system was in operation throughout the factory. But this did not mean that Dodge and his associates considered scientific management perfect or immutable. Alford wrote that "some parts of the system as originally introduced have been abandoned or superceded by something entirely different."[47] Probably the most important modifications occurred in the planning department. Between 1908 and 1912 the number of men employed there was reduced by 40 percent.[48] The Link-Belt managers also abolished the job of "speed boss" after Barth completed his work and introduced slide rules.[49] They altered many of the original accounting forms and retained (or reverted to) the premium in some departments.[50] Finally, they went beyond Taylor in the personnel area, introducing a modest welfare program and, ultimately, a company union.[51] The latter, created in 1915 over Taylor's objections, was designed to encourage "our men to take an interest in the determination of base rates and piece rates so as to . . . disarm organized labor."[52] Dodge and his associates insisted, however, that they had not deviated from Taylor's philosophy and objectives.

The Tabor reorganization, like the Link-Belt effort, was also an outgrowth of Taylor's personal contacts in the Philadelphia engineering community. Since 1890 Tabor had been a leader in the development of molding machines—labor-saving foundry devices. Until the turn of the century the company had merely marketed its products; it contracted the manufacturing out to firms like the Sellers Company. But in 1900 the Tabor family persuaded Wilfred Lewis to leave Sellers and become president and part owner of Tabor. One of Lewis's first moves was to establish a factory in downtown Philadelphia.[53] To his dismay, he soon discovered that his engineering expertise was of limited value in production management. Rather than improving the firm's financial position, the factory recorded substantial losses.

Three problems plagued the company. First, the factory was old and dilapidated, and the machinery, according to Barth and Hathaway, was little better.[54] This deficiency reflected the company's limited resources rather than Lewis's mistaken judgment, but it seriously hindered operations, even after the introduction of scientific management. Second, the plant was poorly managed, partly because of Lewis's inexperience and partly because of his efforts to economize by minimizing "nonproductive" or indirect labor costs. In 1904 the company employed 105 production and only five clerical workers.[55] Finally, the workers were dissatisfied. They formed a union and struck in 1901, demanding shorter hours and higher pay. Lewis agreed to reduce the work day in return for a promise to maintain production at existing levels.[56] By early 1902 these difficulties had reduced the company to near bankruptcy.

In desperation Lewis turned to Taylor for financial assistance. Taylor agreed to buy Tabor stock in return for the opportunity to introduce scientific management, an arrangement that Lewis quickly accepted. Barth began at the Tabor plant in early 1903 and retained overall responsibility for several years. Taylor also spent some time there in 1903, though his determination to retire, his preoccupation with Boxly, and the preparation of "Shop Management" limited his contribution. At one point he apparently hoped that Barth could handle the mechanical work while Lewis, with a copy of "Shop Management," did the rest.[57] These ad hoc arrangements proved unsuccessful. Both managers and workers objected to the disruption of their routine, and production costs increased rather than decreased. Faced with the possible failure of the company and a severe blow to his reputation, Taylor "insisted upon his right to direct the introduction of his system . . . without obstruction or interference."[58] From that time until Hathaway's arrival in late 1904 he and Barth spent more time at Tabor. The company's losses decreased, and the threat of failure lessened.[59]

In 1910 Hathaway described how he and Barth had introduced scientific management at Tabor. "In the first place," he noted, "[we] went over all of our machines" and "got them in as good condition as possible." Then they "looked after" the belting and introduced Taylor's belt maintenance methods. "The next thing we did was to provide the shop with a plentiful supply of small tools, such as bolts and clamps. . . . We supplied them [the workers] with cutting tools of standard shapes, and steel of a quality that we knew would do the work." He and Barth also "installed a toolroom and equipped it with tools," rearranged the store-rooms, and set up a planning office adjacent to the drafting department. To operate the planning office, they appointed a production or order-of-work clerk; a route clerk; a cost clerk; a balance of stores clerk; an "instruction-card man . . . [who] writes up an instruction card, stating the best method" and appropriate times based on slide rule and time studies; a move man "who does nothing but move the material"; and a time study man. They also trained functional foremen: gang bosses, speed bosses, inspectors, and repair bosses. Finally, they introduced time study and an incentive wage, either the task and bonus or the differential piece rate, depending on the job.[60] Their work was thoroughly conventional and orthodox, in accord with Taylor's post-1901 teachings. The only possible exception was the accounting system, which Hathaway did not mention. This omission, however, was more likely a result of Hathaway's declining interest in accounting techniques than any actual deviation from Taylor's methods.[61]

The workers' response to these changes was gratifying to Taylor, particularly since Tabor had a history of labor unrest. Lewis recalled that the "Kickers were gradually converted or discouraged, better discipline was established and a few of the men were soon earning 30 percent more wages than they could command elsewhere."[62] A new type of complaint became common:

> if there is anything on the instruction card that they consider unfair they register their first kick. If they find that the method they have is superior they kick. If they believe they have an easier way of doing it that would not require as much physical effort they would bring it to us. If anything interferes with them, then, no matter how trifling it may be, there is another kick. If they think they can not make the time they kick to have it demonstrated to them.
>
> They demand that when they are supposed to work under ideal conditions that the conditions must be furnished, and unless they are furnished they kick.[63]

Like the Link-Belt workmen, the Tabor employees supposedly objected when they were unable to earn the bonus or "high" rate.[64] Yet to Taylor the most convincing evidence of the beneficial effect of scientific management was their loyalty to the company. In 1910 when a city-wide machinists' strike closed all the plants in the area, only one Tabor employee left his job.[65]

Other effects of scientific management were equally impressive. Tabor broke even in 1906 and made a profit in 1907, largely because of cost reductions.[66] By 1910 the company had doubled its 1904 output with no addition to the plant or machinery. Materials moved "from the Stock room to the shopping room . . . like the course of a river."[67] The number of office and managerial employees increased to more than twenty, while the production force declined to approximately seventy-five.[68] Workers who became functional foremen and planning office clerks received high wages; those who remained in their former jobs often earned substantial bonuses.

Taylor's methods thus saved Tabor between 1903 and 1908 and contributed to its survival over the next half century, despite intense competition, inferior facilities, and managerial deficiencies in other areas of the business. More than a decade after Taylor's death Lewis reported that he and his associates had "deviated" from Taylor's system "only in methods of application and in mechanisms employed."[69] They assigned one man to perform the duties of several functional foremen in slack periods; simplified the planning operation, notably the bulletin boards, "balance" of stores, and route sheets; and developed standardized instruction cards and time study sheets. Their experiences suggested that scientific management was no panacea for the ills of a manufacturing firm, but could make a substantial difference in the performance of the factory and the behavior of the employees.

The reorganization process and impact of scientific management at Link-Belt and Tabor were virtually identical, obvious consequences of Taylor's presence and direct or indirect participation in the work. At both plants improvements in the physical setting and machinery occupied Barth and his assistants for nearly two years and preceded other aspects of the system. When he had made substantial progress in those areas, Barth introduced the Taylor production and cost systems— especially the planning department and functional foremen. Finally, Barth revised the traditional methods of work and pay with time study, an incentive wage, and ultimately the differential piece rate. As a Tabor time study man indicated to a congressional committee, the incentive wage "is only a small part of scientific management. Time study in its entirety is only one feature. . . . Scientific management can be used without the employment of any piece-work bonus system."[70]

Shop Reform, 1906–1915

In the decade and a half after Taylor's retirement the Bethlehem veterans and post-1901 recruits undertook similar efforts for other firms. Gantt was the only one of these men who had developed a large consulting practice before 1906, but as Taylor's promotional campaign succeeded, Barth, Cooke, Hathaway, and the others also attracted substantial numbers of clients. C. B. Thompson maintained that they introduced scientific management in more than two hundred institutions, including 181 factories, during Taylor's lifetime.[71] With possibly one or two exceptions their work was less complete than Barth's and Hathaway's at Link-Belt and Tabor. Thompson, for example, was able to obtain information on only 120 of the 181 factories. Of that group only 69 were "successes."[72]

The "successes"—the firms that were most affected by the expert's work—were a heterogeneous group.[73] The largest number were machinery plants, small job-order shops like Smith and Furbush, large machinery works like the Santa Fe and Canadian Pacific shops and the New England Butt Company, and mass production factories like Yale and Towne, Pullman, Remington Typewriter, and Winchester Arms. Next most numerous were textile factories, giant manufacturers like the Amoskeag Company and Cheney Brothers, and small companies like Sayles Bleachery, Brighton Mills, and Joseph Bancroft and Sons. Taylor's disciples also reorganized printing and publishing plants and clothing factories. Conversely, they did relatively little work in the heat-using industries, where large batch and flow manufacture restricted the area of managerial discretion and thus the potential for "inefficiency." The disciples succeeded (and failed) in small and large factories alike; the notion that scientific management was particularly suited to small shops is erroneous and misleading. The crucial factor was neither technology nor plant size, but, as Taylor insisted, the managers' commitment to change. No matter the industry or size of plant, if the managers were not sufficiently committed, if they could not resist the temptation to interfere, a successful reorganization was most unlikely.

The experiences of twenty-five of the best-known firms that introduced scientific management indicate that Link-Belt and Tabor were useful models for understanding the disciples' work.[74] In nearly every case the expert devoted most of his time initially to the improvement of tools and machinery. Gradually he shifted his attention to the organization of the factory and then, after substantial progress had been made in that area, introduced the labor features of scientific management—instructon cards, time study, and an incentive wage. In most instances his innovations had a greater impact on the manufacturing process and shop organization than on the activities of production workers.[75]

There were, of course, many variations. Some plants required more preliminary work than others. The Pullman plant, where Barth worked periodically from 1913 to 1919, was practically a model factory before he started. The Cheney Brothers factory at South Manchester, Connecticut, one of Gantt's jobs, was equally advanced. Taylor was uneasy when his followers accepted such assignments, fearful that an expensive reorganization would not appreciably improve the plant's performance. He apparently discouraged one client, the McElwain Company of Boston, on these grounds.[76] On the other hand, a few firms, like the Eastern Manufacturing Company, adopted scientific management in a desperate effort to stem losses or even avoid bankruptcy. The condition of the factory obviously affected the amount of time and energy the expert devoted to the technical and organizational aspects of scientific management.

The disciples' personal interests and biases also accounted for significant variations in the application and ultimately the effects of scientific management. Barth and Hathaway were traditional engineers; they emphasized machine performance and postponed, even neglected, Taylor's labor measures. They typically devoted their time to the first phase of the reorganization effort, leaving the managerial and labor features of scientific management to subordinates. Barth was the more extreme of the two; he relied almost exclusively on Dwight Merrick for time studies and the incentive wage. Gantt and Cooke shared the biases of Barth and Hathaway, but were more sensitive to the labor implications of scientific management. Their approach was also a reflection of their respective specializations, textile and printing and publishing plants, which were technically less demanding than machine shops. As noted earlier, Gantt became more and more preoccupied with the task and bonus system and, though his work remained relatively orthodox, increasingly saw himself as a social reformer rather than a technician.

Though none of these efforts was as thorough as the Link-Belt and Tabor reorganizations, their effects were roughly similar. The most frequent omissions were measures affecting the workers—functional foremanship and the incentive wage, in particular. Apparently the disciples introduced the full complement of specialized supervisors at only one of the twenty-five companies (the Plimpton Press of Norwood, Massachusetts) either because they discounted the value of Taylor's innovation or feared further disruption of the managerial hierarchy. They omitted the incentive wage for quite different reasons. The need to reorganize the machinery, establish a planning office, and revamp the tool and stores areas before the system could operate effectively often led them to postpone the installation of the task and bonus or differential piece rate, which they considered essential, until it was too late. In nearly one-third of the factories their activities evoked such opposition that their services were terminated before they had an opportunity to introduce the incentive wage. Where the system operated "three years or more . . . 50 to 85 percent of the employees [earned] bonuses ranging from 10 to 60 or 70 percent."[77]

Thus, it appears that scientific management had no more dramatic effect on these workers than it had on the Link-Belt or Tabor employees. Insofar as it led to a rearrangement of the shop, modified the foreman's authority, reduced delays, and increased output, it had a profound impact on the wage earner—as it did on everyone concerned with the operation of the factory. Otherwise, the effects of scientific management on the workers were minimal. They were largely confined to employees who worked under one of the Taylor incentive wage plans—probably less than a half of the production employees in the twenty-five plants. Of that minority some received the bonus or "high" rate prematurely, before the necessary preliminary steps had been introduced or completed. In a few cases this was a sign of driving and may have led to overwork and excessive fatigue, not to mention "soldiering." The residual group—workers who received the bonus or differential piece rate in shops that had been properly systematized— earned higher wages for steadier work. The surviving evidence suggests that they recognized their elite status and favored scientific management.

In most cases, then, scientific management as applied by Taylor in the 1890's and as applied by his disciples after 1901 had somewhat different effects on the workers. Taylor introduced the differential piece rate whenever it seemed expedient; as a result, a relatively large proportion of workers at the Manufacturing Investment Company, the Johnson Company, and Simonds worked under it during the 1890's. His disciples, faithful to the "Bethlehem model," delayed the introduction of the incentive wage, in many instances permanently. Ironically, Taylor came under attack for his treatment of the worker at a time when scientific management had less effect and presumably less ill effect relative to the total number of production workers who might have been affected than at any time since the 1880's.

It is difficult, often impossible, to determine the changes that plant executives made after the disciples departed. Certainly the experiences of firms like Midvale and Link-Belt suggest that many of them did not maintain the disciples' original procedures and standards. If opposition to the system can be taken as a rough index of the likelihood of such revision, the modifications must have been frequent and substantial. In a few firms the top executives themselves were opponents. In at least four instances scientific management was introduced in the course of a power struggle between the younger and older members of the management group or as part of a larger reorganization program after the younger men had taken over.[78] More frequently, the plant managers, especially those at the lower levels, viewed Taylorism with considerable apprehension and skepticism. The combined pressures of high costs, disrupted routine, and the antagonism of those who were demoted or censured obviously took their toll. The foremen, in particular, were unhappy at the erosion of their powers.

The managers' objections varied widely, depending on individual situations, with one significant exception. Executives of mass production machinery firms like Remington Typewriter, Winchester Arms, and Yale and Towne were uniformly skeptical of functional foremanship and the planning department. They recognized the need for more expert supervision, but questioned the compatibility of functional management and the coordinated flow of hundreds of thousands of parts through the plant. With somewhat less unanimity they also doubted that Taylor's planning department was consistent with the principle of clearly defined managerial responsibility and authority. Their response was to retain Taylor's innovations, but to make the functional supervisors and planning clerks staff rather than line officials. By 1915 these firms typically had engineering, inspection, time study, "standards," and "labor" departments that offered advice and services to the line managers. The conventional foreman remained, but with severely limited powers.[79] By World War I scientific management had created the prototypes of mid-twentieth-century precision-manufacturing operations.

As might be expected, scientific management as applied by Taylor's less conventional followers and competitors had somewhat different effects on the factory and its employees. Yet the variations were not necessarily a result of the individual's incompetence or deliberate rejection of Taylor's methods. At the Santa Fe Railroad shops, Emerson's first and most ambitious effort to apply scientific management, he faithfully followed Taylor's prescriptions. He standardized equipment and operations "to better every shop condition making for improved efficiency," installed a new cost system, devised an intricate "dispatching system" or planning department, and reorganized the toolrooms. He also altered the method of supervision (exactly how is not clear, although he opposed functional foremanship) and introduced time study and a bonus wage, his "Individual Effort System."[80] Since he had little prior experience with machine tool operations, his machine shop work presumably would not have impressed Barth or Hathaway. But in other respects Emerson's work at the Santa Fe differed little from that of the more orthodox disciples.

The same generalization applies to Frederick A. Parkhurst's reorganization of the Ferracute Machine Company after Oberlin Smith, the owner, had rejected Hathaway's more costly proposal. Parkhurst may have settled for a less elaborate planning office, but otherwise his work appears thoroughly orthodox and complete.[81] Gilbreth likewise demonstrated his familiarity with scientific management at the New England Butt Company between 1911 and 1914, his one attempt to introduce the complete Taylor system.[82]

Thus, the deficiencies Taylor and his followers detected in Emerson's and later Gilbreth's work were usually the results of deliberate strategies or innovations rather than lack of ability or unfamiliarity with scientific management. Emerson's desire for wealth and social position overshadowed his mastery of Taylor's methods, just as it had apparently compromised earlier achievements. When Emerson started his management consulting business in 1907, his goal was to exploit the reputation and contacts he had acquired at the Santa Fe; neither he nor Samuel Emerson ever mentioned any objective other than immediate profit in their letters. In practice this meant that they abandoned Taylor's system for what Emerson later called "efficiency" work. In most cases this was no more than a common sense approach to factory organization coupled with time study and an incentive wage.[83] The Emerson strategy often succeeded: plant performance improved, the managers—who were only marginally affected—did not object, and the workers made higher wages. In other instances, particularly when the workers were union members, it failed.[84] At the American Locomotive Company, Emerson's labor reforms provoked labor disturbances in at least three plants in early 1908 and led to the repudiation of time study and the incentive wage.[85]

Though he shared many of Emerson's personal characteristics, Gilbreth also remained at heart an orthodox disciple except on the subject of time study. At New England Butt he introduced the standard reforms but added other features—a "betterment" room, a photographic department, and his "route model"—that grew out of his interest in motion study.[86] Gradually these innovations—"Gilbrethiana," as Hathaway called them in derision—overshadowed scientific management.[87] Gilbreth's independent course became increasingly apparent as his relationship with Taylor deteriorated. By 1919 an assistant could write that the managers of the Pierce-Arrow Company, one of Gilbreth's clients, were angry. "They think you are trying to reorganize the whole plant"—to introduce scientific management instead of the motion study methods that Gilbreth had promised.[88]

Although motion study was applicable to a wide range of activities, Gilbreth used it primarily as a substitute for the time study techniques that Taylor and Thompson had developed. This approach meant that Gilbreth's work, like Emerson's, had a relatively greater impact on the employees than the activities of the conventional disciples. The nature of that impact, however, is difficult to ascertain. It appears that the workers did not interpret motion study as a "speed-up" technique; at least there were no notable labor disturbances at the plants Gilbreth reorganized, and Gilbreth always maintained that the employees appreciated his efforts. On the other hand, he was an astute handler of men, especially union workmen, and paid increasing attention to nonindustrial applications of motion study. Possibly he avoided Emerson's difficulties for these reasons. In any event, the question is only marginally relevant, for Gilbreth's interest had taken him to the periphery of the scientific management movement by the time of Taylor's death.

In general, then, Taylor successfully imposed his convictions on his followers. No matter what he said or wrote for public consumption, his followers knew what he required and acted accordingly. Those who for whatever reason did not accept his approach soon ceased to be members of the Taylor circle. Yet the disparity between Taylor's pronouncements and the disciples' work caused growing difficulties in his relations with the uninitiated, especially the managers and employees of the government arsenals and shipyards where scientific management was introduced after 1906. Though the results of these undertakings were generally consistent with Taylor's expectations, the experiences anticipated several of the problems that would appear when Taylor and his doctrines emerged outside the parochial world of the factory and engineering society.

The Public Sector: Reform and Reaction

Taylor's rise in the 1880's and 1890's was closely associated with the emergence of the late-nineteenth-century armaments industry, particularly the reorientation of the eastern steel manufacturers. Government contracts created opportunities for Taylor at Midvale and Bethlehem and brought his methods to the attention of a variety of influential men, from William C. Whitney to the Army and Navy inspectors stationed at Midvale and Bethlehem. By 1906 many of the officers who had observed him in the 1890's had risen to important commands. Their recollections, coupled with Taylor's growing prominence, resulted in several plant reorganizations and the promise of many more. These activities, in turn, helped to project Taylor and scientific management into public affairs. The introduction of Taylorism at a private company had little impact outside the firm; the introduction of scientific management at a shipyard or arsenal often had wide-ranging external implications.

This difference resulted from variations in the management of private and public manufacturing plants and from the operation of the military services. The military plants had lower overhead costs because of their public status and higher direct labor costs because of liberal civil service benefit programs.[89] The officer-managers generally had less authority and managerial expertise. The Army's Ordnance Department, which operated the arsenals, had a permanent body of industrial managers; the Navy was less fortunate. The amalgamation of the line and staff corps at the end of the nineteenth century created endless confusion in the shipyards.[90] A line officer always commanded the facility, while the naval constructors, or engineering officers, had de facto responsibility for the operation of the yard. The arsenal and shipyard managers also had comparatively little control over the workers. Government factories were often unionized, and civil service procedures prohibited many traditional antiunion activities. Though civil service regulations also circumscribed the unions' potential services to the employees, contemporary engineers, including many military officers with experience at shipyards and arsenals, believed that the union influence, coupled with the officers' inability to hire and fire at will, resulted in widespread efforts to restrict output and stifle innovation.[91]

Although military observers at Midvale and Bethlehem had been impressed with Taylor's work, the first officer to introduce scientific management was Navy Constructor Holden A. Evans, who had had no direct contact with Taylor. In 1905, while serving at the Norfolk yard, Evans made several improvements that attracted the attention of Admiral Washington Capps, the head of the construction bureau. As a result, Capps transferred Evans to the Mare Island yard near San Francisco and made him the de facto head of manufacturing. Evans interpreted this promotion as official encouragement for even more sweeping changes. He read "Shop Management" and, more important, discovered that his master mechanic, Lorin V. Ester, had worked at the Tabor Company.[92] Between mid-1906 and 1908 he made the Mare Island facility the first "scientifically" managed government plant.

Evans first introduced Taylor's refinements of systematic management. He developed a more detailed cost system, reorganized the machine tools, supplied the men with additional tools, and installed Taylor's belt maintenance methods. He also established a central tool-grinding department and improved the operation of the toolrooms. Navy regulations prevented a thorough reorganization of the stores department, but he implemented most of Taylor's stores control techniques. He set up a planning department to control production in the machine shop and later in other areas of the plant. His planning office operated much like the ones Barth installed at Link-Belt and Tabor, though with fewer clerks. Evans also created a full complement of functional foremen except for the disciplinarian.[93]

Like Barth, Hathaway, and the other orthodox disciples, Evans postponed Taylor's labor measures until he had completed the other changes. In the interim the Mare Island planning department issued only general instructions to the men; the gang bosses continued to perform their traditional functions. Evans also delayed the introduction of time study and an incentive wage. He wrote that his "constant aim" was to "get the shops up to maximum efficiency" under day work and "at the same time collect data which will make it easy to go to one of the more efficient systems of paying labor."[94]

While he was "collecting data," Evans systematically eliminated ineffective or uncooperative workers. At Simonds and Bethlehem, Taylor had encouraged less than "first class" men and women to leave by a variety of means, including wage reductions; Evans was less subtle. He set out to purge the plant of incorrigible, incompetent, and redundant employees. Despite civil service regulations, he devised a technique to rid the shipyard of supervisors who resisted his instructions, and he forced production workers to compete for positions. In the sail-making department, for example:

> it was soon evident to the men themselves that it would be necessary to reduce the force . . . and the first cut brought out the fact that it is difficult to obtain work in this district. With still further improvement a second small reduction was necessary, and this left about half the original force. These men are all excellent mechanics, who can produce a large output. The majority of these owned their homes in, and had strong ties binding them to, the vicinity, and they knew that if they lost their jobs they would have to leave their homes to obtain work. This brought about keen competition between the men, and resulted in a very large output.[95]

He replaced skilled machinists with helpers wherever possible and rearranged the boiler shop "so the work shoved the men; each operation had to keep ahead of the operation behind, and if this was not the case it immediately showed up."[96] According to a local Machinists union official, he also "threatened to fill the yard with Negro mechanics and to make good that threat, has a Negro machinist now in his employ."[97]

Evans's policy again underlined the fact that in its preliminary stages scientific management was compatible with a variety of labor policies. If Dodge's paternalism represented one extreme, the ruthless winnowing of the Mare Island employees symbolized the other. Since neither Taylor nor his disciples had developed a clearly defined procedure for dealing with employees during the transition period, the character and objectives of the expert or plant manager determined the workers' fate. Though neither Dodge's nor Evans's approach was a necessary concomitant of scientific management, both were options under scientific management.

During Evans's reorganization of the Mare Island shops the workers were remarkably subdued. They protested, but took no direct action to halt his activities.[98] Indeed, many of them seemed oblivious to the entire process. The Machinists' official wrote that the Mare Island employees were "lukewarm union men . . . utterly indifferent to the situation."[99] Though the documents provide no ready explanation for these attitudes, it is possible the workers were confused rather than indifferent. Because of their union backgrounds they were aware of certain potential threats and prepared to react. Several unions represented at the plant had taken stands against the Halsey premium plan and presumably would have struck if Evans had attempted to introduce an incentive wage. But Evans did not interfere with the existing wage system; his innovations were of a more mundane and, from the employees' perspective, traditional character. It is likely that the workers perceived him simply as another "driving" superintendent. Layoffs between jobs had been common in the past, so there was nothing new in Evans's reduction of the shipyard labor force.[100] As the Machinists leader noted, the unions wanted a replacement for Evans who was "more in sympathy with the upholding of the dignity of labor."[101] Yet without an obvious challenge like the premium the union leaders found it impossible to arouse or unify the workers.

In late 1907 Evans decided to use time studies and the task and bonus to increase the output of various laborers—scalers, caulkers, and riveters—who had been unaffected by his previous efforts. He first ordered his assistants to time men scaling the hull of an Army transport ship.

> Ten different men were put on this work and stop watch times taken. The average time of these men was taken as a basis for obtaining the piece work rate. If these men worked all day at the rate when timed, they would scale something over 400 sq. ft. per

day. I allow one-half of the time for periods of rest, unavoidable delays, going to the water closet, and similar delays, making the daily task as 200 sq. ft.[102]

He then proposed a 50 percent bonus for men who completed the task. As he explained to Admiral Capps, "it will require severe bodily exertion and fatigue to produce these results, and I fully concur in the statement made by Mr. Taylor that where this is the case it is necessary to pay 50% more than the regular wages to obtain the best results." Paraphrasing Taylor, he concluded that the high wage would attract "active, strong and ambitious laborers" and ultimately produce "the best body of laborers in this section of the country."[103] Capps approved Evans's request in September, and the men accepted the plan. Evans also put the caulkers, a union group, on the task and bonus without incident. He reported that the men "make large wages, are perfectly contented, and never give the management the slightest trouble."[104] When he announced his plan to the unionized riveters, however, they balked, refusing to work. Surprised by their truculence, Evans "called a mass meeting of the strikers and met them face to face." He emphasized that "nobody would suffer and most would benefit." "In spite of the arguments of the union officials," he recalled, the riveters then voted to return to work under the task and bonus.[105]

Shortly after this incident Admiral Caspar F. Goodrich, Taylor's old colleague and friend, emerged as a second and more influential spokesman for scientific management in the Navy. The reasons for his sudden initiative are not clear; he had known of Taylor's work since the 1890's, but had never indicated an interest in scientific management, much less a desire to reform the shipyards. Possibly the combination of Taylor's growing reputation and his strategic position as commander of the New York Navy Yard spurred him to action. In any event, by early 1908 he had convinced the Navy to appoint a commission to establish specifications for the tool steel used in the shipyards. The Tool Steel Board's first action was to solicit Taylor's views.[106] Goodrich also persuaded his superiors to create a special toolroom at the Philadelphia Navy Yard to make high speed steel tools for all the Atlantic navy yards. On Taylor's recommendation the Navy selected Hathaway to set up the toolroom. By December 1908 Hathaway was making "very rapid and successful progress."[107]

Goodrich also installed some features of scientific management in the New York yard. At first he proceeded slowly and deliberately. "I feel," he wrote, "that it is wiser to restrict my activities to improving machines and tools, rather than attempt a radical change in organization."[108] In early 1909 he obtained permission to hire Barth as a consultant "not . . .

to introduce any system but to [provide] advice."[109] By March he had altered the layout of the machine shop and toolroom and may have introduced a rudimentary planning department.

In the meantime, however, he had made an uncharacteristically bold proposal that profoundly affected the subsequent history of scientific management in the Navy, as well as his and Evans's careers. In late 1908 Goodrich submitted a navy yard reorganization plan that called for the appointment of a single manager who would have the power to run the yard like a private factory and to introduce scientific management. Evans, operating independently, suggested a similar plan in November 1908. Truman Newberry, the Secretary of the Navy, liked their ideas and moved to implement them in early 1909, at a time when he expected to retain his office in the new Taft administration. The line officers were shocked, partly because the reorganization theatened to deprive them of their customary shore duty and partly because it promised to upset the prevailing balance between line and staff officers. In the following years they fought and ultimately eliminated scientific management from the Navy, not because they opposed Taylor's ideas per se, but because scientific management had spawned the obnoxious Goodrich-Evans-Newberry reorganization scheme.

As long as Newberry remained in office, Goodrich and Evans made progress. Taylor conferred with the secretary in December and reported that Newberry would "look upon this work as the most important during the next administration."[110] Barth began his duties in New York, and Evans became the formal head of the manufacturing departments at Mare Island. In February, however, President-Elect William Howard Taft, responding to various pressures, appointed Newberry ambassador to Russia and made George von L. Meyer, a Massachusetts politician and former postmaster general, secretary of the Navy. The line officers reacted immediately. By April, Goodrich reported to Taylor that a "fierce war" was being waged "against all the improvements in the Navy Yards which were inaugurated by Mr. Newberry."[111] The Navy bureaucracy forced Goodrich to resign the following month and reassigned Evans to an obscure Seattle post shortly thereafter.[112] The line officers scrapped Hathaway's tool-making operation and "devastated" Mare Island. They "wiped every trace of records and data out of existence, and went back to the original system of incompetent foremen, giving orders by word of mouth."[113] Taylor contemplated various counter-moves before offering to pay Evans's salary for a year while he studied scientific management in Philadelphia. Meyer's rejection of this plan seemingly marked a complete reversal of the policy Newberry had initiated in 1909.

In January 1911 Taylor called on President Taft to protest Meyer's decision. The president gave him little satisfaction, but Taylor talked at length with Charles D. Norton, Taft's secretary, who apparently persuaded Taft to contact Meyer.[114] The Navy secretary's views underwent a hasty change. Though one of Taylor's informants reported that "Mr. M. intends to do only enough to justify himself with Mr. Taft," the secretary appeared to have developed a sincere interest in Taylor and his work.[115] He named Gantt, Emerson, and Charles Day to draft a report on Navy yard reorganization.[116] In early April he entertained this group and Taylor at battleship exercises off the Virginia coast and became quite friendly with Taylor. The latter was skeptical but optimistic: "He has been very suddenly converted to the principles of scientific management, and really appears to be genuinely in earnest. Of course I cannot look into his mind or his motives, but he seems to be genuine."[117] A month later the secretary visited Taylor in Philadelphia, listened to his lecture, and toured the Tabor and Link-Belt shops. In the interim Taylor was able to inform Evans that he would be given "congenial employment, of the kind to which you are well suited."[118]

For the next few months Evans's situation improved markedly. He was assigned to Bath, Maine, as an inspector and then to the Watertown Arsenal to study the installation of scientific management there.[119] He had two congenial interviews with Meyer, who appointed him to the Vreeland Board, an advisory body that was studying shipyard management. Meyer then assigned Evans to the Norfolk Navy Yard because Virginia was a Democratic state and the workers' protests, transmitted through their political representatives, would have little effect on the Republican administration in Washington.[120] In early October, Evans arrived in Norfolk to make that base the Navy's showcase.

Before he could begin his work, however, the secretary again bowed to the line officers' entreaties and revoked his orders. Evans submitted his resignation in disgust, and Meyer, under pressure from the Navy establishment, accepted it. To indicate his continued dedication to efficiency, Meyer then ordered certain reforms in the management of the Norfolk yard. Taylor was apparently correct when he wrote that these changes, supposedly derived from a British efficiency plan, were "in reality . . . just as near as they could get to our system."[121] Meyer's reforms included a planning department similar to Taylor's; indeed, the forms and instruction cards were so similar that the workers recognized them as part of the Taylor system and struck in early 1912.[122] Meyer quickly disavowed any desire to introduce an efficiency plan in the Navy yards.

The Army reformers operated in a radically different environment for a variety of reasons. The Ordnance Department was a separate staff department, charged with manufacturing weapons and ammunition, and was therefore insulated from the intra-service rivalries that plagued Evans and Goodrich. Within the department many officers were acquainted with Taylor and his ideas as a result of his work at Midvale and Bethlehem. Two generations of Watertown Arsenal officers, for example, were familiar with the Taylor grinding machine, which had been installed there in the 1890's.[123] Above all, General William Crozier, head of the department, was a Taylor devotee who did not interpret the Navy situation as an indictment of scientific management or waver in his determination to improve the arsenals' performance. It is not surprising that Taylor viewed the Army plants as one of the most promising fields for the application of scientific management.[124]

There remained, however, one important potential obstacle. The arsenal workers' unions wielded considerable influence, due largely to Crozier, who looked upon the arsenals as his personal responsibility and was sensitive to any criticism of them. As a result, the workers and their representatives played a more prominent role in the introduction of scientific management in the arsenals than they had in the shipyards.[125]

Crozier first became interested in scientific management as a result of Taylor's growing reputation as an engineer who understood the labor problem. In December 1906 he guided Taylor and an ASME delegation on a tour of the Army's Sandy Hook Proving Ground. Crozier and Taylor talked informally about the possibility of reorganizing the arsenals and corresponded frequently in the following months. At that time Crozier's primary interest was a piece rate system for the Watertown and Watervliet, New York, arsenals, which used "the old time method of daily wages."[126] Although he soon discovered the true nature of Taylor's system, he continued to think of it as an answer to the arsenals' particular labor problems. This emphasis led him to select Watertown because of its high labor costs and to defer substantive action until after the election of 1908, when the workers' political influence would be minimal.[127]

In the interim, a related incident underlined the need for caution. The contacts between Taylor and Crozier in late 1906 and early 1907 had awakened considerable interest among the ordnance officers, many of whom felt embarrassed professionally by the arsenals' poor reputations. Several, who either did not know or understand the reasons for Crozier's decision to postpone the installation of scientific management, acted unilaterally. Colonel C. G. Wheeler, at Watertown, contacted Gantt about the possibility of working there. Colonel Frank Hobbs, at

Rock Island, went even further. In September 1908 he independently introduced time study in the Rock Island shops: "I had the officers . . . studying how they were going to do it for four or five months. [P]ossibly for busy men this was a rather short time, but I thought the sub-division into elements was sufficient for a first trial and would give much information for future application." He acknowledged that time study was not scientific management and "would not have all of the good results . . . of Taylor's system," but "it would surely make for . . . very much good."[128] To the employees, however, time study was both a threat and a prelude to the obnoxious premium plan, the bête noire of the metal trades unions. They protested to their congressman, and Crozier immediately ordered a halt to Hobbs's activities. Hobbs was angry but eager "for the work to go on."[129]

Pushed by his impatient subordinates, Crozier contacted Taylor again in early 1909. The "principal difficulty," he wrote, was "in arranging such method of payment of workmen as will not result in pressure by the Unions upon members of Congress."[130] He would not shirk a confrontation with the unions, "but a fight is apt to be expensive, and I think it ought to be possible to attain our object without one."[131] Taylor answered with two persuasive arguments. He noted, quite appropriately, that the workmen would not be directly affected for many months.[132] He also repeated his standard response to questions about worker resistance. As soon as the men understood that "time study will mean higher wages for them, they will welcome it and help you in every way with it, instead of opposing it."[133] To support this claim, he asked Dodge and Lewis to write Crozier attesting to their employees' contentment under scientific management. Crozier was apparently reassured, though he remained wary of the unions' potential for trouble.[134]

Convinced that government manufacturing plants offered the greatest immediate opportunity for advancing scientific management, Taylor devoted considerable time and resources to the Watertown reorganization. He promised Crozier that if both Barth and Hathaway were too busy to take the job, "I will see that something else is postponed."[135] At the general's request he accompanied Barth on an initial tour of the Watertown facility in April 1909. His report was predictably optimistic: output would double, and there would be "very little trouble from the standpoint of the workmen in introducing our whole scheme of management."[136] By "very little trouble" he did not mean that the workers would accept scientific management without objection. His letters to Barth indicate that he expected protests and interpreted Crozier's concern as an indication that the Army would not take the responsibility for replacing ineffective employees. Barth would have to do "what I have done in many cases in the past, namely . . . get the necessary men to do the work at the Arsenal."[137]

Barth began his activities at the arsenal in mid-June and worked there intermittently for three years. He treated the Watertown assignment like any other job, with one exception. He started with the machine shop, but reversed his customary sequence—apparently in deference to Taylor's desire for quick results—and introduced the managerial features of scientific management before he had completed the physical reorganization of the shop. His first important step was to establish a planning department, which began to operate in December 1909 and became increasingly elaborate in the following years. As early as August 1909 he suggested that Wheeler send one or more men to Tabor or Link-Belt to learn time study techniques.[138] He also introduced the Taylor belt maintenance methods, a tool-forging and grinding department, and the Taylor toolroom and storeroom systems. The results of these preliminary reforms tended to confirm Taylor's and Crozier's expectations. When Hathaway visited the arsenal in early June 1910, he reported that "the routing seemed to be working perfectly and the store room and tool room, both of which are models in appearance, are almost done."[139]

Having demonstrated that scientific management could achieve immediate results, Barth returned to his preferred approach. On his first visit he had supplied the officers with forms to record "the elements of the various machines, showing their speeds, feeds, and the general design of the machine."[140] In October 1909 he studied their reports and recommended several changes in the use of the machinery. In February 1910 Wheeler noted that they were making progress on "a systematic study of all machine tools with a view to standardizing them."[141] In April, largely to educate the officers, Barth conducted a series of competitive tests of different tool steels and in the following months devoted more and more of his time to improvements in machine tool operations. By the winter of 1910–11 he was ready to make slide rules for the arsenal machines.[142] At Barth's urging, Taylor assigned Merrick to begin time studies at the arsenal in May 1911.

By that time Barth had nearly completed his work. He had reorganized and improved the machinery, belting, and tools and had installed a planning department complete with bulletin boards, the Taylor cost system, and a corps of clerks. Because he had not finished his machine tool improvements, he did not introduce speed bosses until late 1911, but the gang bosses and inspectors performed their duties as Taylor had defined them. Finally, he had ordered time studies in anticipation of a shift to the incentive wage. According to the officers, production had increased substantially and unit costs had declined. Though there had been no wholesale discharges comparable to the Mare Island reductions, some ineffective or unnecessary workers had been laid off.[143] By 1911 the Watertown machine shop had become a model plant, as Hathaway had predicted.

Crozier was so pleased with Barth's activities that he summoned prominent officers from other arsenals to a special meeting at Watertown in December 1910 to consider the introduction of scientific management in their plants. For nearly a week the men studied every facet of the Watertown operation. They inspected different departments and watched the employees perform their duties. "The course of each important paper was followed from its origin to the point where it ceased to be operative. The blank forms used at the other arsenals were examined and compared."[144] Barth visited the arsenal during this period and joined the group for an afternoon session. Only one officer criticized the system, and even he seemed satisfied with Barth's replies.[145] At the end of the sessions the officers recommended the adoption of the Taylor stores and cost systems "at all the arsenals," approved the idea of "having the grinding and care of tools done in central tool rooms," endorsed Taylor's belt maintenance procedures, and urged the establishment of planning departments, particularly in plants "where labor is paid for at a daily rate."[146] They considered various ways of introducing these measures at the other arsenals, including the employment of outside experts; in the end, however, they decided merely to send officers and workers to Watertown to observe the Taylor system in operation. This decision, which had a significant impact on the installation of scientific management at the other plants, reflected the officers' desire to retain control of their operations, their enthusiasm for Taylor's methods notwithstanding.

The beginning of time studies at Watertown and the adoption of scientific management techniques at other arsenals were decisive steps in the emerging confrontation between scientific management and organized labor. Evans's and Hobbs's activities had already alerted the metal trades union leaders to the relationship between the Taylor system and the incentive wage. Merrick's work and the extension of Taylor's methods to other arsenals represented, from their perspective, a dramatic escalation of the effort to impose the premium in government plants. Leaders of the Machinists Union responded with protests at Watertown and Washington in June 1911.[147]

Despite these actions the Watertown machinists accepted Merrick and the bonus.[148] As Taylor had predicted, their familiarity with scientific management overcame their instinctive opposition to the incentive wage. Only when the arsenal officers, eager to assert their independence of Barth and impatient at Merrick's slow pace, attempted to introduce the Halsey premium and then time study in the foundry did the arsenal employees react. The molders, unaffected by Barth and Merrick's work until that time, struck against time study in August.[149] The walkout, which lasted a week, united the arsenal workers in opposition to time study and the incentive wage and caused an uproar in Washington that continued long after the strike had been forgotten.

In the meantime, the Rock Island employees had insured that the Watertown strike would have a significant effect on Congress. Recalling Hobbs's abortive effort to impose the premium in 1908, they protested to their congressmen as soon as Hobbs announced, in early 1911, that he planned to implement aspects of the Taylor system at Rock Island. Hobbs did not mention time study; neither the conference report nor his written plans for the Rock Island Arsenal included the introduction of time study or the incentive wage.[150] But the workers, like the union leaders, assumed that scientific management was an incentive wage system and persuaded Iowa Representative Irwin S. Pepper to introduce a bill calling for an investigation of the Taylor system. The House Committee on Labor conducted hearings in late April, but Congress took no action until the molders' strike.[151] That event led to a full-scale investigation, five years of public controversy over time study in the arsenals and much anguish for Taylor and his supporters.[152]

Remarkably, the controversy had almost no effect on the arsenals until 1915, when Congress forbid the use of Army appropriations for time study work. At Watertown the introduction of scientific management proceeded without further interruption. Barth worked at the arsenal until June 1912, devoting most of his time to the machines and slide rules. He probably would have stayed longer if Crozier and Wheeler had not become impatient with his perfectionist approach to machine shop operations.[153] Merrick remained an additional year, timing workers and setting rates in the foundry, smith shop, and woodworking shop. He and his assistants—arsenal employees that he had trained—also set rates for most of the laborers. By the time of his departure even the windows were washed "scientifically."[154] For their part the workers adopted a contradictory, expedient approach to scientific management. Publicly they continued to oppose time study and the bonus; in the plant, however, they worked under the Taylor system with few objections. Outside observers commented on the high morale of the arsenal employees.[155] Crozier and Wheeler soon concluded that the workers had accommodated themselves to the system and registered protests only in deference to their union leaders. One of the molders—the man who had precipitated the 1911 strike—probably summarized their position more accurately when he told Barth that "our concern is not for the present. As things go now, here, nothing could be nicer; our concern is for the future."[156]

In other respects the arsenal experience was similar to that of private firms where comparable efforts were undertaken. Materials costs declined by approximately 50 percent, and output per man doubled, as Taylor had predicted.[157] Despite the continuing dispute over time study and the incentive wage, the workers behaved much like the Link-Belt or Tabor employees. The officers also tinkered with the system, discarding certain features and introducing "short cuts" in others.[158] Merrick was shocked at their method for setting rates and preparing instruction cards when he visited the plant in 1914.[159]

This flexibility was even more apparent at the other arsenals, where scientific management was wholly the work of the officers. Despite their official endorsement of the system at Watertown in December 1910, the arsenal commanders had widely differing views on the applicability of Taylor's methods to their particular institutions. Hobbs predictably sought to introduce the entire system except for time study and the bonus in his machine shop, foundry, and forge shop. If he had not died in 1911, Rock Island might have become a second Watertown. Colonel George Montgomery, the Frankford Arsenal commander, also planned an extensive reorganization. On the other hand, Colonel S. L. Blunt, the Springfield commander, proposed only minor changes in his stores, belting, and cost systems.[160] From 1910 to 1915, while Barth and Merrick were completing their work at Watertown and the unions were escalating their attack on time study in Washington, these men, their associates, and their subordinates introduced their versions of Taylor's methods virtually unnoticed.

Montgomery was the most aggressive and independent of the arsenal commanders. He immediately adopted many of the Watertown innovations, including—in apparent contravention of Crozier's orders—the premium.[161] Possibly sensing trouble, Crozier employed Barth in November 1911 to assist Montgomery. Barth's reaction to Montgomery's initiatives was predictable: it was impossible, he wrote, to duplicate "another man's work without first being instructed in the principles behind [it]."[162] He praised the new stores system, the arsenal's purchasing methods, cost system, and toolroom, but criticized Montgomery's efforts to systematize belting and tool making, dismissed the planning room as "mere beginnings now," and condemned the premium, since "no real time study has been made" and since the premium rate was not high enough to evoke additional effort. This assessment began a stormy two-year relationship between the men. Montgomery charged that Barth "waited" for difficulties to be presented to him, "wasted" time, and made various "inexcusable mistakes."[163] Ostensibly their disagreement centered on the belting system that Barth installed, but the real issues were the leadership of the reorganization effort and the necessary degree of fidelity to Taylor's teachings. During the summer of 1913 Barth resigned in disgust. Taylor persuaded him to return on a temporary basis in 1914, but his relationship with Montgomery did not improve.[164]

The other commanders were less interested and less innovative. Hobbs's successors at Rock Island lacked his enthusiasm or daring and proceeded slowly. Perhaps this was fortunate for Taylor; the Rock Island workers surely would have struck if a vigorous effort had been undertaken. The machinists theatened to walk out in early 1912 when instruction cards were introduced, but backed down when the officers assured them that they did not contemplate time studies or an incentive wage.[165] By that time the arsenal had a planning department, an improved toolroom, and standardized machine tools.[166] Both the commander and master mechanic insisted, however, that these innovations were as much their ideas as Taylor's.[167] Colonel W. W. Gibson, the commander at the Watervliet Arsenal, installed a planning room and an improved belt system in late 1911. But the planning was limited in scope, and Gibson devised many of his own cost and production control forms.[168] In 1914 he proposed to introduce an incentive wage without prior time studies, a suggestion that probably reflected his overall approach to scientific management.

In government, as in private industry, the application of scientific management proved to be a complex and unpredictable process. Though Taylor succeeded in controlling and to some extent systemizing the initial stages, he had little influence over the final outcome or the "improvements" that appeared after the expert's departure. In the shipyards and arsenals political considerations created additional uncertainties. Taylor's role, however, did have one consistent effect. In both private and public institutions his presence insured that the experts did not adopt the opportunistic approach he had used in the 1890's. Even at Watertown, where Taylor was particularly eager to impress Crozier, Barth's concession to expediency was a planning department, not the incentive wage. Ironically, the persistence of the "Bethlehem model" was the least obvious effect of Taylor's activities after 1910. A new public role, reflecting the belated conjunction of scientific management and social reform, soon overshadowed the disciples' efforts at Tabor, Plimpton Press, Watertown Arsenal, and other plants where scientific management affected the work of men and machines.

7

Taylor and the Whole People, 1910–1915

In the first decade of his "retirement" Taylor emerged as the leading spokesman for the engineers' approach to industrial change and the most innovative of the consultants specializing in systematic management. Yet he retained his original identity and audience. He continued to think of himself as a member of the small fraternity of engineers and technically inclined manufacturers who spearheaded the growth of systematic management, and he addressed himself primarily to his fellow engineers. Had he died in 1910 he would likely have been remembered as another William Sellers, Henry R. Towne or Frederick A. Halsey. In the last years of his life, however, Taylor acquired a new identity and an enlarged constituency. Without changing his interests, his promotional strategy, his management system, or even the illustrative stories he used in his papers and speeches, he became a spokesman for the redemptive possibilities of systematic organization and technical expertise in economic and political life. By 1915 he had transcended his profession to become (with Henry Ford and Herbert Hoover) one of a trinity of early-twentieth-century technician-philosophers. The key to this remarkable transformation was Taylor's association with the progressive movement, the pre-World War I crusade that upheld the public interest, the "whole people," against the evils of contemporary society.

The Principles of Scientific Management

In some respects Taylor had always been a reformer. Since the 1880's he had been an unstinting foe of the industrial status quo and a champion of reforms that, he could argue, had greater impact on American society than the better known "reforms" of the politicians, journalists, social workers, and clergymen that are customarily associated with progressive America. Or, as others have suggested, he and his work could be viewed as part of the larger enterprise, an example of the "search for order" that underlay so much progressive activity.[1] Whatever the proper categorization of scientific management before 1910, Taylor also had conventional reform interests. Despite his recurring involvement in the nascent military-industrial complex, he identified closely with the small, owner-operated firms that were characteristic of the fragmented, competitive economy of the nineteenth century. His experiences with the Manufacturing Investment Company, Cramp Shipyard, Bethlehem Steel, and Amalgamated Copper had alerted him to the real or potential evils of the big businesses that seemed to be crowding out the traditional firm. Yet "the day of trusts is here." Taylor had no solution to the problem of corporate power. He was neither a populist, a trust buster, nor a proponent of Theodore Roosevelt's New Nationalism. At best, he attempted to strengthen the position of the traditional firm by substituting scientific management for the seeming disorder and unrest associated with the first factory system.

Taylor's mechanism for achieving this end inadvertently provided his most important link with the progressives. After 1901 the essential figure in the implementation of scientific management was the "expert," the skilled, independent systemizer. More than any conventional consultant, Taylor's expert was a professional, a technician of the highest order. Chosen for his special qualifications and subjected to rigid ethical constraints, he could be trusted to make rational, informed decisions. Until at least 1907, however, Taylor was oblivious to the similarities between his approach to factory reform and the ideas of the businessmen, scientists, engineers, lawyers, and journalists who agonized over the "distended" character of American society. Their answer to the disorganization and inefficiency so apparent in labor-management conflict, big business chicanery, and machine politics, like Taylor's answer to the defects of the factory system, was to elevate a cadre of technicians to positions of power. Experts in business, law, government, and the natural and social sciences, these men and women would supply the harmonizing element lost with the decline of market discipline and face-to-face relationships.[2] Appropriately, it was progressives of this type who recognized the reform implications of Taylor's message and projected him into the public spotlight.

By 1907, thanks to Morris L. Cooke, Taylor's promotional efforts had attracted widespread attention and enticed a growing stream of "pilgrims" to Boxly. Taylor began to complain, not entirely in jest, of becoming a "perennial phonograph."[3] To lessen the demands on his time, he decided to convert the lecture into a short book that he could send to interested businessmen. He initially called this work "The Underlying Philosophy of Scientific Management" and later "The Underlying Principles of Scientific Management."[4] It emerged as *The Principles of Scientific Management*, Taylor's most famous essay. A layman's guide to Taylor's work and possibly an affirmation of the rise of a science of engineering, *The Principles of Scientific Management* was also a reform tract, a progressive manifesto.[5] And this feature was the essential one during Taylor's lifetime. Taylor's declaration of commitment to the insurgent cause was the crucial ingredient in his transformation, the link between his particularistic effort to deal with the challenges of late-nineteenth-century industry and the larger universalistic campaign against waste and inefficiency.

The immediate practical value of the work was obvious. It would prepare prospective clients for Taylor's lecture, legitimize his role as the guarantor of the experts' professionalism, and protect Taylor's interests and reputation at a time when his competitors were increasingly active. Accordingly, he and Cooke devoted many hours to it between 1907 and 1909. Cooke did most of the preliminary work. He transcribed Taylor's lecture, rewrote it, and added material from a manuscript on industrial management he had prepared before Taylor decided to publish his speech. More than 50 percent of the final product was, in fact, Cooke's writing.[6] Taylor, nevertheless, bore the ultimate responsibility for *The Principles of Scientific Management*. He wrote the interpretative sections and struggled to improve the style. He recalled that it was "by far the most difficult piece of writing that I have ever undertaken. I have had to write and rewrite it eight or ten times to get it into form which I thought people would be interested in reading."[7] Clearly there was nothing haphazard or accidental about the structure or language of *The Principles of Scientific Management*.

Taylor's determination to present his ideas in a form "people would be interested in reading" is unmistakable. He used the outline of "A Piece Rate System" once more, but avoided anything that might bore or offend the uninitiated or skeptical reader. He expanded his treatment of the labor problem, jettisoned most of the substantive material that had appeared in his earlier works, added anecdotes from his career, and depicted scientific management as the ultimate antidote to labor unrest. Discarding the "mechanism" of scientific management was no easy task, but Taylor salved his conscience with a short description of his metal-cutting experiments. The result was "Shop Management" in capsule form, a popular guide to the Taylor system.

The chief effect of these alterations was to emphasize two features of the manuscript. The first was the "principles of scientific management," which Taylor made the unifying theme of the work. These principles— the substitution of scientific for "rule of thumb" methods, the "scientific selection and training of the workmen," the combination of "the science and the scientifically selected and trained workmen," and the equal division of work between the management and the workmen[8]—unlike Taylor's more general principles of management, which he had propounded at Bethlehem and explained in "Shop Management," are of uncertain origin. They are sufficiently vague to have been extrapolations of parts of Taylor's lecture, though they do not appear in Cooke's transcription of the talk.[9] Cooke may in fact have been their originator.[10] If so, his contribution was of questionable value. The "principles of scientific management" undoubtedly contributed to the book's popularity, but they also gave it, and Taylor's system, a deceptive unity and simplicity, reinforced the impression that scientific management was an answer to labor unrest and, worst of all, directed critics' attention to the weakest parts of Taylor's work.

Of the four specific principles or achievements of scientific management that Taylor cited, the first was of questionable validity, the second was patently false, the third misleading, and the fourth, though suggesting the actual thrust of scientific management, magnified the effect of the third. As Taylor's pre-1901 experiences showed and as Gilbreth and various critics of Taylor's methods often suggested, there was nothing demonstrably scientific about the labor provisions of scientific management. Taylor's techniques for selecting and training workers were exceedingly primitive, even by the standards of his time. Neither he nor his followers were interested in or sympathetic to the emerging personnel movement, which was based on new and presumably more scientific methods of placement and training. The third and fourth principles made explicit the implied distortion in the others: that scientific management was in essence a way of reorganizing the worker's activity. A realignment of managerial responsibilities was a major feature of Taylor's system, but the central figure in that process was the foreman, not the worker.

The second notable feature of *The Principles of Scientific Management* was Taylor's autobiographical vignettes, expanded and embellished. The "fight" with the Midvale machinists, the story of "Schmidt," and the reorganization of the Simonds inspectors and the Bethlehem laborers accounted for approximately half the text and an even greater proportion of the public attention it commanded in the following years.[11] Taylor viewed these stories as appealing surrogates for the complex details of scientific management. But again, it is not clear why he chose these particular events, apart from the fact he had used them before. Did he consider other incidents—the introduction of the incentive wage at the Manufacturing Investment or Johnson companies, for example? Surely, the substitution of scientific management for the internal contract system at Johnstown would have illustrated the revolutionary potential of his work far more effectively than his treatment of the lowly "Schmidt." In any case, Taylor altered or expanded his accounts whenever it suited his immediate purposes. Though all of the stories had a factual basis, they were, with the possible exception of the Simonds episode, approximations of the actual events.

Taylor's story of "Schmidt," which became the most famous of his anecdotes, was probably the least accurate of the lot. Taylor remembered Henry Noll affectionately as a determined and independent individual, perhaps as a working class version of Frederick W. Taylor. More important, he believed that Noll's experience would make an effective "object lesson." To enhance its effect, he added dramatic language. The sturdy laborer was "stupid and phlegmatic," a man like an "ox."[12] Taylor intended to show that scientific management could redeem such an individual, but critics emphasized his language rather than his moral. In later years his condescending descriptions of Noll and other laborers were grist for the mill of unionists determined to slow the spread of incentive wage systems by depicting Taylor and others like him as insensitive, brutal drivers. As a consequence, Noll assumed a role and significance in the history of scientific management that he had not had in the reorganization of the Bethlehem plan.[13] Having inadvertently called attention to his expedient approach to laborers like Schmidt, Taylor compounded the error by implying that such activities were the essence of scientific management.

Taylor added one new "object lesson," a long, enthusiastic account of Gilbreth's bricklaying system. His reasons for choosing Gilbreth's work rather than Thompson's to illustrate the nonindustrial applications of scientific management are uncertain. Taylor still considered Gilbreth an asset to the movement in 1909 and likely foresaw an expanded role for him, at least for his public relations talents, in future years. In any case, his description was eminently unsatisfactory to Gilbreth.[14]

As an introduction to scientific management, then, *The Principles of Scientific Management* had little to commend it. It was inaccurate in historical detail and, more seriously, in its assertions about the nature of Taylor's contributions and the character of scientific management.[15] Taylor's "principles" had little or no relevance to his work, and his suggestion that time study constituted a "science" was hyperbole at best.[16]

As he and Cooke should have anticipated, his emphasis on labor productivity and the worker created interminable problems for the scientific management movement in subsequent years.[17]

To progressives, however, *The Principles of Scientific Management* was more than a promotional tract or a history of Taylor's relations with subordinates. Though Taylor's focus was shop management, the area of his professional interest, the book's underlying theme was the deficiencies of management generally. And Taylor's statements were sufficiently broad to invite interpretation. His audience of 1911, approaching the work at the high point of reform agitation, read *The Principles of Scientific Management* at several levels.[18] At one level "management" and the "labor problem" referred to the evils of the factory; at another, they were metaphors for the ills of big business and society as a whole. Taylor's solution had the same appealing ambiguity. His call for "science" administered by experts was an appeal for the "mechanism" of scientific management and the services of the expert, but it was also a formula for achieving the progressives' goal of eliminating the evils of American society without fundamentally altering institutions and values. Scientific knowledge, administered by objective, politically neutral experts, would eliminate the waste associated with the factory, the corporation, the government bureau, and the school.

> What really happens is that, with the aid of the science . . . and through the instructions from his teachers [the "experts"] each workman [institution] . . . is enabled to do a much higher, more interesting and finally more developing and more profitable kind of work than he [it] was before able to do.[19]

Taylor was more expansive in his conclusion, a progressive recital of the benefits of reform for the public, the "whole people." While retaining his shop management focus, he spelled out the promise of science and technical competence for American life:

> The writer is one of those who believes that more and more will the third party (the whole people), as it becomes acquainted with the true facts, insist that justice shall be done to all three parties. It will demand the largest efficiency from both employers and employes. It will no longer tolerate the type of employer who has his eye on dividends alone, who refused to do his full share of the work and who merely cracks his whip over the heads of his workmen and attempts to drive them into harder work for low pay. No more will it tolerate tyranny on the part of labor which demands one increase after another in pay and shorter hours while at the same time it becomes less instead of more efficient. . . . The

general adoption of scientific management would readily in the future double the productivity of the average man engaged in industrial work. Think of what this means to the whole country. Think of the increase, both in the necessities and luxuries of life, which becomes available for the whole country, of the possibility of shortening the hours of labor when this is desirable, and of the increased opportunities for education, culture, and recreation which this implies.[20]

Taylor submitted *The Principles of Scientific Management* to the ASME publications committee early in 1910. He maintained privately that he did this for sentimental reasons—"because all of my past writing . . . has been presented to our society."[21] However, he was not oblivious to the fact that the ASME imprimatur would enhance the work's promotional value. He admitted as much when he wrote, in another context, that *The Principles of Scientific Management* dealt with a topic of interest to every engineer.[22] This possibility was also apparent to the members of the society's publications committee, several of whom objected to the manuscript's commercial potential and nontechnical character. Unwilling to accept it, but too embarrassed to reject the work of a former president, the committee stalled. Months passed, and Taylor became increasingly annoyed.[23] In late 1910 he withdrew the manuscript, printed it privately for ASME members, and agreed to publish it in the popular progressive journal, *The American Magazine*.

The Burdens of Notoriety

While the ASME committee deliberated, two unforeseen developments completed Taylor's transformation. The first was the well-known confrontation between the progressives and the railroads, the Eastern Rate Case.[24] In June, Louis D. Brandeis agreed to represent a group of eastern trade associations opposing a railroad rate increase before the Interstate Commerce Commission (ICC). Searching for an effective strategy to counter the railroads' rationale that increased wages required higher prices, Brandeis seized the efficiency issue. If the railroads were properly administered, he argued, they could pay higher wages without raising prices. To document his argument, he turned to Taylor and his followers. The testimony of Gantt, Gilbreth, and, above all, Emerson in October and November 1910 radically altered the character of the hearings. The rate request (ultimately rejected) was nearly forgotten in the ensuing furor over Brandeis's "scientific" alternative that promised to benefit the consumer, the shipper, the worker, and the railroads. The incident, widely reported, sparked the extraordinary "efficiency craze" of the following years and Taylor's emergence as a public figure. The second development, no less significant for Taylor's career, was known only to a handful of his associates and purposely concealed in Taylor's official biography. During the fall of 1910 Louise Taylor revealed the first unmistakable symptoms of involutional depression, a psychological disorder related to menopause that plagued her thereafter.[25] Taylor's final years, the years of his greatest public visability, were devoted overwhelmingly to her care and recuperation.

Ironically, when Brandeis first contacted Taylor about the ICC hearings, Taylor treated his proposals as a routine and not particularly relevant inquiry about scientific management. He wrote James M. Dodge that the evidence Brandeis would present to the ICC "on the subject of efficiency will be so indefinite and vague that it will not be possible to seriously influence the present freight rate controversy."[26] He turned down a request to testify on grounds that he knew so little about railroad shops that he would "injure, rather than help the cause" and had prior commitments.[27] Cooke refused for similar reasons. Only Gilbreth and Gantt among Taylor's closest associates recognized the importance of Brandeis's proposition. They arranged the meetings at which the ICC presentations were planned and Brandeis decided to emphasize the term "scientific management."[28]

Taylor quickly changed his mind when it became apparent that Brandeis's activities would generate favorable publicity about scientific management. The turning point came in early November when four magazine editors contacted Taylor, apparently a result of Brandeis's carefully orchestrated campaign against the railroads.[29] Henceforth Taylor cooperated fully, soliciting the assistance of his colleagues and providing Brandeis with a variety of data. He was amazed at the latter's skill in presenting the case and in publicizing the hearings. In a short time Brandeis had succeeded in "waking up the whole country . . . I have rarely seen a new movement started with such great momentum as you have given this one."[30]

This admiration, coupled with his unhappiness at the ASME, made Taylor more receptive to the Brandeis-inspired editors than he might have been a year before. He listened to their entreaties and weighed the advantages of a lay medium. At first he and Cooke favored *The Atlantic Monthly*, but Ray Stannard Baker, editor of *The American Magazine*, proved highly persuasive. An activist with impressive reform credentials of his own, Baker argued that *The American Magazine* would reach a more diverse and impressionable audience than the *Atlantic Monthly*.[31]

Attracted by this prospect, Taylor authorized Baker to serialize *The Principles of Scientific Management* in the spring of 1911.

The publication of *The Principles of Scientific Management* was an important sequel to the rate case hearings. Widely read, the series linked Taylor with progressive reform and elevated him to the status of a celebrity. Baker's introduction left no doubt about Taylor's role or significance. It was

> to the fine scientific habit of mind . . . that the country must look for its salvation. There have been times in recent years when it seemed as though our civilization were being throttled by things, by property, by the very weight of industrial mechanism, and it is no small matter when a man arises who can show us new ways of commanding our environment.

Baker concluded that Taylor was "a public servant in the best sense."[32] Taylor was beseiged with requests for personal appearances, speeches, and interviews. Overnight he became a public figure.

The acclaim that greeted the ICC hearings and the publication of *The Principles of Scientific Management* coincided with the beginning of Louise's crisis. Since her return to Philadelphia she had suffered periods of ill health. She was often irritable, and her lack of affection for the children is one of her son's most vivid memories.[33] But any conclusion about her physical or mental state before mid-1910 is necessarily speculative. After that time, however, it is clear that she suffered a rapid decline, the result of several factors, including Taylor's growing prominence.[34] Her face became disfigured, and she experienced extended periods of extreme irritability and depression.[35] Increasingly, she refused public contacts and demanded Taylor's constant companionship. His letters between 1911 and 1915 reveal a harassed but devoted husband, at times "almost . . . worried to death."[36]

For Taylor the most distressing feature of Louise's affliction was its cyclical pattern. Periods of intense physical and emotional distress alternated with periods of apparent recuperation. She experienced her first severe "nervous breakdown" (as Taylor called it) in the spring of 1911. She became worse after a long summer vacation at the Equinox House, a resort hotel in Manchester, Vermont. She suffered from depression and insomnia during the winter of 1911–12, but improved the following spring. A trip to Europe started the cycle again. The Taylors spent the summer of 1912 in Plymouth, Massachusetts, where Louise's mother lived. Taylor reported:

> She and I are alone with two of our [servant] girls in the small cottage close to Mrs. Spooner's house, and she will see no one except the doctor and myself for a long time to come. She has

already begun to sleep far better, and realizes that this complete
rest is doing her a lot of good. It is of course monotonous for her,
but that is what is wanted. I am also leading a very monotonous
life, but to me this is infinitely preferable to the continuous worry
and anxiety which I had while we were abroad.[37]

He noted that he was "tied down to Plymouth so closely" that he "was
unable to get away even for one full day at a time."[38]

In the fall a new doctor, Judson Daland, suggested a diagnosis and
treatment that further curtailed Taylor's schedule. Daland believed that
Louise's difficulties were the result of a congenital digestive disorder. To
be near him, they closed Boxly and lived at the Bellevue-Stratford Hotel
in Philadelphia during the winter of 1912–13. Louise improved, as she
had the previous winter. By the spring of 1913 Taylor thought she was
better than she had been "for two or three years" and was "confident of
her complete recovery."[39] A spring vacation in Charleston, South
Carolina, resulted in further improvement, but a European vacation
that summer led to another relapse.

The same pattern of recovery and relapse occurred in 1913 and 1914
and again in 1914 and 1915. Taylor cared for Louise at Plymouth during
the summer of 1913 and at Boxly during the winter of 1913–14. In
January 1914 she was "sicker . . . than she has ever been." He explained
that "we have been obliged to exclude every one from the house . . .
the house is really turned into a rest cure."[40] Because Louise showed
little improvement at Boxly, they left again, first for Atlantic City,
where she made a "steady and rapid gain," and then for the Samoset
House, at Rockland, Maine, where one of her doctors spent his
summers.[41] They returned to Atlantic City in the fall of 1914 and spent
the winter at the Hotel Brighton. Louise suffered a relapse shortly after
their arrival. By November 1914 Taylor was planning "a full year of
complete rest." He confided that "I have to stay very close to Lou all the
time to help cheer her up. She hardly realize[s] how she is dependent
upon even the little attention which I am able to pay her. I have only
been away from her for a day at a time; and then only once or twice
this fall."[42]

Louise's illnesses had a pronounced effect on Taylor's behavior between 1911 and 1915. At last, when success seemed within his grasp, he
was stifled, preoccupied with a seriously but inexplicably ill wife and
unable to press his advantage. Taylor seldom complained, but his
frustration was apparent in other ways, much as it had been in the
waning days of his Bethlehem work. In his dealings with critics he was
abrupt, often antagonistic. In public appearances he was ill-prepared,
repetitious, and easily provoked. To observers unfamiliar with his
personal life he seemed rude and impatient, an unpleasant person.[43]

Apart from his private anxieties, Louise's illness forced Taylor to modify or abandon most of his "retirement" activities. His absence from Boxly forced him to curtail his gardening and grass-growing experiments, the last outlets for his "enthusiasm for invention." He played golf whenever possible, but after mid-1912 even that benign dissipation became more difficult. Taylor continued to give his standard talk whenever he was home, but the effect was different. Because of his restricted schedule and popularity his audiences now often numbered twenty to thirty people, and the sense of personal involvement that the "pilgrims" of earlier years found so compelling was lost. (Link-Belt executives became so exasperated at the "constant interruptions . . . by reason of the number of visitors" that they attempted to restrict the tours to one afternoon per week.[44]) Taylor tried to compensate by devoting additional time to important prospective clients like Richard A. Feiss, a Cleveland clothing manufacturer, and Marcel Michelin, son of a prominent French tire maker, and to less happy visitors like Milton Herrmann, but was never wholly satisfied with these efforts.

Taylor's post-1911 writings also reflected the unprecedented demands on his time. In preparing the opening address for a conference at Dartmouth College on scientific management that Cooke and Harlow S. Person, dean of the college's Amos Tuck Business School, scheduled for October 1911, Taylor revised his presentation for the last time. He condensed *The Principles of Scientific Management*, moved the definition of scientific management (a "mental revolution"), which had appeared inconspicuously near the end of the original manuscript, to the beginning of his paper, and omitted all references to the specific features of scientific management except slide rules and his metal-cutting discoveries.[45] Taylor adopted this approach because Cooke and Person wanted a short, introductory address, not a two-and-a-half hour lecture. As he had done in the past when faced with such a task, Taylor emphasized generalizations and discarded detail.

In subsequent months and years Taylor continued to use the outline he had hurriedly devised in the fall of 1911. His presentations to a special House of Representatives committee investigating scientific management in 1912 and to the U.S. Commission on Industrial Relations in 1914 were almost identical to his Dartmouth lecture. Even his published articles, which he knew would be read by people who had attended the 1911 conference or who were familiar with his testimony, were practically the same.[46] Once again, a course originally dictated by expediency became Taylor's standard approach to scientific management. And again the deletions served to emphasize the labor features of scientific management and to obscure Taylor's more significant organizational and technical innovations.

When Taylor was away from Boxly—which was most of the time after 1911—he improvised as best he could. While staying at Plymouth in July 1912, for example, he talked at length with Frank Barkley Copley, then a magazine writer. Copley's articles on Taylor, published in *The American Magazine* and *The Outlook*, established his claim as a potential biographer.[47] Two years later in Maine, Taylor spent a day with a group of New England progressives—former U.S. Indian commissioner, Robert Valentine, Henry Kendall of Plimpton Press, Felix Frankfurter of the Harvard Law School, and Stanley King of the W. H. McElwain Company. Kendall recalled: "It was really a great day. Mr. Taylor was not obliged to defend his principles or policies. We spent the day questioning him on all sorts of subjects and getting at his underlying theories."[48] Both Copley and Kendall's friends apparently assumed that Taylor's "underlying theories" concerned the worker's role under scientific management. At least they did not object when Taylor devoted most of the discussion to his attitudes toward the incentive wage, collective bargaining, and unions.[49]

After 1911 Taylor's journeys and his proselytizing activities extended beyond the United States. He and Louise spent the spring of 1912 and the summer of 1913 in Europe, ostensibly to aid her recuperation. But as Taylor's reputation spread and as his papers and books were translated into European languages, he also used these trips to promote scientific management. He had had earlier contacts with Henri Le Chatelier, an influential French scientist who became Taylor's chief enthusiast and disciple in Europe. Le Chatelier interested several important European manufacturers, including the Michelins, who contacted Taylor during his European vacations. As a result, some of the largest French factories, notably the Renault and Panhard auto plants, the Michelin works, and the government-operated arsenals, introduced scientific management before World War I.[50] Unfortunately for Taylor, the French manufacturers were no more tractable than their American counterparts. They disregarded his warnings and, like many United States employers, tried to introduce the system too quickly. When the Renault workers struck against scientific management in 1913, Taylor reacted much as he had to the American Locomotive Company strikes of 1909 or the Watertown arsenal walkout of 1911. "If a man [Renault] deliberately goes against the experience of men who know what they are talking about, and refuses to follow advice given in a kind but unmistakable way, it seems to me that he deserves to get into trouble."[51] And, as he might have predicted, such incidents made scientific management as controversial in Europe as it had become in the United States.[52]

A more significant deviation from Taylor's earlier approach was the lecture tours he undertook with increasing frequency after 1910. He had made his first trip in 1909, when he spoke at the University of Illinois, the Cincinnati Metal Trades Association, and the Packard Motor Company in Detroit. The success of this venture encouraged him to accept more outside speaking engagements as substitutes for his Boxly lectures. By late 1911 he was giving the "greater part" of his working time to these appearances.[53] One of his most successful lectures was to 600 Detroit auto plant foremen and superintendents.[54] He was also popular on college campuses. More than 500 students listened attentively to his 1913 lecture at the University of Toronto, and large and enthusiastic audiences greeted him at the University of Wisconsin, the University of Chicago, and Pennsylvania State College.[55] Inevitably there were exceptions. Taylor's greatest disaster occurred in December 1911 when he addressed the Illinois Manufacturers Association. The manufacturers, he reported in dismay, were there "for a good time" and quickly lost interest in his remarks.[56] "One or two occasions such as the Chicago meeting," he added, "would lead me to give up the talking business entirely."[57] Nevertheless, he agreed to extended lecture trips in January 1913, April 1914, and February and March 1915.

Taylor's new situation demanded similar revisions in his relations with his followers. After 1910 he maintained close ties with his principal associates, notably Barth and Hathaway, but had little contact with the others, including a new and enthusiastic generation of disciples. This group included Hollis Godfrey, a scientist, writer, and educator who temporarily assisted Cooke in his public relations work; Royal R. Keely, a professor of mechanical engineering who served an "apprenticeship" at Tabor and began to introduce scientific management in 1912; C. Bertrand Thompson, a professor at the Harvard Business School who became the first historian of scientific management and a practicing consultant; and Holden Evans. Besides these men Taylor approved the appointment of numerous Tabor and Link-Belt employees as assistants to Barth, Hathaway, and other disciples and subsidized the "apprenticeships" of a half-dozen applicants who did not complete their training because of the outbreak of World War I.

Together with his growing public role and Louise's ill-health, the continuous influx of recruits made Taylor increasingly dependent upon Hathaway. The latter, in turn, devoted more and more of his time to consulting work and the coordination of Taylor's activities.[58] Inevitably, as he assigned trainees to outside jobs and accepted responsibility for their performance, Hathaway began to evaluate their work independently of Taylor. Soon his judgments became the "official" estimations of the individual's worth. He played a major part in the Taylor-Gilbreth imbroglio and exercised even greater influence over the new and less important men.

Hathaway's role was largely responsible for friction that developed among Taylor's disciples after 1910. If less outspoken than Barth, he was equally orthodox and suspicious of interlopers. A self-made man, he endorsed Taylor's suggestion that scientific management could be mastered only through on-the-job experience. He often seemed to enjoy denigrating men like Godfrey, Keely, and C. B. Thompson, who had advanced degrees and backgrounds as educators. He wrote, for example, that Godfrey "was brought into the fold . . . for the purpose of undertaking high-brow research work . . . [but] it would be a mistake to start him out on anything of the sort if he can be used to more practical advantage."[59] He viewed Thompson with skepticism and, after Taylor's death, with outright contempt.[60] His most severe criticism, however, was directed at Keely, who, despite a satisfactory performance at Tabor, impressed him as an impractical dreamer and visionary. Eventually he and Barth persuaded Taylor to discard Keely as an incompetent.[61]

The Revolt of the Mechanical Engineers

Taylor's emergence as a progressive also had far-reaching effects outside his immediate circle of family and associates. The many facets of the "efficiency craze" do not warrant reconsideration here, but the impact of Taylor's transformation on the mechanical engineers, the men he was closest to and presumably sought to benefit, suggests the disruptive nature of the reform impulse. One phase of the larger "revolt" that divided the engineering societies, professions, political parties, and legislatures in the years before World War I, the conflict over Taylor's new role was a catalyst in the rise of progressive and anti-progressive camps in the ASME.[62]

At least since Taylor's presidency there had been serious differences within the society over the group's direction and future orientation. Taylor, Cooke, and the disciples sought to make the ASME a forum for the discussion of management problems, while many of their fellow engineers preferred to retain a more esoteric, technical focus. At first the difference was more an irritant than a serious problem. For several years the principal culprits were men like Emerson and Gilbreth who constantly injected their pet schemes into society discussions. Increasingly, however, Cooke became the center of the controversy. Taylor's colleague not only favored the broader approach, he sought to apply Taylor's insights to the reformation of society and to instill in his associates a larger conception of social responsibility. By 1911 many traditional engineers had found common ground with the corporate executives who, at least by implication, were the villains of Cooke's schema. Opposition to "The Principles" was one indication of this informal alliance. In the following years some of the society's most articulate members, including men like John Calder and L. P. Alford, who were practitioners of systematic management but who believed an engineer was primarily a technician and the ASME primarily an organization for the discussion of technical issues, became openly critical of Taylor and scientific management.[63]

By that time, however, Taylor and his followers were the best-known and most vigorous group within the society. The appearance in 1911 and 1912 of two organizations devoted to management problems, the Society to Promote the Science of Management and the Efficiency Society, underlined their ability to fragment the profession if denied access to traditional channels of power and expression. The society's leaders, notably Calvin W. Rice, the secretary, who had close ties to Taylor and the corporate executives, recognized this dilemma and initiated a policy of accommodation. The first manifestation of this effort was the appointment of an ASME committee to study scientific management in early 1912. This group, chaired by James M. Dodge, included other Taylor allies—Henry R. Towne; Wilfred Lewis; Holden Evans; W. B. Tardy, a Navy engineer who was sympathetic to Taylor; W. L. Lyall of Brighton Mills, a Gantt client; and M. H. Vaughan of the Canadian Pacific Railroad, another Gantt client. Its secretary and principal member, however, was Alford, who as editor of the *American Machinist* had indicated serious reservations about Taylor's "principles" of management.[64] The committee report, which Alford wrote, was so ambiguous that Taylor and his contemporaries and more recent historians have variously interpreted it as antagonistic to and supportive of scientific management.[65] Taylor himself alternately dismissed it as "colorless and insipid" and used it in his promotional work.[66]

The ASME also remained open to Cooke. As a result, some of his most notable battles with corporate interests were fought within the society and involved issues such as the presentation of papers and the election of reformers, including himself, to seats on the organization's governing board. By 1914 Cooke had developed a substantial following, as well as many enemies, within the ASME; by 1919, as Edwin T. Layton has written, "the Taylorites momentarily seemed to control the society."[67] Together with the creation of a special management division in 1920, this triumph emphasized the enormous impact of Taylor and his followers on the engineering profession after 1905 and the ability of the ASME to absorb the heretical and often abrasive actions of the management reformers.

In the meantime conflicts among the engineers interested in managerial issues—principally Taylor and his disciples on one hand and his imitators and critics on the other—had resulted in a second type of institutional fragmentation. Taylor's success in associating scientific management with reform prompted the appearance of even more consultants and "systematizers," for the most part men who embraced his tie with the cause of "efficiency," but not his conception of scientific management or the expert's function. As a consequence, there was almost as much disagreement over the type of organizational affiliation management experts should have as over the goals and methods of scientific management itself.

The Society to Promote the Science of Management (after 1915 the Taylor Society) was an outgrowth of Gilbreth's restless imagination and the divisions within the ASME.[68] While gathering data for Brandeis's ICC presentation in late October 1910, Gilbreth perceived the need— and the potential—for a society which would "perpetuate the work begun by Fred W. Taylor" and "promulgate the principles laid down by him." He discussed the idea with Robert T. Kent and then with Cooke, Wilfred Lewis, and Conrad Lauer, a member of Charles Day's firm and a former Tabor employee. Lewis was dispatched to consult Taylor, and Kent prepared a letter to a select group of prospective members. Taylor, on the verge of withdrawing the "Principles" from the ASME, viewed the new organization almost exclusively in terms of his relations with the ASME. He told Lewis that he was "not entirely sure . . . that a separate society of the kind contemplated would do as much good as an organization in the main society."[69] He did see it, however, as a useful lever to win concessions from the ASME. Lewis reported that Taylor "regarded with a good deal of pleasure" the "probability of its stirring up the ASME to take some definite action."[70] Taylor immediately notified Calvin Rice, secretary of the ASME, of the plan, pledged to work against it, and suggested that Gilbreth be added to the ASME publications committee.[71]

Undoubtedly influenced by Taylor's reaction, his followers insisted that the new society operate as a de facto subsidiary of the ASME. In March 1911 Cooke temporarily resigned as a charter member because the draft constitution of the new organization did not include the same membership requirements.[72] The other initiators quickly corrected this defect and sent the constitution to Rice with "a view to some sort of affiliation."[73] Kent recalled:

> We were very rigid in our requirements for membership . . . so jealous were we of our standing that nobody would be admitted unless he could at least qualify for membership in the American Society of Mechanical Engineers. To avoid offending that august body that we hoped to educate . . . we elected as our first president . . . a past president of their society, Mr. Dodge.[74]

Formally organized in December 1911, the Society to Promote the Science of Management included practicing consultants and business-men who were receptive to Taylor's ideas. The businessmen, it was hoped, would finance experimental work, proselytize among their friends, and leave the substantive activities, including the society's programs, to the disciples.[75] Gantt and Hathaway, who had initial reservations, soon joined, and even Taylor consented to an honorary membership in 1914. Gilbreth served as treasurer between 1911 and 1914, although he seems to have been uncharacteristically subdued at the society's meetings. As his relationship with Taylor changed. he gradually withdrew from the society. By 1920, when he returned to attack conventional time study, he was an unwelcome outsider, an example of the "wrong kind" of member.[76]

Yet as the Taylor Society grew, it too became susceptible to the centrifugal forces that affected other phases of the management move-ment. By the time of Taylor's death it had more than fifty members; the society's memorial service for Taylor in October 1915 attracted 250 guests.[77] Under Harlow S. Person, who served as president from 1914 to 1919 and "manager" or executive secretary thereafter, the society expanded even more rapidly. Although applicants were carefully screened, a growing number were acquainted with Taylor chiefly or solely through his writings.

The most obvious manifestation of this transition was the changing focus of the society's programs. In a 1912 report on the society's possible functions, Hathaway argued that the group "should avoid papers by authors who endeavor to cover the whole field of management, result-ing in much going over of the same ground in a superficial way and frequent disagreements in matters of detail." "Every newcomer," he added, "will have a wild desire to write papers on a subject he is little qualified to handle."[78] As long as Hathaway and other disciples dominated the society's program committee, this philosophy prevailed. Meetings were devoted to the details of scientific management. The papers, published in Kent's *Industrial Engineering* after 1914 and the society's *Bulletin* thereafter, were of high quality, but lacked appeal. Gradually, however, men who had less interest in the technical features of scientific management and who took *The Principles of Scientific Management* seriously began to influence the programs. Papers on broader and more controversial topics, especially the labor implications of scientific management, appeared with greater frequency. The works of Robert Valentine and Robert Wolf on collective bargaining and of Richard Feiss on personnel management, published in 1915 and 1916, symbolized the trend. Valentine, Wolf, and Feiss were "newcomers," men of broad perspective who undoubtedly possessed a "wild desire" to transcend the narrow approach preferred by Hathaway, Barth, and the other older, more orthodox disciples.

By comparison, the Efficiency Society lacked a sharply defined focus and eschewed professional standards. Founded at the same time Gilbreth, Kent, and Cooke were perfecting their plans, it was largely the work of H. F. J. Porter, Taylor's former Bethlehem colleague. Porter had gone to the Nerst Lamp Company, a Westinghouse subsidiary, in 1903 and had introduced a suggestion system modeled after one Charles U. Carpenter had installed at the National Cash Register Company. To administer the plan, he established committees of workers and managers which evolved into one of the first company unions.[79] Two years later Porter set up a consulting practice to introduce time study, the incentive wage, and his committee system. "We could travel together," he wrote Taylor, "despite our differences over details."[80] To Taylor, however, their "differences over details" were an insurmountable barrier to cooperation, much less a working partnership. As far as he was concerned, Porter operated in the labor reform tradition of paternalistic employers and theorists who sought to increase productivity through "unsound" schemes.[81] Their relations worsened in 1907 when Porter hired several Tabor time study men to help him reorganize the Nelson Valve Works in Philadelphia.[82] Well before the appearance of Porter's organization Taylor had added his former colleague to his growing list of "fakirs."

This background largely determined Taylor's response to the Efficiency Society. Despite numerous pleas he refused to play any role in the group or to allow Porter to use his name.[83] He explained that "in matters of management he [Porter] and I stand at the two very extremes. He repudiates all of those things which I stand for, and I do not at all believe in the principles which he advocates."[84] In the following years his denunciations of the Efficiency Society and its "great army of cranks and charlatans" became more strident.[85] As a result, the society, which had over 800 charter members and became the most important institutional manifestation of the post-1910 "efficiency enthusiasm," operated wholly apart from and often in opposition to the Taylor movement.[86]

The Limits of Reform

The turmoil associated with the rise of progressivism in the ASME underlined the seriousness of the division between reformers and anti-progressives and the importance both groups attached to reform issues. Still, the differences are easily exaggerated. Taylor, Cooke, and other reformers antagonized their colleagues with their novel ideas and assumptions, but they remained engineers. Like the progressive businessmen they so closely resembled, they had limited reform interests.[87] They were highly sensitive to economic issues, especially the dangers of corporate power and of labor-management conflict in modern society. They were also critics of contemporary politics and politicians and, in some cases, proponents of political reforms. But they were ambivalent on the proper role of government. They favored greater technical expertise and more nonpolitical government activity, but opposed the regulation of business and increased public expenditures. Finally, their attitudes toward social and humanitarian issues differed little from those of anti-progressive engineers. They clung to the belief that technological innovation would eradicate poverty and injustice and that government or labor union involvement in industry was irresponsible and counterproductive. On such issues they clearly broke ranks with many of their fellow reformers.

Taylor was a devotee of this circumscribed approach to reform. He was hostile to big business, critical of politicians, and skeptical of humanitarian gestures, particularly those that involved workers.[88] His labor "reforms" were premised on the assumption that men worked for money and would improve themselves if offered appropriate financial incentives. Interference with this fact of life by government, social workers, unions, or well-meaning employers like John Patterson would only postpone the solution of the poverty problem. Taylor's narrow conception of reform was also apparent in his relations with educators and trade unionists, groups that commanded much of his attention during the last years of his life.

As a result of his new prominence, the heads of many of the leading technical schools invited Taylor to lecture or to serve on advisory boards. To the educators' consternation and occasional embarrassment, he took these commitments seriously and literally, offering abundant criticism but little money. Taylor's approach to education reflected divergent, even conflicting, memories of his formative years, in particular a realistic recollection of his haphazard formal education and a romanticized conception of his subsequent rise to prominence, a view that emphasized determination, self-discipline, and triumph over adversity. As a result, Taylor became an uncompromising opponent of modernity, including virtually all the innovations of educational reformers.[89]

Taylor first articulated an educational philosophy in 1906 in the process of preparing an address to commemorate the opening of an engineering building at the University of Pennsylvania.[90] He had per-

ceived a disturbing problem: young engineering graduates disliked the
routine activity of the industrial firm, while manufacturers disliked the
condescending manner and uncooperative behavior of the graduates.
Both attitudes, he believed, were results of mistaken policies by
universities. Taylor then attacked progressive educational practices,
notably the elective system, the absence of enforced discipline, and
"the idea . . . that it is the duty of the teacher to make the subject
interesting rather than [the students'] . . . duty to learn whatever comes
their way."[91] He added, almost as an afterthought, an idea derived from
his own experiences that later became the cornerstone of his educational theory:

> I am going to suggest that college students be obliged, say at the end
> of their first year, to work in competition with men working for
> their living for a period of six months. The college boys to keep the
> same hours and have the same work that is given to ordinary work-
> men. I believe this will tend, by giving them a foretaste of their life's
> work, to give them a more earnest purpose in their college course,
> and also to appreciate the necessity of rigid discipline.[92]

Harvard president Charles W. Eliot's reminder that colleges sought to
produce "men having personal initiative and the faculty of independent
thought" rather than "men of automatic action like soldiers, sailors, and
factory operatives" had no more effect than Gilbreth's warning that time
study was unscientific.[93]

In the following years Taylor repeated his arguments with growing
stridency. In speeches and papers he attacked the elective system and
boosted his plan for a period of practical experience designed to
inculcate discipline (as opposed to the new "cooperative" engineering
plans introduced by reformers to familiarize students with the practical
problems of industry). He accused Alexander C. Humphreys, president
of Stevens, of "missing the great opportunity to put Stevens ahead of all
other Engineering Colleges" by not adopting his recommendation for a
half year of shop work.[94] He criticized Edwin Gay, dean of the Harvard
Business School, for requiring an undergraduate degree as a prerequisite for admission, and increasingly he emphasized the training of
ordinary workmen rather than college men as scientific management
practitioners. When Ira N. Hollis, dean of the Harvard Engineering
College, asked him to serve on the college's advisory committee, he
warned that he disagreed with the Harvard program and would continue to push his ideas.[95] Hugo Diemer, a professor at Penn State,
recalled that Taylor was "relentless in his criticism of the shortcomings
of the average college student."[96]

Although Taylor's ideas on education changed few minds, at least among men like Eliot and Humphreys, his agitation was not in vain. Stripped of its anti-intellectual, anti-progressive overtones, his emphasis on real world activity rather than books and theory affected the operation of one of the most important professional schools, the Harvard Graduate School of Business Administration. Shortly after the school opened in September 1908, Dean Gay organized a course on industrial management that featured luminaries of the systematic management movement, including Taylor, who lectured annually between 1909 and 1914. Gay coordinated the work himself until 1911; C. Bertrand Thompson succeeded him; and Selden O. Martin directed it in 1914, Taylor's last year. At first the course featured lectures on the principles of management by Charles Buxton Going, editor of the *Engineering Magazine*, then talks on cost accounting, production management, labor problems, and finally scientific management. In 1913 Thompson reversed the sequence because of the students' "lack of familiarity with the practical details of factory management."[97] Henceforth Going's lectures came after the other topics with the exception of scientific management, which remained the final subject, and capstone, of the course. In 1911 Gay added an advanced course on scientific management, which featured the introduction of Taylor's methods at the Rindge Manual Training School in Boston.[98] He sought, unsuccessfully, to persuade Taylor to teach the course.

Taylor recognized the potential value of his Harvard appearances for the diffusion of scientific management and accorded them a high priority. Besides his lectures—typically his standard speech, a talk on industrial discipline, and a more general discussion of his refinements of systematic management—he arranged for the disciples to participate in the course. Barth followed Taylor's appearances with lectures on specific features of scientific management—routing, mnemonic symbols, or the preparation of slide rules.[99] In 1911 or 1912 Taylor convinced Gay to add Gantt and Sanford Thompson to describe the labor features of scientific management and Cooke and Hathaway to help with the advanced course. He also prepared an original paper for one of his 1909 presentations, surely a compliment to Gay and the school. His paper, "An Outline of the Organization of a Manufacturing Establishment under Modern Scientific or Task Management," was probably his last statement on industrial management that deviated from his standard formula for publicizing his work.[100] It emphasized the major features of scientific management, notably the planning department and functional foremanship. It also included Taylor's only recorded effort to define in detail the duties of managers above the shop level.[101] His prescriptions

—that the president should free himself from routine, that the financial, sales, and advertising departments should be organized along functional lines, and that the "exception principle" should define the activities of the top managers—were less arresting than the fact that he deigned to make these efforts in his Harvard talk.

Taylor, nevertheless, insisted that his work at Harvard was no more meaningful or significant that his other promotional activities. After persuading Gay to include the disciples in the Harvard courses, he advised them not to let their commitments to the school interfere with their regular work.[102] He endorsed Hathaway's calculated slights of C. B. Thompson, after the latter had become a practicing consultant.[103] And when Gay asked Taylor to join the faculty he replied:

> I find every minute of my time taken up here in working in the interest of scientific management. I am quite sure that you do not realize the amount of missionary work that has to be done in this interest. I think it is a fact that, in the course of a year, I am conducting in Philadelphia here an even larger school for scientific management than the one which you have at Cambridge; and the scholars who come here are in almost all cases men who have already been tried out in competition with their fellows, and who have risen to the top. . . . I have found it absolutely necessary, in order to properly instruct men of this type, to have establishments close at hand which are running under scientific management, and the owners of which are willing to have people come into them for instruction. For this kind of teaching, Philadelphia is also the best place in the country.[104]

It was Taylor's well-known feud with union leaders, however, that most clearly revealed the limitations of his progressivism. If his associations with Eliot, Humphreys, and Gay exposed his hidebound orthodoxy in educational matters, his conflict with the unionists—which had originated in the Mare Island, American Locomotive Company, and Rock Island incidents and become a cause célèbre after the Watertown Arsenal strike—underlined his insensitivity to social justice issues. He had never shared his father's concern for the disadvantaged or the labor reformers' concern for the worker. His business ambitions, his identification with the engineering profession, and his career in the machinery industry had foreclosed any but an expedient view of the labor problem. Ray Stannard Baker's observation that Taylor made "the machines serve the man, not the man the machines" simply reflected his unfamiliarity with Taylor's work.[105] After 1910, as Taylor became more dependent on the labor problem to promote scientific management, he became more discrete. Yet his outlook and priorities did not change. He was equally pleased with the achievements of the humanitarian Dodge and the driver Holden Evans and continued to criticize fellow progressives who saw in personnel work or labor legislation more promising antidotes to unrest.

Given the strength of the progressive impulse, Taylor was fortunate to escape censure for as long as he did. While he remained primarily a technician and spoke primarily to other technicians, he enjoyed a deceptive immunity. But after 1910 he attracted a growing legion of critics. His offensive references to men like Henry Noll and his characterization of scientific management as a solution to the labor problem—tactics that attracted large and often sympathetic audiences —antagonized labor reformers and others devoted to social justice causes. Rebuttal came from many quarters, but union leaders, shrewdly claiming to speak for all workers, proved to be his most effective opponents.[106] By 1911 Taylor's statements and the Watertown strike had almost single-handedly revived the Machinists' anti-incentive-wage campaign. He was naturally chagrined. Like nearly all engineers and most progressives, he viewed the unionists as self-serving opportunists whose actions promised to thwart the will of the whole people. Together with his other problems, this view dictated an impatient, often hostile response to their charges.

Taylor's greatest professional challenge of 1911 was the arsenal conflict. The Watertown strike and the Machinists' attack on scientific management had little direct impact on the operation of the arsenals, but they worried Taylor.[107] The protests, after all, were aimed more at him than at the Ordnance Department, and he stood to lose far more in terms of reputation and influence than Crozier or the arsenal commanders. He responded by insisting, with predictable vigor, that his reforms benefited the workingmen and that collective bargaining was irrelevant and undesirable.

Given this approach, Taylor's efforts to deal with the union leaders were inevitably unsuccessful. In early 1911, before the union offensive had begun, he and Gilbreth met John Mitchell, president of the United Mine Workers, and Hugh Frayne, an American Federation of Labor organizer, at the home of Anne Morgan, daughter of the famous financier. Taylor was cautiously optimistic about the results of the session:

> We had to make it perfectly clear that what we were doing was not
> speeding up the men, but teaching them and helping them through
> the services rendered by the management. . . . I have no doubt
> whatever that we can do no more than modify the hostility of these

> labor leaders. . . . They are, of course, afraid that our system will render unions less necessary. This was evident from the beginning.[108]

Since he made no attempt to disabuse them of their suspicions, he soon discovered that he had done little to "modify" their antagonism. Taylor made other efforts to educate the labor leaders, but always on his terms. He argued that scientific management made collective bargaining unnecessary, "but if it were needed we should not hesitate to have it."[109] For their part, the union leaders remained unconvinced. By 1914 they publicly avowed a willingness to reconsider their position if the engineers acknowledged the desirability of collective bargaining; privately they remained resentful and suspicious of Taylor and scientific management.[110]

As Taylor indicated, however, he did not expect to win the union leaders to his side, only to modify their hostility and neutralize their opposition. To achieve these goals, he intensified his public relations efforts to counteract their charges and, more specifically, attempted to affect the outcomes of government investigations of scientific management. Both activities were distasteful, the latter probably more than the former. If possible, Taylor had even less regard for politicians than labor leaders. But with the help of his politically astute disciples he vigorously defended the labor provisions of scientific management and helped postpone congressional action against time study and bonus payments.

As soon as the House of Representatives' investigation of the Watertown incident was announced in September 1911, Taylor made plans to influence it. He studied the backgrounds of the House committee members, invited them to Philadelphia, compiled lists of companies they might tour, and, in general, spared no effort "to make the best possible showing."[111] When the hearings began in October, he traveled to Boston and other cities to monitor them. He believed that he was the only observer who had attended all the hearings.[112] When witnesses favorable to scientific management appeared, he coached them. His own testimony, in January 1912, was the high point of the hearings.[113] By that time he had become optimistic about the results. The committee was "impartial and fairminded"; the workers who came to testify against scientific management "have been enlightened"; and "the teeth of the labor leaders have been drawn so their demeanor before the Committee is now quite mild and respectful."[114] Shortly thereafter he abandoned his role as lobbyist to care for Louise, but Hollis Godfrey proved an able replacement. The committee report, issued in March, criticized time study, but did not recommend congressional action. Taylor considered it "all that we could expect."[115]

Taylor adopted a similar approach to the investigations of the U.S. Commission on Industrial Relations between 1913 and 1915. He contacted the members, provided them with information on scientific management, enticed John R. Commons and Mrs. J. Bordon Harriman, two prominent members, to visit Philadelphia and tour Link-Belt, and testified before the commission. Taylor also coordinated the testimony of other proponents of scientific management, advised the commission staff on the selection of a man to aid Professor Robert Hoxie's study of scientific management, and provided information, particularly the names of firms, to Hoxie. Yet Taylor's role in the investigation was less prominent than it had been in 1911 and 1912, partly because scientific management was only one of many topics the commission studied and partly because nationally prominent union leaders, politically adept and at least superficially conciliatory toward scientific management, represented the labor side, while Brandeis and Robert Valentine, as well as Taylor and his immediate followers, spoke for the management position. Brandeis and Valentine adopted a more flexible attitude toward the unions, anticipating the reconciliation that would occur in the following years.

Still, Taylor found the commission investigation, like his other political activities, a source of continuing anxiety. He devoted much of his time between 1913 and 1915 to the hearings and the Hoxie study and to the numerous problems that grew out of them. Valentine, who had been selected as the management expert to assist Hoxie and who strongly favored collective bargaining, was a special source of concern.[116] Equally disturbing was the exceedingly slow pace of the Hoxie inquiry and the commission deliberations. Taylor remained involved and optimistic to the end, but received little satisfaction for his efforts.[117] He was distressed when Congress prohibited the use of stop-watches and bonus payments in government facilities in early 1915. Perhaps it was fortunate that he died before learning of a second adverse development, Hoxie's critical report, *Scientific Management and Labor*.

By the winter of 1914–15 Taylor was emotionally and physically exhausted. Louise's relapse in late 1914 had been a major blow, and the congressional action against time study supposedly left him "much depressed."[118] He wrote that he was "so overwhelmed" that he had "hardly been able to do anything for several weeks."[119] He was unable to work "for the lack of time and also for lack of heart."[120] Under these circumstances his health deteriorated. He had had a severe bronchial infection in 1913 and may have suffered from diabetes.[121] On his lecture trip to Cleveland and Youngstown in late February and early March 1915 he caught a cold that persisted after his return to Atlantic City. On March 9 he wrote that "as long as temperature and a bronchial cough continues I do not dare go out of doors very much."[122] A week later, however, he and Louise traveled to Philadelphia to visit his sister. The day after their arrival he entered Medico-Chirurgical Hospital with pneumonia. His condition worsened rapidly and, despite his doctors' assurances of recovery, he died on March 21, the day after his fifty-nineth birthday.

Finis: The Completion of a Legend

Taylor's premature death was a personal tragedy that had relatively little effect on the application of scientific management or the growing identity between "efficiency" and reform. By 1915 Taylor was important primarily as a symbol, a point of reference for others. He may have been the "father" of scientific management, but he presided over a burgeoning, uncontrollable family. His approach and standards remained benchmarks for other consultants and manufacturers, but scientific management was no longer the well-defined entity it had been in 1901 or even in 1910. It was a mark of Taylor's success that the factory revolution and the progressive efficiency movement, as practical, transforming forces in the industrial plant and society, had transcended him and his circle.

On the other hand, the timing of Taylor's death had a profound effect on the subsequent treatment of his career and contributions. By the spring of 1915 Taylor and the disciples were almost wholly preoccupied with their critics, the unionists in particular. They were defensive and suspicious, an isolated, embattled minority—or so they perceived themselves. In this context Taylor's death was a devastating blow. Lacking perspective on contemporary events, his loyal followers sensed a new vulnerability, a possibility that, in his absence, his reputation and movement might be discredited by critics or eclipsed by the likes of Emerson and Gilbreth. With growing anxiety they plotted their response.

After Taylor's funeral at Cedron on March 24, Barth, Cooke, Hathaway, Sanford Thompson, and Clarence M. Clark met to consider the future. Their first step was to form the Frederick W. Taylor Cooperators, an organization of relatives and associates that was to direct the disciples' strategy in the following years. The Cooperators' initial project, organized in conjunction with the Taylor Society, was an elaborate memorial service at Boxly on October 23. Two hundred and fifty friends and professional admirers attended. Pleased with the success of this effort, the Cooperators and other associates met at the Adelphia Hotel the following morning to plan their next move. After an extended discussion, they agreed that an authorized biography would be a valuable weapon in their continuing struggle to defend Taylor's reputation. They weighed the merits of commissioning an outside writer versus a member of the Taylor circle and decided that a professional author would be the better choice. "We . . . would appeal to a larger class of readers and thus tend to spread abroad the principles of Scientific Management."[123] The group then named a committee of Cooke, Thompson, and Clark to employ an appropriate author. Guided by Cooke, the committee selected Frank Barkley Copley.

Copley began his work in 1916 and at first encountered few problems. He had access to Taylor's voluminous papers and to the men and women who had worked with Taylor throughout his career. Copley found Taylor's disciples eager to talk. Carl G. Barth, generally unapproachable to strangers, "just opened his heart and mind, and dumped out everything to use or not to use in accordance with my discretion."[124] Louise Taylor was equally enthusiastic. Despite her illness, she was voluble, even ebullient. Soon she began to send him gifts and favors. Copley wrote that there was "a world . . . of pathos in her gratitude." Yet he was uncomfortable; the attention, he noted, is a "little embarrassing."[125]

As his work progressed, Copley's sense of unease grew. Despite the outward friendliness of Taylor's associates, he found himself subject to numerous pressures. The Cooperators wanted a useful biography, one that would aid them in their defense of Taylor. Copley understood this and intended no concessions to the labor reformers or unionists. But there were other complicating factors. The Cooperators, he discovered, were only the most loyal and orthodox of Taylor's followers; other men, less friendly, had played major roles in Taylor's career. How would he treat them? Even among the Cooperators there were divisions. The Clarks, in particular, had little use for Cooke, who was leading a widely publicized attack on the Philadelphia Electric Company, with which they were closely identified.[126] The most serious problem, however, was Louise Taylor. Despite her initial enthusiasm, she was unstable and unpredictable. One day she would be friendly and receptive; the next day she would be despondent or irritable. Copley had to be wary of every word in her presence.

Mindful of these real or potential difficulties, Copley returned to New York in February 1917 and began to work on his manuscript. He wrote steadily during the spring and summer and, as he reported, "got off to a very good start."[127] Louise Taylor visited him at least once and expressed her support for the project. Copley wrote that she was "not the most stable person in the world; but I now believe she is genuinely well disposed towards Mary [his wife] and me personally."[128] After the summer of 1917 Copley worked on the manuscript on a part-time basis, completing it in mid-1919. In the interim he sent his finished material to Clark and Cooke and received, as he recalled, "many kindly, complimentary and encouraging statements."[129]

Louise Taylor, Cooke, Clark, Thompson, and Harlow S. Person read the draft during the summer of 1919 and suggested various improvements. Their comments confirmed Copley's earlier misgivings. Person charged that the manuscript "does not bring out the *greatness, the soul, of the man.* It is not a work of interpretation."[130] Louise elaborated: "I want to feel in reading the book that I am following the development of the man, as he struggled with the various problems as they daily faced him, so that one will fully realize the heroic efforts he made to try and make clear to the world the need of science and of a better understanding of human relations."[131] Thompson concurred.[132] They also insisted that Copley delete potentially controversial passages, derogatory references to Taylor's critics, profanity, and "initimate personal and family matter."[133]

To insure that Copley made the necessary changes, they hired an outside expert, Professor Henry G. Pearson of Harvard University, to oversee the project. After several meetings in early 1920 Pearson prepared a summary of their objections and a detailed outline for Copley to follow in rewriting the manuscript.[134] Copley was furious, particularly at Pearson's refusal to give him the readers' detailed comments. "Can I be blamed," he fumed, "for suspicioning that the intention is to give me . . . only such part of them as someone considers is good for me?"[135]

Copley's relations with the Cooperators deteriorated rapidly in the following months. At the May 1920 meeting of the Taylor Society, Copley met Thompson and Pearson to go over the manuscript. Pearson called parts of the work "superficial" and suggested that Copley spend several months reading Taylor's published works. Thompson proposed to write a memorandum, noting—in Copley's words—"such things as I could do and such principles as I must follow in preparing the final manuscript."[136] Later, at the evening banquet, Louise Taylor attacked Copley for supposedly refusing to consider the readers' comments. So shocked that his "brain largely went out of action," Copley returned to New York and issued an ultimatum to Clark: Pearson must "disappear from the job completely and permanently," and the readers must deal with him personally, or he would resign. If he continued, he must not be restricted "by anyone standing over me and attempting to tell me what to do." In return, he would "do everything I conscientiously can do to meet the wishes of Mr. Taylor's relatives and professional associates."[137]

Reluctantly, the Cooperators complied. Pearson played no further role in the project, and the readers consulted Copley directly. In turn, Copley agreed to cut the work drastically, revise several chapter titles, and accept certain substantive changes involving "Mr. Taylor's attitude towards unions."[138] Nevertheless, there were additional disputes in late 1920 and a major crisis in the fall of 1922. Thompson wrote in despair that "it would be impossible to publish it [the biography] under Copley's name without his approval. On the other hand, it would be impossible to publish it without his name because it would not be accepted by any publisher."[139] Finally, Thompson negotiated a new compromise: "Mrs. Taylor would indicate the personal parts of the book which she absolutely required cutting out and . . . Copley would accept these provided that efforts were made . . . to have her accept certain portions which [Thompson believed] . . . should be left in." Thompson would attempt to reconcile other differences and would send the suggested changes to Copley, who would discuss them with Harlow Person and Ida Tarbell, the journalist, "and their decision would be final."[140] In this fashion the biography was completed and published in 1923. *Frederick W. Taylor, Father of Scientific Management* became the authoritative source on Taylor's life and work.

It is difficult to gauge the precise effects of Copley's ordeal. Clearly his problems did not change the basic thrust of his work; his *Outlook* article had been sympathetic, even effusive, in its portrayal of Taylor. And there was undoubtedly reason for much of the criticism. Even in its final form the biography is diffuse, redundant, and too long by at least one-half. Nevertheless, Copley's correspondence suggests that the Cooperators influenced the book in several ways. First, they insured that Copley's interpretive statements were consistent with Taylor's post-1911 promotional campaign, in particular, his emphasis on the reorganization or rationalization of work. Given Copley's assumptions about scientific management and the environment in which he worked, there was little likelihood of any other approach. The result was a distortion of the character and significance of Taylor's early career. Second, the Cooperators guaranteed that Copley took the "principles" of scientific management seriously. Following Taylor's post-1911 lead, his associates insisted that Taylor's greatest contribution was his "philosophy" of management, most succinctly summarized in the "principles." Person's chief complaint of 1919 was that Copley's draft did not reflect Taylor's "soul." If Copley was to satisfy his employers, he had little choice but to make the "principles" an important feature of his story. Third, the Cooperators had a major, perhaps a decisive, effect on Copley's account of Taylor's post-1901 career. By insisting that he emphasize the "principles" and by systematically excising controversial material, the Cooperators insured that Taylor's strategy for promoting scientific management, his conception of the expert's role, his contentious relations with Emerson and Gilbreth, and to some degree, his emergence as a reformer, would remain obscure. Lastly, the Cooperators influenced Copley's account of Taylor's personal life. The biography carefully noted Taylor's idiosyncrasies, particularly those that suggested an interest in order and organization, but virtually nothing else of an intimate or personal character. As might be expected, Taylor's family life received only the most superficial and idealized treatment. Louise appeared as a devoted and reticent helpmate; her disabilities and treatments, which more than anything related to scientific management had influenced Taylor's behavior and activities after 1910, were scarcely mentioned.

Ironically, the "revised" biography never served its intended purpose. By 1923 the furor of Taylor's last years had waned. The more vocal progressives had lost their audiences; the unionists had mellowed; and Emerson and the other imitators had gone their separate ways. Taylor's reputation was secure, his fame probably greater than ever. Judged by its original goal, the biography was a costly mistake. Yet it served another, ultimately more important purpose. Thanks to the Cooperators and Louise Taylor, the book reinforced the supposed lessons of *The Principles of Scientific Management*. Together they created the intellectual framework that circumscribed the discussion of Taylor's contributions in the following decades. As a result, Taylor's achievements as an inventor, engineer, manager, and reformer received less attention than his more modest contributions to the "solution" of the labor problem. Like Taylor before them, Copley and the Cooperators had bowed to the exigencies of the moment in portraying the rise of scientific management. The cumulative effect was to divorce Taylor from his milieu and foreclose the possibility of a realistic portrayal of his innovations, not to mention his preeminent role in the emergence of modern industry.

8
Epilogue:
Taylor and the Managerial Revolution

In "Shop Management" Taylor wrote, in a lightly veiled reference to his own rise, that "good manners, education and even special training and skill . . . count for less in an executive position than the grit, determination and bulldog endurance that knows no defeat."[1] In fact, Taylor's successes had everything to do with his "education . . . special training and skill," while his difficulties often resulted from a "determination and bulldog endurance" that alienated clients, allies, and friends. Taylor was a notable inventor, a pioneer consultant, an influential publicist, a progressive reformer, and a controversial public figure, but his signal contribution transcended these roles. He demands our attention because he was a key member of the group that by virtue of "education . . . special training and skill" transformed industrial management and, to a lesser degree, industrial society between the 1870's and World War I. In the process he helped make the factory as fascinating and controversial as the big business corporation.

The "most important change," as L. P. Alford noted in a contemporary assessment of the factory revolution, was the rise of "an attitude of questioning, of research, of careful investigation . . . of seeking for exact knowledge and then shaping action on discovered facts."[2] Though this tendency was by no means confined to industry or even economic affairs, Taylor was a leading exemplar and symbol of it. In industrial and engineering circles he signified the transition from nineteenth- to twentieth-century techniques. Committed to the "fraternity of mechanicians" and the small competitive enterprise, he achieved prominence because he embraced the spirit and methodology

198

of the modern scientific investigator and the large bureaucratic organization. In later years he became a celebrity because he dramatized the possibilities and pitfalls of the new order. Supporters and detractors alike agreed with Ray Stannard Baker that it was "no small matter when a man arises who can show us new ways of commanding our environment."[3]

Taylor's larger role was, in turn, based on his contributions to the transformation of industrial management. More than any other contemporary engineer, he perceived the interrelated character of the new management systems and the need for disciplined, comprehensive change if the manufacturer and the industrial sector were to attain the optimum results. This approach was a source of frequent conflict and debate, not least because of Taylor's "determination and bulldog endurance." But it also provided a standard that growing numbers of technicians were to embrace in the following years.

The tangible results of Taylor's work were more limited during his lifetime. The firms that introduced scientific management as he prescribed it became the world's most meticulously organized factories. The much larger group that adopted fragments of the Taylor system also shared the benefits of his insights.[4] By the second decade of the twentieth century Taylor's metal-cutting discoveries had revolutionized machine tool practice. His innovations in production management—methods for managing tools, materials, machines, supervisors, and workers—were less popular, at least in the precise forms he recommended. Thousands of plants introduced elements of scientific management, but few firms created formal planning departments or issued detailed instruction cards to machine workers.

Even fewer embraced functional foremanship. This was unfortunate, for in functional supervision Taylor had a technique that might have offset the adverse social impact of centralized management and the "machine model." Together with modern personnel management, it might have restored the positive environment of the nineteenth-century precision machinery plant. But functional foremanship had little chance. A logical extension of systematic management, it nevertheless contradicted the hallowed notion of individual accountability and the newer concept of line and staff organization. For Taylor it was largely an afterthought; for his associates and clients it was at best an indication of his thoroughness, at worst an embarrassing symbol of his inflexibility.

On the other hand, Taylor's approach to the factory worker was immensely popular. This is to say, manufacturers combined time study with the "rule of thumb" personnel measures that he favored. The effects varied widely and defy simple generalization. Where scientific management was introduced in toto, the workers generally shared the benefits of the new order; in a much larger number of plants time study simply reinforced the status quo. If relatively few were helped it also seems likely that few were harmed. Students of Taylor's work, including sophisticated observers like Robert Hoxie, often confused traditional driving methods with scientific management and reached negative, even alarmist conclusions about the effects of his innovations. In retrospect, however, their concern appears exaggerated. Whatever the experts' or the manufacturers' inclinations, the exigencies of implementing scientific management often served as effective if inadvertent buffers against driving. Equally important, the deficiencies of time study and the unpopularity of Taylor's incentive wage plans insulated workers against their potential ill effects. If studies of American factories in the 1920's are even reasonably accurate and representative, time study in practice was no more oppressive than the "rule of thumb" techniques of the nineteenth century.[5] Certainly it had little effect on worker efforts to restrict production.[6] Though the incentive wage remained popular, no more than a handful of employees ever worked under the differential piece rate or task and bonus systems.[7]

As the preceding chapters have indicated, Taylor's efforts to publicize his labor measures diverted attention from his more meaningful alterations of machine practice and managerial procedure. But they also had a second unanticipated effect: they diverted attention to the work of the labor reformers. Taylor's contention that scientific management increased labor productivity, improved morale, and prevented strikes was only one step from Patterson's contention that welfare work "pays." Taylor did not anticipate or applaud this effect, but he was powerless to stop it.

In the years following Taylor's death, labor reform became the concern of a substantial proportion of the nation's businessmen, largely because of the World War I industrial boom. After 1915 manufacturers responded to burgeoning demand, escalating turnover, and growing unrest by embracing the ideas of the pioneer labor reformers. Welfare work spread rapidly, and welfare workers, in the guise of "employment managers," encroached on the foreman's formerly sacrosanct powers to hire, fire, and train. Soon the personnel experts had introduced additional activities—intelligence tests, job analyses, and foreman training programs to name only the most significant—that further enhanced their roles. Finally, the wartime upsurge of militant trade unionism and a powerful alternative, company unionism, underlined the importance of the specialists' services. By 1920 there were 4,000 to 5,000 employment managers and several hundred businesses that had reasonably advanced programs.[8] The last bastion of the nineteenth-century fore-man's power had been breached, and a new relationship, based on managerial control of the worker, became the basis of personnel work in the post-war manufacturing plant. Compared to the gradual spread of systematic and scientific management, labor reform took the country by storm.

The final irony of Taylor's career was that the war experience also ended many of the conflicts that seemed so important during his life-time. Most notably, it lessened tensions between big business and the progressive engineers. In part this was due to the redirection of the reform impulse from domestic to foreign issues, in part to the passing of men like Taylor whose business careers had antedated the trusts. But the most important factor was the changing character of corporate management. By 1915 professional managers had succeeded financiers and speculators in top management positions and, together with a new generation of middle managers, had created centrally controlled, bureaucratic enterprises. Middle managers were often production specialists committed to the spirit, if not the letter, of scientific manage-ment.[9] The war boom accelerated this change. By the 1920's big business executives had become champions and promoters of the new factory system. The contrast between corporate and shop management, so evident to engineers like Taylor and in later years to writers like Thorstein Veblen, seemingly disappeared.[10] Appropriately, perhaps, the modern manufacturing plant of the post-war decade attracted almost as much attention and controversy as the corporation had during the progressive period.

A similar process occurred in the factory. By the end of the war scien-tific management and personnel work had achieved a degree of popu-larity and acceptability that earlier proponents would not have fore-seen in their most euphoric moments. Predictably, industrialists began to view them as compatible, even complementary movements. By 1920, thanks to the efforts of men like Cooke and the new generation of professional employment managers, they had converged. Though pro-duction management and personnel management remained separate entities in theory and often in practice, the mutual isolation and antag-onism that had characterized their pre-war development had ended.

No comparable deus ex machina hastened the resolution of other con-flicts. The divisions among the disciples healed slowly; indeed, the most notable dispute, the "war" between Taylor's followers and Gilbreth, ended only with Gilbreth's death in 1924. By that time, however, the growing respectability of systematic management and the appearance of experts who had little direct contact with Taylor made it appear little more than a personal vendetta. The struggle between Taylor's followers and the unions had a similar history. During and after World War I, Cooke, Feiss, and other proponents of scientific management negotiated a truce with the unions based on mutual acceptance of time study and collective bargaining. By the late 1920's the nation's most prominent labor leaders had become exponents of the "humanized" Taylor system.[11] Yet this development, too, was soon obscured by larger events. The Depression raised doubts about the ability of either the engineers or the AFL leaders to speak for industrial employees. By the mid-1930's the workers demanded more than scholarly conferences and "labor management cooperation." It was not that they rejected the initiatives of the 1920's; they rejected the limited context in which the issues had been addressed and demanded a more thorough reexamination of their relations with industrial managers. Their activities were of sufficient moment to constitute a final, distinctive chapter in the development of the new factory system.

It has been the thesis of this study that Taylor's life provides the best introduction to the formative period of the modern factory, indeed to the turbulent history of the American industrial enterprise in the most critical years of its evolution. Taylor's reactions to his environment—his creative responses to the apparent deficiencies of the factory system and contemporary society, his disavowal of the big business corporation and the initiatives of the labor reformers—seem paradoxical by later standards, but they provide a forceful commentary on the concerns of the pre-war generation, especially that select group of individuals who, by virtue of "education . . . special training and skill," created the new factory system. America's engineer of paradox illuminated the revolutionary age in which he lived. Belatedly, it is time to recognize the precise nature of his contributions.

Reference Matter

Notes

Preface

1 For a discussion of "systematic management" see Joseph A. Litterer, "Systematic Management: The Search for Order and Integration," *Business History Review* 35 (1961): 461–76; and Litterer, "Systematic Management: Design for Organizational Recoupling in American Manufacturing Firms," *Business History Review* 37 (1963): 369–91.

2 Taylor's innovations in production management, including time study and the "differential" piece rate, obviously affected the workers, and Taylor often characterized them as labor reforms. But it is misleading to associate these measures with workers, and particularly with reform. The labor reform movement had a different origin and *modus operandi*. See Chs. 1 and 6.

3 Thompson wrote *The Theory and Practice of Scientific Management* (Boston, 1917) and the obscure but extremely useful *The Taylor System of Scientific Management* (New York, 1917). He also edited a valuable anthology of early articles, *Scientific Management* (Cambridge, Mass., 1914).

4 Harry Braverman, *Labor and Monopoly Capitalism* (New York, 1974), Chs. 4–5; William E. Akin, *Technocracy and the American Dream* (Berkeley, 1977), Ch. 1; David Noble, *America by Design* (New York, 1977), Ch. 10; Sudhir Kakar, *Frederick Taylor: A Study in Personality and Innovation* (Cambridge, Mass., 1970). See below, Ch. 2, n. 25, for objections to the Kakar biography.

Chapter 1
The Factory Revolution

1 See Alfred D. Chandler, Jr., *The Visible Hand: The Managerial Revolution in American Business* (Cambridge, Mass., 1977).

2 See Louis Galambos, *The Public Image of Big Business in America, 1880–1940* (Baltimore, 1975), Chs. 3–4.

3 The critical change was the shift from hand to machine work. The transition from mill to factory was often gradual and indistinct.

4 Alfred D. Chandler, Jr., "Anthracite Coal and the Beginnings of the Industrial Revolution in the United States," *Business History Review* 46 (1972): 141–81. For the factory system in Britain see Sidney Pollard, *The Genesis of Modern Management* (London, 1965).

5 See Daniel Nelson, *Managers and Workers: Origins of the New Factory System in the United States, 1880–1920* (Madison, 1975), Ch. 2.

6 For iron and steel see Peter Temin, *Iron and Steel in Nineteenth Century America: An Economic Inquiry* (Cambridge, Mass., 1964); for the shoe industry see "The Boot and Shoe Industry as a Vocation for Women," U.S. Bureau of Labor Statistics *Bulletin* 180 (1915); Blanche Evans Hazard, *The Organization of the Boot and Shoe Industry in Massachusetts before 1875* (Cambridge, Mass., 1921); and Alan Dawley, *The Industrial Revolution in Lynn* (Cambridge, Mass., 1977).

7 The best source for these discussions is the leading trade journal of the industry, *The American Machinist. Iron Age, Iron Trades Review*, and after 1890 *Engineering Magazine* also contain frequent comments on factory organization.

8 This is obviously a rough distinction, a partial guide to the reality of American industry in the nineteenth century. Two complicating factors were of special importance. First, in all factories there were many nonmachine workers who were only indirectly affected by the basic manufacturing process. Second, there were many plants that combined heat-using and mechanical processes. This was the case at Midvale Steel and Bethlehem Iron, two of Taylor's most important employers. For Taylor, at least, this was a matter of no consequence. He treated Midvale and Bethlehem as machinery manufacturers, not as iron and steel mills. See Chs. 2 and 4.

9 See Frank T. Stockton, *The International Molders Union of North America* (Baltimore, 1921); and Jesse S. Robinson, *The Amalgamated Association of Iron, Steel and Tin Workers* (Baltimore, 1920).

10 Charles H. Fitch, "Report on the Manufacture of Interchangeable Mechanism," U.S. Department of the Interior, *Tenth Census, 1880, Manufactures* (Washington, D.C., 1883), 48–49; and W. Paul Strassman, *Risk and Technological Innovation* (Ithaca, 1958), 130.

11 The concept of the "American System" has received a much needed reexamination in David Houndshell's important study, "From the American System to Mass Production: The Development of Manufacturing Technology in the United States, 1850–1920" (Ph.D. diss., University of Delaware, 1978). Houndshell argues that armory methods were adopted in only a handful of factories that had direct ties to the arms industry, in short, that there were important gradations even in the precision machinery complex. Houndshell's distinction is obviously relevant to a discussion of the social implications of manufacturing systems. Yet in this context I believe that the older, less precise meaning of American System is adequate. Indeed, I have not rigorously distinguished between "precision machinery manufacture" and "machinery manufacture" except to exclude custom and job shops doing "general machine work." Though Taylor never worked in the small arms industry, he often operated in a social environment that closely resembled that of the genuine American System plants. For distinctions between machinery plants see Charles Day, "Metal Working Plants, Their Machine-Tool Equipment," *Engineering Magazine* 39 (June 1910):366–67.

12 Fitch, "Interchangeable Mechanism," 61.

13 Ibid.

14 Daniel Nelson, "The American System and the American Worker," in *The American System of Manufactures*, ed. Otto Mayr, forthcoming.
15 Ibid., 12–13.
16 See *Tenth Census, 1880, Manufactures*, xvii.
17 Massachusetts Bureau of Statistics of Labor, *Thirteenth Report*, 1883, 306.
18 The following discussion of foremanship is based on Nelson, *Managers and Workers*, Ch. 3.
19 George S. Gibb, *The Whitesmiths of Taunton* (Cambridge, Mass., 1946), 284.
20 Massachusetts Bureau of Statistics of Labor, *Thirteenth Report*, 1883, 306.
21 Quoted in Thomas L. Norton, *Trade Union Policies in the Massachusetts Shoe Industry, 1919–1929* (New York, 1932), 47.
22 Henry Roland, "Six Examples of Successful Shop Management, IV," *Engineering Magazine* 19 (Sept. 1900):897.
23 This is not to suggest that such internal factors were the sole causes of unrest and violence. But employers' policies clearly bore a major share of the responsibility. For the relationship between the employer's role and labor violence see H. M. Gitelman, "Perspectives on American Industrial Violence," *Business History Review* 47 (1973):1–23.
24 See Norman Ware, *The Industrial Worker*, 1840–60 (Boston 1924); and David Montgomery, *Beyond Equality: Labor and the Radical Republicans, 1862–72* (New York, 1967).
25 See Gitelman, "Perspectives on Industrial Violence."
26 See, for example, Philip Taft and Philip Ross, "American Labor Violence: Its Causes, Character, and Outcome," in *The History of Violence in America*, ed. Hugh Davis Graham and Ted Robert Gurr (New York, 1969), 281–344.
27 In the heat-using industries, production limitations were often written into union contracts. Employers, however, were always uneasy with such stipulations and often looked upon them as a prime reason for eliminating the unions as soon as possible. See Robinson, *Amalgamated Association*, 114.
28 See Sidney Fine, *Laissez Faire and the General Welfare State* (Ann Arbor, 1956); and Galambos, *The Public Image*, Chs. 3–4.
29 Chandler, *The Visible Hand*, Ch. 8.
30 The most acute student of the factory revolution was Horace L. Arnold, an obscure journalist who wrote (under his own name and that of Henry Roland) for *Engineering Magazine*. Arnold and the publishers of *Engineering Magazine* wrote from an engineering perspective.
31 *History of the Baldwin Locomotive Works, 1831–1923* (Philadelphia, 1923), 82.
32 Harold C. Passer, *The Electrical Manufacturers* (Cambridge, Mass., 1953), 302–5.
33 Charles M. Riply, *Romance of a Great Factory* (Schenectady, 1919), 77.
34 Richard B. DuBoff, "The Introduction of Electric Power in American Manufacturing," *Economic History Review* 20 (1967):510.
35 See Monte Calvert, *The Mechanical Engineer in America, 1830–1910* (Baltimore, 1967); and Edwin T. Layton, Jr., *The Revolt of the Engineers* (Cleveland, 1971), Ch. 2.

36 See Seymour Melman, "The Rise of Administrative Overhead in the Manu-
    facturing Industries of the United States, 1899–1947," *Oxford Economic
    Papers* 3 (1951):90–91.
37 See Calvert, *Mechanical Engineer*, Ch. 9; Layton, *Revolt*, Ch. 3; and Edwin
    T. Layton, Jr., "American Ideologies of Science and Engineering," *Tech-
    nology and Culture* 17 (Oct. 1976):688–701.
38 Nelson, *Managers and Workers*, Ch. 6. There was, of course, a much larger
    group of critics who often commented on the factory and labor issues. For
    their views and activities see Fine, *Laissez Faire*. However, their influence on
    the operation of the factory was minimal. It consisted of (1) creating a climate
    of public censure that indirectly encouraged sensitive manufacturers to insti-
    tute reforms, usually welfare programs, and (2) encouraging the public
    regulation of employment and working conditions. Also see James B. Gilbert,
    Work without Salvation (Baltimore, 1977).
39 The labor reformers' perspective and approach are summarized in Carroll
    Wright's classic "Report on the Factory System of the United States,"
    Tenth Census, 1880, Manufactures, 533–610.
40 Joseph A. Litterer, "Systematic Management: Design for Organizational
    Recoupling in American Manufacturing Firms," *Business History Review*
    37 (Winter 1963):370.
41 Ibid.
42 Henry P. Kendall, "Types of Management: Unsystematized, Systematized
    and Scientific," in Dartmouth College Conferences, *Addresses and Discus-
    sions at the Conference on Scientific Management Held Oct. 12, 13, 14, 1911*
    (Hanover, 1912), 120.
43 Samuel Paul Garner, *Evolution of Cost Accounting to 1925* (University, Ala.,
    1954), 98, 114–15.
44 Ibid., 187–88.
45 Litterer, "Systematic Management," 376–83.
46 Ibid., J. Slater Lewis, *The Commercial Organization of Factories* (London,
    1896); and Horace L. Arnold, *The Complete Cost Keeper* (New York, 1912).
47 Frederick W. Taylor to Henry R. Towne, Aug. 8, 1896, Frederick W. Taylor
    Papers (Stevens Institute of Technology, Hoboken, N.J., File 63A.
48 Henry Roland, "Six Examples of Successful Shop Management, III," *Engi-
    neering Magazine* 12 (Dec. 1896):402.
49 Henry R. Towne, "Gain Sharing," American Society of Mechanical Engi-
    neers *Transactions* 10 (1889):618.
50 Roland, "Six Examples, III," 404–6; and Henry R. Towne, "Discussion,"
    ASME *Transactions* 8 (1887):290–92.
51 Henry R. Towne, "Discussion," 644–46.
52 *American Machinist* 22 (Mar. 9, June 29, 1899):516, 179; and Frederick A.
    Halsey, "Discussion," ASME *Transactions* 41 (1919):170.
53 Frederick A. Halsey, "The Premium Plan for Paying for Labor," ASME
    Transactions 22 (1891):758.
54 Ibid., 763. Halsey uses a day rate in his example.
55 Ibid., 761.

56 See *American Machinist* 22 (Mar. 9, 1899):179.
57 See Horace B. Drury, *Scientific Management: A History and Criticism* (New York, 1915), 48–49.
58 See Sumner Slichter, *Union Policies and Industrial Management* (Washington, D.C., 1941), 305–8.
59 James O'Connell, "Piece-Work Not Necessary for Best Results in the Machine Shop," *Engineering Magazine* 19 (June 1900):373–74. Also see International Association of Machinists *Proceedings of Eighth Convention*, 1899, 336, 390–91, 403–4; Mark Perlman, *The Machinists* (Cambridge, Mass., 1961), 43; and Sumner Slichter, *Union Policies*, 306–8.
60 See Milton J. Nadworny, *Scientific Management and the Unions, 1900–1932* (Cambridge, Mass., 1955), Ch. 2.
61 Nelson, *Managers and Workers*, Chs. 5–6; and Stuart D. Brandes, *American Welfare Capitalism* (Chicago, 1976).
62 "What is Welfare Work?" National Civic Federation *Monthly Review* 1 (Aug. 1904):5.
63 Nelson, *Managers and Workers*, Ch. 6.
64 Samuel Crowther, *John H. Patterson, Pioneer in Industrial Welfare* (Garden City, 1923), Ch. 12.
65 Paul Monroe, "Possibilities of the Present Industrial System," *American Journal of Sociology* 3 (June 1902):414–15.
66 Gertrude Beeks to Stanley McCormick, Nov. 3, 1902, McCormick Papers (State Historical Society of Wisconsin, Madison), Series 3B, Box 27.
67 See Daniel Nelson, "The New Factory System and the Unions: The NCR Company Dispute of 1901," *Labor History* 15 (Winter 1974):89–97.
68 Henry Eilbert, "The Development of Personnel Management in the United States," *Business History Review* 33 (1959):345–64.
69 Charles U. Carpenter "The Working of a Labor Department in Industrial Establishments," *Engineering Magazine* 25 (April 1903):5–6.
70 Charles Henderson, *Citizens in Industry* (New York, 1915), 278–80.
71 "How the Welfare Department Was Organized," National Civic Federation *Monthly Review* 1 (June 1904):13–14.

Chapter 2
Formative Years, 1856–1889

1 Anthony F. C. Wallace, *Rockdale* (New York, 1978), 359. Also see Bruce Sinclair, *Philadelphia's Philosopher Mechanics* (Baltimore, 1974).
2 Nathaniel Burt, *The Perennial Philadelphians* (Boston, 1963), 67–77; and E. Digby Baltzell, *Philadelphia Gentlemen* (Glencoe, 1958), 264–67.
3 Interview with Robert P. A. Taylor, Providence, Rhode Island, June 17, 1974. Compare Taylor with Sidney George Fisher, a contemporary. Nicholas B. Wainwright, ed., *A Philadelphia Perspective: The Diary of Sidney George Fisher Covering the Years 1834–1871* (Philadelphia, 1967).

4 Edwin T. Freedley, *Philadelphia and Its Manufactures* (Philadelphia, 1858), 59–60.

5 Frederick B. Tolles, ed., *Slavery and "The Woman Question:" Lucretia Mott's Diary, 1840* (Philadelphia, 1952), 13, 44; and Betty Fladeland, *Men and Brothers: Anglo-American Antislavery Cooperation* (Urbana, 1972), 265. Also see Frank Barkley Copley, *Frederick W. Taylor, The Father of Scientific Management*, 2 vols. (New York, 1923), 1:41.

6 Birge Harrison Recollections, Frederick W. Taylor Papers (Stevens Institute of Technology, Hoboken, N.J.), File 14K.

7 Ibid.; and Edward W. Hocker, *Germantown, 1683–1933* (Germantown, 1933), 227–41.

8 Copley, *Taylor*, 1:51.

9 The Unitarian Society of Germantown, *Register of Families* (Germantown, n.d.).

10 Copley, *Taylor*, 1:51; for similar experiences see Logan Pearsall Smith, *Unforgotten Years* (Boston, 1939), Ch. 2.

11 Copley, *Taylor*, 1:64.

12 Franklin Taylor to Frederick W. Taylor, Nov. 14, 1872, Taylor Papers [no file number].

13 Harrison Recollections, Taylor Papers, File 14K.

14 See Sudhir Kakar, *Frederick Taylor: A Study in Personality and Innovation* (Cambridge, Mass., 1970), 18–19.

15 See Baltzell, *Philadelphia Gentlemen*, 301–7; and Myron R. Williams, *The Story of Phillips Exeter* (Exeter, 1957), 46.

16 See John Mason Kemper, *Phillips Academy at Andover, A National Public School* (New York, 1957), 14–19.

17 Williams, *Phillips Exeter*, 64.

18 Franklin Taylor to Frederick W. Taylor, Nov. 14, 20, 1872, Taylor Papers [no file number].

19 Franklin Taylor to Frederick W. Taylor, Apr. 24, 1873, Taylor Papers [no file number].

20 Emily Taylor to Frederick W. Taylor, Sept. 29, 1873, Taylor Papers [no file number].

21 Frederick W. Taylor, "The Principles of Scientific Management," in Dartmouth College Conferences, *Addresses and Discussions at the Conference on Scientific Management Held October 12, 13, 14, 1911* (Hanover, 1912), 371; and Frederick W. Taylor, *Scientific Management* (New York, 1947), 258–59.

22 Emily Taylor to Frederick W. Taylor, Dec. 10, 1873, Taylor Papers [no file number].

23 For a more speculative and melodramatic interpretation see Kakar, *Taylor*, 20–44.

24 Emily Taylor to Frederick W. Taylor, Feb. 22, 1874, Taylor Papers [no file number].

25 Compare this assessment with Kakar, *Taylor*, Ch. 3. My objection to the Kakar account is not that it is wrong; the meager data make it impossible to say that any interpretation is wholly accurate or inaccurate. My complaint is

that it is unsupported and misleading. Kakar grasps at straws, building his case on miscellaneous statements made, in many instances, thirty years after the events. The result is a strong and probably exaggerated emphasis on the exotic and sensational. Taylor may have been an obsessive-compulsive personality, and he may have experienced an identity crisis, but the documents do not show it. At best they are inconclusive.

26 Monte Calvert, *The Mechanical Engineer in America, 1830–1910* (Baltimore, 1967), Ch. 4. Also see the series on the "old man" by W. S. Rogers, "Sketch of an Apprenticeship," *American Machinist* 13–14 (Aug. 1890–Mar. 1891).

27 See James S. Whitney, "Apprenticeship," Philadelphia Social Science Association, Mar. 21, 1872.

28 Frederick W. Taylor, "Success," Taylor Papers, File 8B.

29 Taylor, "Testimony," 112.

30 Copley, *Taylor*, 1:78.

31 Ibid., 89.

32 Ibid., 143.

33 Frederick W. Taylor, "A Comparison of University and Industrial Methods and Discipline," 7, Taylor Papers, File 76A.

34 Taylor, "Success," 22, Taylor Papers, File 8B; and Frederick W. Taylor, "Why Manufacturers dislike College Students," *Proceedings of the Society for the Promotion of Engineering Education* 17 (1909):85.

35 Sam Bass Warner, Jr., *The Private City: Philadelphia in Three Periods of Its Growth* (Philadelphia, 1968), 61: Diane Lindstrom, *Economic Development in the Philadelphia Region, 1810–1850* (New York, 1978), Ch. 2.

36 J. Thomas Scharf and Thompson Westcott, *History of Philadelphia*, 3 vols. (Philadelphia, 1884), 3:2253.

37 For Clark's business career see Vincent Carosso, *Investment Banking in America* (Cambridge, Mass., 1970), 11; Fritz Redlich, *History of American Business Leaders: A Series of Studies*, Vol. 2, *The Molding of American Banking: Men and Ideas* (New York, 1951), 71–72, 350; and Scharf and Westcott, *History*, 3:2101.

38 L. T. C. Rolt, *A Short History of Machine Tools* (Cambridge, Mass., 1965), 175; Joseph W. Roe, *English and American Tool Builders* (New Haven, 1916), 247–51; Calvert, *Mechanical Engineer*, 9–10; and Scharf and Westcott, *History*, 3:2263–65.

39 See W. Ross Yates, "Samuel Wetherill, Joseph Wharton and the Founding of the American Zinc Industry," *Pennsylvania Magazine of History and Biography*, 98 (Oct., 1974):469–514; and Yates, "Joseph Wharton's Nickel Business," *PMHB*, 101 (July, 1977):287–321.

40 B. S. Stephenson, "Eminent Men of the Iron World, II, Jos. Wharton," *Iron Trade Review* 40 (Apr. 4, 1907):546–50; and Dumas Malone, ed., *Dictionary of American Biography* (New York, 1936), 20:29–30.

41 Lorin Blodget, "The Social Conditions of the Industrial Classes of Philadelphia," Philadelphia Social Science Association, Nov. 8, 1873.

42 Copley, *Taylor*, 1:106–7.

43 Russell Davenport, "A Farewell to Midvale," *Iron Age* 42 (Aug. 2, 1888):161.

44 See H. L. Gantt, "Recent Progress in the Manufacture of Steel Castings," ASME *Transactions* 15 (1894):266–70.

45 Davenport, "A Farewell," 161.

46 Ibid.

47 Ibid.

48 Ibid.

49 Ibid. Also see advertisements in *Iron Age* 23 (June 19, 1879):6.

50 Copley, *Taylor*, 1:114.

51 "Annual Review of the Manufacturing and Iron Industries of Eastern Pennsylvania," *Iron Age* 23 (Jan. 23, 1879):17.

52 See Copley, *Taylor*, 1:Ch. 7; Kakar, *Taylor*, Ch. 4.

53 Taylor, "Testimony," 80.

54 Frederick W. Taylor, *The Principles of Scientific Management* (New York, 1911), 49–50.

55 Ibid.

56 See Charles Shartle to William A. Fannon, May 2, 1886, Taylor Papers, File 14H; and International Association of Machinists *Monthly Journal* 6 (Nov. 1894):430–31.

57 Taylor to Morris L. Cooke, Dec. 2, 1910, Barth Papers (Harvard Business School, Boston, Mass.), Drawer 2.

58 Copley, *Taylor*, Vol. 1.

59 Wilfred Lewis, "The Versatile Genius of Taylor," Nov. 25, 1915, Taylor Papers, File 14S.

60 Taylor to Cooke, Dec. 2, 1910, Barth Papers, Drawer 2; Alexander C. Humphreys to Kempton P. A. Taylor, July 23, 1915, Taylor Papers, File 14O.

61 Copley, *Taylor*, 1:332. Elizabeth Madiera, a family member, recalls that Taylor "babied" Louise. Interview, Bryn Mawr, Pa., September 13, 1979.

62 Copley, *Taylor*, 1:119. He was informally appointed chief engineer in 1884. He actually acquired the title in 1888.

63 Taylor, "Success," 7–8, Taylor Papers, File 8B.

64 Taylor to Cooke, Dec. 2, 1910, Barth Papers, Drawer 2.

65 Patent 404,126.

66 Patents 568,174; 400,143; 424,939.

67 Taylor, "Success," 20, Taylor Papers, File 8B.

68 Copley, *Taylor*, 1:196–98.

69 Patents 359,369; 368,693; 417,525; 420,614; 428,703; 429,162; 448,276.

70 Carl G. Barth, "Introduction," Taylor Papers, Notebook 1 (1933).

71 Taylor, "On the Art of Cutting Metals," ASME *Transactions* 28 (1906):33–34. Taylor's statement also suggests, of course, that his efforts to prevent soldiering had been unsuccessful.

72 Ibid.; and Barth, "Introduction," Taylor Papers, Notebook 1.

73 See, for example, "The Application of the Indicator to Machine Tools," *American Machinist* 13 (Aug. 14, 1890):8; and F. J. Miller, "Cutting Tools," *American Machinist* 10 (Mar. 26, 1887):7 (Apr. 9, 1887):3, (Dec. 3, 1887):2.

74 Barth, "Introduction," Taylor Papers, Notebook 1.

75 Taylor to Barth, Dec. 18, 1913, Taylor Papers, File 113D.

76 Taylor, "Art of Cutting Metals," 37–38.

77 Taylor, "Shop Management," ASME *Transactions* 24 (1903):1444; and L. P. Alford, *Henry Laurence Gantt: Leader in Industry* (New York, 1934), 63–65. Gantt recalled in 1917: "The name by which our office went was the 'fish house.' There were two of us there, one very tall man, and he was called the 'big fish' and I was the 'little fish.' That is the amount of respect that was being shown these methods after seven years" (Gantt, "Discussion," *Bulletin of the Taylor Society* 3 [Feb. 1917]:11).

78 Taylor, "Art of Cutting Metals," 38.

79 Shartle to Fannon, May 2, 1916, Taylor Papers, File 14H.

80 Copley, *Taylor*, 1:165.

81 Taylor, "A Piece Rate System," ASME *Transactions* 16 (1895):880.

82 William A. Fannon Recollections, April 20, 1916, Taylor Papers, File 14H.

83 See George F. Steele to James Deering, April 28, 1894, Taylor Papers, File 70G. Taylor cited various dates. I have generally followed the account which appeared in "A Piece Rate System," his first "history" of scientific management.

84 Towne's description of his elementary production control plan appeared in 1882, and Halsey supposedly devised the premium in 1884.

85 Taylor, "Discussion," ASME *Transactions* 7 (1885–86):475–76.

86 Barth, "Introduction," Taylor Papers, Notebook 2.

87 Taylor, "Shop Management," 1396.

88 Steele to James Deering, April 28, 1894, Taylor Papers, File 70G. Also see Copley, *Taylor*, 1:221, 266.

89 Taylor, "Records from Midvale," Taylor Papers, Notebook 1; and Steele to James Deering, April 6, 1895, Taylor Papers, File 70G.

90 Shartle to Fannon, May 2, 1916, Taylor Papers, File 14H.

91 Taylor's accounts of his labor measures include several different dates. See Taylor, "A Piece Rate System," 869; Copley, *Taylor*, 1:226–28; and Taylor, "Shop Management," 1396.

92 Copley, *Taylor*, 1:231.

93 Taylor, "A Piece Rate System," 869.

94 Ibid.

95 Ibid. 876.

96 According to George F. Steele, Taylor's goal was to have the worker "busting himself all day long." Steele to James Deering, Feb. 28, 1894, Taylor Papers, File 70G. Also see Taylor, "A Piece Rate System," 874.

97 Taylor, "Testimony," 264–66.

98 Steele to Deering, Feb. 28, 1894, Taylor Papers, File 70G. Also see Fannon Recollections, Taylor Papers, File 14H.

99 Fannon Recollections, Taylor Papers, File 14H; and Copley, *Taylor*, 1:334.

100 Taylor, "Records from Midvale," Taylor Papers, Notebook 2; Taylor, "Shop Management," 1445; and Taylor, "A Piece Rate System," 876.

101 Taylor, *Principles of Scientific Management*, 55.

102 Taylor, "Report of Conversation by and Questions Put to Mr. F. W. Taylor, June 4, 1907," Taylor Papers, File 791. Also see Taylor, *Principles of Scientific Management*, 54–55.

103 Taylor, "A Piece Rate System," 871.

104 Steele to James Deering, April 28, 1894, Taylor Papers, File 70G. There were also serious methodological deficiencies. See Ch. 4, below.
105 Taylor, "A Piece Rate System," 870.
106 Shartle to Fannon, May 2, 1916, Taylor Papers, File 14H.
107 Henry Roland, "Six Examples of Successful Shop Management," *Engineering Magazine* 12 (Feb. 1897):836; and U.S. Congress, Commission on Industrial Relations, *Final Report and Testimony*, 64th Cong., 1st Sess. (Washington, D.C., 1916), 3:2857.
108 Taylor, "A Piece Rate System," 875.
109 Taylor, "Testimony," 42.
110 Taylor, "Shop Management," 1404.
111 Frank B. Copley, "Frederick W. Taylor, Revolutionist," *Outlook* 3 (Sept. 1, 1915):42.
112 Davenport, "Farewell to Midvale," 161; and Taylor, "A Piece Rate System," 879–81.
113 Steele to Deering, April 28, 1894, Taylor Papers, File 70G.

Chapter 3
Years of Revelation, 1890–1898

1 C. Bertrand Thompson to Frederick W. Taylor, Oct. 24, 1913, Frederick W. Taylor Papers (Stevens Institute of Technology, Hoboken, N.J.), File 52G.
2 Caspar F. Goodrich, "Memorial" [1915], Taylor Papers, File 14J.
3 Wilfred Lewis Recollection, July 26, 1915, Taylor Papers, File 14S.
4 See Charles Thomas Davis, *The Manufacture of Paper* (Philadelphia, 1886), 242–44, 260–74; and David C. Smith, *Papermaking in the United States (1691–1969)* (New York, 1970), 135–36, 166–75.
5 "Manufacturing Investment Company," Aug. 22, 1891, William C. Whitney Papers (Library of Congress), Vol. 65. Taylor wrote that "all my spare cash has gone into the M. I. Company" (Taylor to Ernest N. Wright, May 1, 1891, Taylor Papers, File 69A). Also see David C. Smith, *A History of Lumbering in Maine, 1861–1960* (Orono, Me., 1972), 251.
6 Frank B. Copley, *Frederick W. Taylor, Father of Scientific Management*, 2 vols. (New York, 1923), 1:336–37, 372–73.
7 Taylor to A. L. Smith, Jr., Dec. 29, 1891, Taylor Papers, File 70F; and Copley, *Taylor*, 1:374.
8 William A. Fannon Recollections, Apr. 20, 1916, Taylor Papers, File 14H.
9 Caspar F. Goodrich, *Rope Yarns from the Old Navy* (New York, 1931), 138–39.
10 Copley, *Taylor*, 1:376; and Taylor to Sanford E. Thompson, May 12, May 16, 1891, Taylor Papers, File 124A.
11 Goodrich to William C. Whitney, Jan. 1891, Whitney Papers, Vol. 63. For the potential pitfalls of the Mitscherlich process see Davis, *Manufacture of Paper*, 244–45, 263–73, 289–90; and Smith, *Lumbering in Maine*, 251.
12 Copley, *Taylor*, 1:383.
13 Taylor to Charles Warren Hunt, Feb. 26, 1898, Taylor Papers, File 125E.

14 Taylor to Whitney, Aug. 27, 1891, Whitney Papers, Vol. 65; and Taylor to Smith, July 11, 1892, Taylor Papers, File 70F.

15 Unsigned Memo, Taylor Papers, File 13.

16 Taylor to R. D. Evans, May 1, 1891, Taylor Papers, File 70A. They were "obliged to double both the steam and the water power of the mills and double, practically, all of the machinery in the mill" (Taylor to George W. Hammond, May 18, 1893, Taylor Papers, File 70E). See also Charles N. Glaab and Lawrence H. Larsen, *Factories in the Valley, Neenah-Menasha, 1870–1915* (Madison, 1969), Ch. 5.

17 Glaab and Larsen, *Factories in the Valley*, Ch. 5; and Gordon A. Bubolz, ed., *Land of the Fox, Saga of Outagamie County* (Appleton, 1949), 159–60.

18 Smith to Taylor, May 19, May 20, July 11, Aug. 9, 1892, Taylor Papers, File 70F.

19 Taylor to Hammond, May 18, 1893, Taylor Papers, File 70E.

20 Ibid.

21 Taylor to J. K. Griffith, June 8, 1893, Taylor Papers, File 60B.

22 Taylor to Hammond, May 18, 1893, Taylor Papers, File 70E. See also Taylor to Griffith, June 8, 1893, Taylor Papers, File 60B.

23 "Cost of Emptying and Filling a Digester," Nov. 7, 1892, Taylor Papers, File 36. For pulp loading see "Piece Work Rates for Loading Pulp," July 5, 1893, Taylor Papers, File 36.

24 Taylor, "A Piece Rate System," American Society of Mechanical Engineers *Transactions* 16 (1895):902–3.

25 Taylor to Hammond, May 18, 1893, Taylor Papers, File 70E.

26 William A. Fannon Recollections, Apr. 20, 1916, Taylor Papers, File 14H.

27 Taylor to Whitney, Aug. 27, 1891, Whitney Papers, Vol. 65.

28 Taylor to George F. Steele, Oct. 28, 1891, Taylor Papers, File 70G.

29 Copley, *Taylor*, 1:386; and Taylor to Hammond, May 18, 1893, Taylor Papers, File 70E.

30 Copley, *Taylor*, 1:379–81. Also see Benjamin Frick to Smith, Dec. 9, 1891, Taylor Papers, File 70F.

31 Taylor to Smith, Oct. 20, 1892, Taylor Papers, File 70F.

32 Goodrich to Whitney, Jan. 4, 1891, Vol. 63; Apr. 21, 1891, Vol. 64; May 20, 1891, Vol. 65; Whitney Papers.

33 Goodrich suggested a New York club for Taylor if he was "clubable." Goodrich to Whitney, Oct. 17, 1891, Whitney Papers, Vol. 66.

34 Taylor to Hammond, May 18, 1893, Taylor Papers, File 70E. The *Paper Trade Journal* reported that the change in management was "said to be due to difficulties in the administration of the company's affairs" (*Paper Trade Journal* 22 (June 3, 1893):487). Smith reports that the Madison mill was closed from mid-1893 to mid-1894. The Manufacturing Investment Company failed in 1899 (Smith, *Lumbering in Maine*, 252).

35 Copley, *Taylor*, 1:386.

36 He calculated his loss at $25,000 (Taylor to Hammond, May 18, 1893, Taylor Papers, File 70E; and Taylor to Goodrich [ca. Sept., 1896], Taylor Papers, File 60A).

37 Taylor to John H. King, June 14, 1893, Taylor Papers, File 61B.

38 Taylor to Holden A. Evans, Oct. 23, 1911, Taylor Papers, File 187F.

39 Taylor Scrapbooks, Vol. 2, Taylor Papers.

40 Benjamin Frick to Taylor, Apr. 26, 1892, Taylor Papers, File 70D.

41 Taylor to Smith, Apr. 13, 1892, Taylor Papers, File 70F.

42 William D. Halsey to Taylor, July 12, 1893, Taylor Scrapebooks, Vol. 3, Taylor Papers.

43 Taylor to Hammond, Aug. 25, 1893, Taylor Papers, File 70E.

44 Taylor, "System of Book Keeping and Returns as Introduced," Taylor Scrapbooks, Vol. 2, Taylor Papers.

45 Secretary, Midvale Steel, to Taylor, Mar. 11, 1889, Sept. 7, 1890, Taylor Papers, File 37.

46 Copley, *Taylor*, 1:424.

47 *American Machinist* 17 (Nov. 29, 1894):11.

48 George F. Simonds, "Anti-Friction Ball Bearings," *Iron Age* 52 (Oct. 26, 1893):754.

49 "Simonds Manufacturing Company's Chicago Plant," *Iron Age* 53 (Feb. 6, 1893):283.

50 Taylor to Griffith, July 13, 1891, Taylor Papers, File 60B.

51 Taylor to Griffith, June 8, 1893, Taylor Papers, File 60B.

52 Taylor to Hammond, Aug. 25, 1893, Taylor Papers, File 70E.

53 Copley asserted that Taylor worked for the William Deering Company, Copley, *Taylor*, 1:445. In addition, he must have devoted much of his time during the summer and fall of 1893 to the preparation of "Notes on Belting," which was based on the voluminous records kept by Taylor and Gantt at Midvale from 1884 to 1893.

54 Taylor to A. J. Moxham, Feb. 21, 1896, Taylor Papers, File 45. "It enables the manager to know exactly what part of his shop he must drive at for an increase in products and where he can afford to pay liberal wages . . . and where he can only reduce costs by reducing wages" (Taylor to W. A. Donaldson, Sept. 23, 1896, Taylor Papers, File 45). The system is explained in detail in Royal R. Keely, "Overhead Expense Distribution," *Industrial Engineering and Engineering Digest* 13 (July 1913):301–03.

55 Copley, *Taylor*, 1:447.

56 Ibid., 446–47.

57 Leighton Lee to Taylor, Aug. 10, 1898, Taylor Papers, File 34.

58 Copley, *Taylor*, 1:440.

59 Ibid., 433.

60 Frederick W. Taylor, "On the Art of Cutting Metals," ASME *Transactions* 28 (1906):39.

61 Copley, *Taylor*, 1:439.

62 Taylor to Lee, Aug. 12, 1898, Taylor Papers, File 34.

63 Steele to James Deering, Apr. 28, 1894, Taylor Papers, File 70G.

64 Steele to Taylor, Oct. 29, 1896, Taylor Papers, File 70H.

65 Taylor to Steele, May 28, 1895, Taylor Papers, File 70H.

66 Taylor to A. O. Fox, Sept. 9, 1896, Taylor Papers, File 38; and Taylor to Steele, Oct. 20, 1896, Taylor Papers, File 70H.

67 Copley, *Taylor*, 1:393–94. Because of the paucity of information on this

subject, it is impossible to determine whether these combinations were pools or merged firms. Presumably Taylor's antipathy to big business would not have prevented him from acting as referee or mediator for a pool.

68 Taylor, "A Piece Rate System," 860.

69 Ibid., 862–81.

70 Taylor to Steele, June 26, 1896, Taylor Papers, File 70H.

71 Taylor to Charles Warren Hunt, Feb. 26, 1898, Taylor Papers, File 125E.

72 Sanford E. Thompson to Taylor, Dec. 27, 1895, Taylor Papers, File 124A.

73 Ibid.

74 Taylor to Thompson, Mar. 28, 1896, June 3, 1896, Taylor Papers, File 124B; and Taylor, "Shop Management," ASME *Transactions* 24 (1903): 1424–28.

75 Thompson to Taylor, Feb. 1, 1896, Taylor Papers, File 124A.

76 Taylor to Thompson, Feb. 17, 1896, Taylor Papers, File 124B.

77 Taylor to Thompson, Jan. 8, 1896, Taylor Papers, File 124A.

78 See ibid.; and Thompson to Taylor, Feb. 13, 1896, Taylor Papers, File 124B.

79 Taylor to Thompson, Oct. 16, 1896, Taylor Papers, File 124C.

80 Taylor to Thompson, Feb. 22, 1896, Taylor Papers, File 124B.

81 Taylor to Thompson, Jan. 27, 1896, Taylor Papers, File 124B.

82 See Taylor to Thompson, Mar. 11, 1896, Taylor Papers, File 124B.

83 Taylor to Thompson, Mar. 26, 1896; and Thompson to Taylor, Mar. 31, 1896, Taylor Papers, File 124B.

84 Thompson to Taylor, Oct. 16, 1896, Taylor Papers, File 124C.

85 A. O. Fox to Taylor, Aug. 6, 1895, Taylor Papers, File 38. Taylor also introduced some elements of a planning department ("General Directions for Issuing Orders for Work," Carl G. Barth Papers [Harvard Business School, Boston, Mass.], Drawer 2).

86 Taylor to A. J. Moxham, Feb. 10, 1896, Taylor Papers, File 45.

87 Alfred D. Chandler and Stephan Salsbury, *Pierre S. DuPont and the Making of the Modern Corporation* (New York, 1971), 29; and Tom Johnson, *My Story* (New York, 1913), 29–30.

88 *Iron Age* 53 (Jan. 18, 1894): 115; and Chandler and Salsbury, *Pierre S. DuPont*, 26.

89 "The Steel Motor Company," *Street Railway Journal* 11 (Aug. 1895): 547. See also George T. Hanshett, "Electric Railway Motors," *Street Railway Journal* 13 (Dec. 1897): 835.

90 Chandler and Salsbury, *Pierre S. DuPont*, 29–30; and Johnson, *My Story*, 29–33. Also Pierre S. DuPont to Arthur J. Moxham, Feb. 5, June 6, 1894, Pierre S. DuPont Papers (Eleutherian Mills Historical Library, Wilmington, Del.), File 26, Box 1.

91 "Why the Johnson Company Went to Lorain," *Iron Trade Review* 28 (Jan. 3, 1895): 9–10; and "The Johnson Plant at Lorain," *Iron Age* 55 (May 9, 1895): 973.

92 "Memorandum to Stockholders of the Johnson Company," Mar. 24, 1896, Pierre S. DuPont Papers, File 26, Box 1; and Michael Massouh, "Tom Loftin Johnson, Engineer-Entrepreneur (1869–1900)" (Ph.D. diss., Case Western Reserve University, 1970), 172–73.

93 "Memorandum to Stockholders of the Johnson Company," Mar. 24, 1896.

Pierre S. DuPont Papers, File 26, Box 1; and *Johnstown Tribune*, Mar. 4, Apr. 16, 1896.

94 Taylor to Caspar F. Goodrich, June 3, 1896, Taylor Papers, File 60A.

95 Ibid.

96 Taylor to Steele, Oct. 14, 1896, Taylor Papers, File 70H.

97 Taylor to Steele, Feb. 26, 1895, Taylor Papers, File 70H.

98 Ibid.

99 Taylor to Steele, Sept.? 1896, Taylor Papers, File 70H.

100 Taylor to Steele, Nov. 20, 1896, Taylor Papers, File 70H.

101 Taylor to Moxham, Feb. 21, 1896, Taylor Papers, File 45.

102 Taylor to Goodrich, June 3, 1896, Taylor Papers, File 60A.

103 Taylor to Donaldson, Sept. 23, 1896, Taylor Papers, File 45.

104 Ibid.

105 Taylor to Steele, Oct. 14, 1896, Taylor Papers, File 70H; and Taylor to T. Coleman DuPont, Nov. 2, 1896, Taylor Papers, File 45.

106 Taylor to T. Coleman DuPont, Dec. 12, 1896, Taylor Papers, File 45.

107 Taylor to W. A. Harris, Jan. 15, 1897, Taylor Papers, File 45.

108 Taylor to Sanford E. Thompson, June 3 and 6, 1896, Taylor Papers, File 124C.

109 Taylor to George W. Hammond, July 2, 1896, Taylor Papers, File 70E.

110 Taylor to Donaldson, Aug. 23, 1896, Taylor Papers, File 45.

111 Taylor to Fox, Oct. 22, 1896, Taylor Papers, File 38.

112 Moxham to Pierre S. DuPont, July 18, 1896, Pierre S. DuPont Papers, File 26, Box 1; Moxham to Taylor, July 9, 1896, Taylor Papers, File 45; and Chandler and Salsbury, *Pierre S. DuPont*, 31–33.

113 Taylor to Steele, Oct. 14, 1896, Taylor Papers, File 70H.

114 "Memorandum to the Stockholders of the Johnson Company," Apr. 3, 1897, Pierre S. DuPont Papers, File 26, Box 1.

115 Taylor to Moxham, Feb. 21, 1896, Taylor Papers, File 45.

116 Taylor to W. A. Harris, Jan. 15, 1897, Taylor Papers, File 45.

117 Taylor to T. Coleman DuPont, Oct. 21, 1896, Taylor Papers, File 45.

118 See Taylor to T. Coleman DuPont, Apr. 6, 1896, Taylor Papers, File 45.

119 Taylor to T. Coleman DuPont, Nov. 2, 1896, Taylor Papers, File 45.

120 Taylor to T. Coleman DuPont, Apr. 6, 1896, Taylor Papers, File 45.

121 Taylor to T. Coleman DuPont, Nov. 2, 1896, Taylor Papers, File 45.

122 R. T. Lane to Taylor, Feb. 3, 1899, Taylor Papers, File 45.

123 "Report in Progress Made in Manufacture of the Simonds Rolling Machine Company," July 1, 1907, Taylor Papers, File 42.

124 "Permanent Rates," Dec. 29, 1892, Taylor Papers, File 42.

125 "Report in Progress," July 1, 1907, Taylor Papers, File 42.

126 Ibid.

127 Taylor, "Shop Management," 1384.

128 But see "Making Balls for Bearings," *American Machinist* 19 (Oct. 1, 1896): 20.

129 Frederick W. Taylor, *The Principles of Scientific Management* (New York, 1911), 88.

130 "Report in Progress," July 1, 1907, Taylor Papers, File 42.

131 Ibid.
132 Taylor to A. H. Couden, Nov. 22, 1897, Taylor Papers, File 42.
133 Ibid.
134 Ibid.
135 Wilfred Lewis to Frances Mitchell, Nov. 25, 1915, Taylor Papers, File 14S.
136 See Taylor to Conden, Nov. 22, 1897; Taylor to Charles L. Humphreys, Oct. 27, 1897; and Charles J. Harrah to Walter A. Simonds, Oct. 22, 1897, Taylor Papers, File 42.
137 "Report in Progress," July 1, 1907, Taylor Papers, File 42.
138 Taylor to Griffith, June 10, 1898, Taylor Papers, File 60B; Taylor to Alfred Bowditch, June 9, 1898; and Taylor to H. L. Gantt, June 11, 1898, Taylor Papers, File 42.
139 Taylor, "Shop Management," 1385.
140 Thompson, "The Effect of Shorter Hours on Labor," Taylor Papers, File 42.
141 Taylor, "Shop Management," 1385.
142 Taylor, *Principles of Scientific Management*, 89–90.
143 Compare Taylor, "Shop Management," 1384–85; Taylor, *Principles of Scientific Management*, 95; and Thompson, "The Effect of Shorter Hours," Taylor Papers, File 42.
144 Thompson, "The Effect of Shorter Hours," Taylor Papers, File 42.
145 Ibid.
146 Taylor, "Shop Management," 1384; and Taylor, *Principles of Scientific Management*, 94.
147 Taylor, "Shop Management," 1384.
148 Taylor, *Principles of Scientific Management*, 94.
149 Taylor, "Shop Management," 1383; C. Bertrand Thompson, *The Theory and Practice of Scientific Management* (Boston, 1917), 47; and Horace B. Drury, *Scientific Management: A History and Criticism* (New York, 1915), 125.
150 H. L. Gantt, *Work, Wages, and Profits* (New York, 1910), 82–84.
151 Taylor, "Shop Management," 1385–86; and Taylor, *Principles of Scientific Management*, 96.
152 Taylor to Clarence M. Clark, June 6, 1898, Taylor Papers, File 42.
153 See "A New System for the Manufacture of Steel Balls," *American Machinist* 23 (Nov. 1, 1900):1035–39.
154 Taylor to Bowditch, June 9, 1898, Taylor Papers, File 42.
155 Taylor to Alfred Jones, June 27, 1898, Taylor Papers, File 42.

Chapter 4
Years of Achievement, 1898–1901

1 H. F. J. Porter, " How Bethlehem Became an Armament Maker," *Iron Age* 110 (Nov. 23, 1922):1340.
2 Walter B. Herrick, Jr., *The American Naval Revolution* (Baton Rouge, 1966),

65; Mark D. Hirsch, *William C. Whitney* (New York, 1948), 326–27; B. S. Stephenson, "Eminent Men of the Iron World II, Jos. Wharton," *Iron Trade Review* 40 (Ap. 4, 1907):548; and Porter, "How Bethlehem," 1340.

3 Russell W. Davenport, "Production of Heavy Steel Forgings in the U.S.," *Enginerring News* 28 (Nov. 23, 1893):418.

4 Ibid.

5 Robert Hessen, *Steel Titan: The Life of Charles M. Schwab* (New York, 1975), 43–44; and Joseph Frazier Wall, *Andrew Carnegie* (New York, 1970), 645–48.

6 "Armor for the Navy," *Iron Age* 46 (Dec. 11, 1890):1046; Charles Oscar Paullin, *Paullin's History of Naval Administration, 1775–1911* (Annapolis, 1968), 400; and Herrick, *American Naval Revolution*, 66, 70–80.

7 Herrick, *American Naval Revolution*, 81.

8 "The Bethlehem Hammer," *Iron Age* 52 (July 13, 1893):60,62. Also see "The Bethlehem Armor and Gun Plant," *Iron Age* 47 (Mar. 26, 1891):577.

9 "The Bethlehem Armor and Gun Plant," 577.

10 Davenport, "Production of Heavy Steel Forgings," 418.

11 "The Bethlehem Hammer," 60–62.

12 Ibid., 62.

13 Hessen, *Schwab*, 45–48; and Herrick, *American Naval Revolution*, 146–47.

14 For speculation regarding Schwab's role see "Armor Plate Frauds," *American Machinist* 17 (Apr. 26, 1894):8; and "The Armor Plate Frauds," *American Machinist* 17 (May 21, 1894):8.

15 Herrick, *American Naval Revolution*, 182–83.

16 "The Cost and Price of Armor Plate," *Iron Age* 59 (Jan. 21, 1897):20.

17 Paullin, *Paullin's History*, 475. On Apr. 20, the day President McKinley approved an ultimatum to Spain, Joseph Wharton reported that "our armor plate affair [is] in good shape" (Wharton to Robert P. Linderman, Apr. 20, 1898, Joseph Wharton Papers [Swarthmore College, Swarthmore, Pa.], Series 4, Box 13).

18 Hessen, *Schwab*, 96.

19 See "Armor Plate Bids Rejected," *Iron Trade Review* 33 (Aug. 16, 1900):10; and *Report of the Industrial Commission on the Relations and Conditions of Capital and Labor* (Washington, D.C., 1901), 14:354–55.

20 Paullin, *Paullin's History*, 475–76; and "Armor Plate Contract Let," *Iron Trade Review* 33 (Jan. 22, 1900):15.

21 Charles J. Harrah wrote that Linderman had asked to inspect the Midvale plant. "As we always adapt our exhibition to the level of the visitor's mental ability," he proposed to emphasize Taylor's reorganization of the unskilled yard laborers (Charles J. Harrah to Frederick W. Taylor, Mar. 3, 1898, Frederick W. Taylor Papers [Stevens Institute of Technology, Hoboken, N.J.], File 71G). See also Wharton to Linderman, Apr. 10, 1900, Wharton Papers, Series 4, Box 14.

22 Taylor to Russell W. Davenport, July 6, 1890, Taylor Papers, File 32.

23 Davenport to Taylor, June 14, 1898, Taylor Papers, File 57C.

24 H. F. J. Porter to Taylor, June 30, 1897, Taylor Papers, File 63C.

25 Davenport to Taylor, Nov. 22, 1897, Taylor Papers, File 57C.

26 Taylor to Davenport, Jan. 3, 1898, Taylor Papers, File 57C.

27 Taylor to Linderman, Jan. 3, 1898, Taylor Papers, File 33.

28 Taylor to Linderman, Jan. 19, 1898, Taylor Papers, File 32.

29 Linderman to Taylor, Jan. 6, 1898, Taylor Papers, File 32.

30 Taylor to Henry L. Gantt, June 2, 1898, Taylor Papers, File 119B; and Taylor to J. K. Griffith, June 10, 1898, Taylor Papers, File 60B.

31 Taylor to Gantt, June 2, 1898, Taylor Papers, File 119B.

32 Taylor to Caspar F. Goodrich, Apr. 3, 1899, Taylor Papers, File 60A1.

33 Taylor to Alfred Jones, June 27, 1898, Taylor Papers, File 42.

34 Taylor to Gantt, June 2, 1898, Taylor Papers, File 119B.

35 Taylor to Linderman, n.d. [ca. late May, 1898], Taylor Papers, File 32.

36 Taylor to Linderman, June 21, 1898, Taylor Papers, File 2.

37 Ibid.

38 In early June, Taylor had written that he had hoped to "help Davenport," but found him preoccupied "following up Government contracts" (Taylor to Griffiths, June 10, 1898, Taylor Papers, File 60B).

39 Taylor to Linderman, June 21, 1898, Taylor Papers, File 32.

40 Taylor to Linderman, Aug. 8, 1898, Taylor Papers, File 32.

41 Ibid.

42 Taylor to Linderman, Aug. 16, 1898, Taylor Papers, File 32.

43 Taylor to Linderman, Feb. 27, 1899, Taylor Papers, File 32.

44 Taylor had recommended the establishment of a tool-dressing department complete with special hammers, dies, and grinding machines. Taylor to Linderman, May 29, 1899, Nov. 30, 1898, Nov. 3, 1898, Taylor Papers, File 32; and H. L. Gantt, *Work, Wages, and Profits* (New York, 1913), 105–6.

45 Taylor to Linderman, May 29, 1899, Taylor Papers, File 32.

46 E. B. Lewis to E. P. Earle, June 8, 1899, Taylor Papers, File 33; and Gantt to Taylor, June 7, 1899, Taylor Papers, Notebook 7.

47 Taylor to Linderman, May 29, 1899, Taylor Papers, File 32.

48 Gantt to Taylor, June 7, 1899, Taylor Papers, Notebook 7; and Joseph Welden to Taylor, June 27, 1899, Taylor Papers, File 33.

49 Welden to Taylor, June 27, 1899, Taylor Papers, File 33.

50 Ibid.

51 See *Hearings before Special Committee of the House of Representatives to Investigate the Taylor and Other Systems of Shop Management* (Washington, D.C., 1912), 3:1583; Frederick W. Taylor, "Shop Management," ASME *Transactions* 24 (1903):139; and Taylor's testimony in *Hearings before Special Committee.* Taylor's "Testimony" is more readily available in Frederick W. Taylor, *Scientific Management* (New York, 1920) (see 246).

52 "Duties of a Gang Boss, Standing Order No. 1," Mar. 22, 1901; "Duties of a Speed Boss, Standing Order No. 2," Mar. 22, 1901, Carl G. Barth Papers (Harvard Business School, Boston, Mass.), Drawer 2.

53 E. A. Lucey, "Life Work of H. L. Gantt," ASME *Transactions* 42 (1920):414.

54 Maunsel White to Davenport, Jan. 5, 1900, Taylor Papers, File 32.
55 Ibid.; and Frederick W. Taylor, "On the Art of Cutting Metals," ASME *Transactions* 28 (1906): 51.
56 For detailed accounts see White to Davenport, June 6, 1900, Taylor Papers, File 32; Taylor, "Art of Cutting Metals," 51–52; and L. T. C. Rolt, *A Short History of Machine Tools* (Cambridge, Mass., 1965), 199–200.
57 Patents 683,580; 668,269; 668,270; 709,526; 722,770; 735,423; 781,851; 735,424; 735,425; 735,361.
58 See "The Taylor-White Tool Steel Process," *Iron Trade Review* 33 (Aug. 9, 1900): 17; and "The Taylor-White Steel Process," *Engineering Record* 42 (Aug. 4, 1900): 97.
59 Taylor told Goodrich that it "increased the output per tool from 31 to 137 pounds per hour" (Taylor to Goodrich, June 16, 1900, Taylor Papers, File 60A1). See also H. L. Gantt, "A Bonus System of Rewarding Labor," ASME *Transactions* 23 (1902): 351.
60 See Fred J. Miller, "Metal Working Machinery," in U.S. Department of Commerce and Labor, Bureau of the Census, *Manufactures, 1905*, (Washington, D.C., 1908), 4: 232–33.
61 Harless D. Wagoner, *The U.S. Machine Tool Industry from 1900 to 1950* (Cambridge, Mass., 1966), 9–10.
62 Taylor to Joseph Wharton, Feb. 6, 1900, Taylor Papers, File 32; Wharton to Robert P. Linderman, Feb. 15, 1900, Wharton Papers, Series 4, Box 14; and "Memo on Foreign Sales," Jan. 10, 1901–July 1, 1901, Taylor Papers, File 33.
63 See C. L. H. Ruggles to Frank H. Phipps, Aug. 6, 1900, Records of Inspector of Ordnance, E. 165S, RG 156, National Archives.
64 Taylor to Goodrich, June 16, 1900, Taylor Papers, File 60A2.
65 "The Taylor-White Process of Treating Tool Steel," *American Machinist* 23 (Aug. 9, 1900): 756; (Aug. 16, 1900): 19; "The Taylor-White Steel Process," 17; "The Taylor-White Process Tool Steel," *Iron Age* 66 (Aug. 2, 1900): 19; and "The Taylor-White Steel Process," 97.
66 Dwight V. Merrick to Kempton P. A. Taylor, Aug. 16, 1915, Taylor Papers, File 13T.
67 See Taylor to W. H. Wahl, Aug. 26, 1902, Taylor Papers, File 5.
68 Taylor to W. H. Wahl, Mar. 11, 1901, Taylor Papers, File 5.
69 Frank Barkley Copley, *Frederick W. Taylor, Father of Scientific Management*, 2 vols. (New York, 1923): 24–33.
70 "A Brief Review of Mr. Barth's Connection with the Scientific Management Movement," Taylor Papers, File 113D.
71 See Taylor to Linderman, Feb. 2, 1899, Taylor Papers, File 32.
72 Taylor to Linderman, May 29, 1899, Taylor Papers, File 32.
73 Taylor to Linderman, Feb. 27, 1899, Taylor Papers, File 32.
74 Taylor to Linderman, May 29, 1899, Taylor Papers, File 32.
75 Taylor to Linderman, Oct. 5, 1899, Taylor Papers, File 32.
76 Ibid.
77 "Taylor's Records from Bethlehem Steel Co.," Taylor Papers, Notebook 6. Taylor gave these principles a prominent place in "Shop Management," but subordinated them to his more famous "principles" in later writings.

78 Sanford E. Thompson to Taylor, Apr. 5, 1898, Taylor Papers, File 124D.

79 Frederick W. Taylor, *The Principles of Scientific Management* (New York, 1911), 140.

80 Charles D. Wrege and Amedeo G. Perroni, "Taylor's Pig-Tale: A Historical Analysis of Frederick W. Taylor's Pig Iron Experiments," *Academy of Management Journal* 17 (Mar. 1974): 14; and George F. Steele to Taylor, Mar. 23, 1895, Taylor Papers, File 70G.

81 Taylor to Sanford E. Thompson, Feb. 3, 1899, Taylor Papers, File 124D.

82 Wrege and Perroni, "Taylor's Pig-Tale," 12.

83 The following account is based on James Gillespie and Harley C. Wolle's, "Report on Establishment of Piece Work in Connection with Loading of Pig Iron at the Works of the Bethlehem Iron Company," June 17, 1899, Taylor Papers, File 32.

84 Ibid.

85 "Employees of the Bethlehem Iron Company with Their Salaries and Wages," Taylor Papers, File 32.

86 Gillespie and Wolle, "Report on Establishment of Piece Work," June 17, 1899, Taylor Papers, File 32.

87 Ibid.

88 Ibid.

89 Ibid.

90 Ibid.

91 Taylor, *Principles of Scientific Management*, 43–48. For details of Noll's life see Wrege and Perroni, "Taylor's Pig-Tale," 9, 15.

92 Gillespie and Wolle, "Report on Establishment of Piecework," June 17, 1899, Taylor Papers, File 32.

93 Ibid.

94 Ibid.

95 Frederick W. Taylor, "Conversation" [1907], Taylor Papers, File 79I.

96 Ibid. Also see Taylor, *Principles of Scientific Management*, 57, 60–61; and Barth to Taylor, Sept. 30, 1899, Taylor Papers, Notebook 6.

97 Wrege and Perroni, "Taylor's Pig-Tale," 20–21. In December 1899 Taylor ordered additional time studies of pig iron handling, which he confused with the earlier work of Gillespie and Wolle. These figures, rather than the ones Barth studied, were apparently the basis for Taylor's "rest" figure of 58%. In addition, Taylor now set the "high" rate at $1.85 per day, rather than $1.68. The reason for this change is not clear from the records, but it meant the laborers earned 4¢ to 7.3¢ per ton. Taylor later used the $1.85 figure in all his references to pig iron handling, suggesting, incorrectly, that "first class" men had earned a 60% premium from the beginning. See Barth, "Report on Fixing of Rates for Loading Pig Iron by Half Pigs on Buggies in the Yards," May 29, 1900, Taylor Papers, Notebook 6.

98 A. B. Wadleigh, "Report on the Unloading of Stock for the Blast Furnaces," Jan. 25, 1900, Taylor Papers, Notebook 6.

99 Taylor, "Shop Management," 1358.

100 Taylor, "Conversation," 38.

101 Gantt to Davenport, Nov. 22, 1899, Taylor Papers, Notebook 6.

102 Taylor, "Conversation" (1907), 36–37, Taylor Papers, File 79I.
103 I found no mention of Taylor's work in the *South Bethlehem Globe* for the period from 1898 to 1901. Professors Wrege and Perroni had no better luck with the *South Bethlehem Globe* or the *Bethlehem Star* (Wrege and Perroni, Taylor's Pig-Tale," 18).
104 Taylor, "Conversation" [1907] 37, Taylor Papers, File 79I.
105 Taylor to Sanford E. Thompson, Mar. 22, 1900, Taylor Papers, File 124E. Thompson also reviewed Wadleigh's data. His comments suggest that it was complete and comparable to the information Thompson was collecting. See, e.g., Thompson to Taylor, Apr. 22, 1902, Taylor Papers, File 125A.
106 Taylor, "Testimony," 51–59; Taylor, "Shop Management," 1360–61; and Taylor, *Principles of Scientific Management*, 65–72.
107 Taylor, "Testimony," 60.
108 Ibid., 59.
109 See Taylor, "Shop Management," 1362–63.
110 Taylor, *Principles of Scientific Management*, 72.
111 H. F. J. Porter, "The Get Together Club, No. One," *Social Service* 3 (Apr. 1901):103.
112 To counter union charges of worker exploitation, Taylor, Wadleigh, and U.S. Army ordnance officials located and examined Noll in 1913. See William Crozier to Taylor, Nov. 21, 26, 1913; and Taylor to Crozier, Dec. 4, 31, 1913, Taylor Papers, File 185D.
113 Taylor, "Shop Management," 1362; Taylor, "Testimony," 65; and Wadleigh to Taylor, Apr. 10, 1901, Taylor Papers, Notebook 6.
114 Gantt, "Bonus System," 351, 359.
115 Ibid., 351.
116 Ibid., 357. Gantt's figures on output (his p. 360) are suspect.
117 Ibid., 343.
118 Ibid., 368.
119 Ibid., 367.
120 Gantt, *Work, Wages, and Profits*, 107.
121 Gantt, "Bonus System," 360.
122 Ibid., 354.
123 Taylor to Linderman, Apr. 4, 1901, Taylor Papers, File 32.
124 Gantt, "Report on Task Work," May 13, 1901, Taylor Papers, File 32.
125 "The Bethlehem Steel Company," *Iron Age* 67 (June 13, 1901):24a.

Chapter 5
Taylor and American Industry, 1901–1911

1 Taylor's testimony in *Hearings before Special Committee of the House of Representatives to Investigate the Taylor and Other Systems of Shop Management* (Washington, D.C., 1912). Taylor's "Testimony" is more readily available in Frederick W. Taylor, *Scientific Management* (New York, 1920) (see 248–49).

2 Interview with Robert P. A. Taylor, Providence, Rhode Island, June 17, 1974; see also Taylor's will, June 18, 1910, Register of Wills, Philadelphia, Pennsylvania.
3 Taylor to Holden A. Evans, Nov. 9, 1909, Taylor Papers (Stevens Institute of Technology, Hoboken, N.J.), File 187D.
4 Interview with Robert P. A. Taylor, June 17, 1974.
5 Taylor's expense reports, Bethlehem Steel Company, Taylor Papers, File 33.
6 Frank Barkley Copley, *Frederick W. Taylor, Father of Scientific Management*, 2 vols. (New York, 1923), 1:393–94.
7 Memo on Taylor-White Sales, Taylor Papers, File 33.
8 See Taylor to George F. Steele, June 19, 1899, Taylor Papers, File 70H.
9 E. H. Mumford to Taylor, Apr. 11, 1903, Taylor Papers, File 162B.
10 Taylor to Caspar F. Goodrich, Jan. 15, 1901, Taylor Papers, File 60A1.
11 Ibid. The Flat Top Coal Land Association was a Clark promotion (see Joseph T. Lambie, *From Mine to Market: The History of Coal Transportation on the Norfolk and Western Railway* [New York, 1954], 237–38.
12 For Greene's career see C. L. Sonnichsen, *Colonel Greene and the Copper Skyrocket* (Tucson, 1974). See also Ira B. Joralemon, *Copper* (Berkeley, 1973), Ch. 6; Marvin D. Bernstein, "Colonel William C. Greene and the Cananea Copper Bubble," *Business Historical Society Bulletin* 26 (Dec. 1952):179–98; Marvin D. Bernstein, *The Mexican Mining Industry, 1890–1950* (Albany, 1964), 56–59; and David M. Pletcher, *Rails, Mines, and Progress: Seven American Promoters in Mexico, 1867–1911* (Ithaca, 1958), 236–51.
13 See Isaac F. Marcosson, *Anaconda* (New York, 1957), Ch. 5.
14 Taylor to A. B. Wadleigh, Oct. 8, 1902, Taylor Papers, File 70H.
15 Taylor to Steele, Nov. 19, 1901, Taylor Papers, File 70H. For a more dispassionate evaluation see Walter Harvey Weed, "Notes on Certain Mines in the States of Chihuahua, Sinaloa and Sonora, Mexico," *Transactions of the American Institute of Mining Engineers* 32 (1901):428–35.
16 Taylor to Steele, Nov. 19, 1901, Taylor Papers, File 70H.
17 Ibid.
18 Ibid.
19 Sonnichsen, *Colonel Greene*, 106–7; and Maunsel White to Taylor, July 31, 1902, Taylor Papers, File 84F.
20 Wadleigh to Taylor, June 5, 1902, Taylor Papers, File 67A; and Sonnichsen, *Colonel Greene*, 106–24.
21 Taylor to White, Feb. 17, 1902, Taylor Papers, File 84F; see also Taylor to Francis T. Chambers, Feb. 17, 1902, Taylor Papers, File 85A. Taylor was apparently not the only dissatisfied investor. A few months later the editor of the *Engineering and Mining Journal* wrote that the Cananea mines "have had a chequered career, in which suspicious methods, stock manipulation, and extravagant management have all played their part" (*Engineering and Mining Journal* 75 [March 28, 1903]:469).
22 Taylor to Wadleigh, Oct. 6, 1902, Taylor Papers, File 67A.
23 Ibid.
24 Ibid.

25 See Sonnichsen, *Colonel Greene*, 177–206; Bernstein, "Colonel William C. Greene," 189–93; and Herbert O. Brayer, "The Cananea Incident," *New Mexico Historical Review* 13 (Oct. 1938): 387–415.
26 Taylor to Chambers, Mar. 11, 1902, Taylor Papers, File 85A.
27 Wadleigh to Taylor, Mar. 10, 1902, Taylor Papers, File 67A.
28 Wadleigh to Taylor, June 8, 1902, Taylor Papers, File 67A.
29 Wadleigh to Taylor, July 24, 1906, Taylor Papers, File 68B.
30 Wadleigh to Taylor, Mar. 10, 1902, Taylor Papers, File 67A.
31 Wadleigh to Taylor, June 5, Mar. 10, 1902, Taylor Papers, File 67A.
32 Wadleigh to Taylor, Mar. 9, 1904, Taylor Papers, File 67A.
33 Taylor to Wadleigh, Oct. 8, 1902, Taylor Papers, File 67A.
34 Taylor to White, Oct. 29, 1902, Taylor Papers, File 84F.
35 Taylor to Wadleigh, Oct. 29, 1902, Taylor Papers, File 68B; and Taylor to Sanford E. Thompson, Oct. 29, 1902, Taylor Papers, File 68B.
36 Taylor to Chambers, Jan. 28, 1908, Taylor Papers, File 85A.
37 Taylor to Steele, Mar. 11, 1901, Taylor Papers, File 70H; and Taylor to Joseph Morgan, June 18, 1900, Taylor Papers, File 69A.
38 Taylor to Steele, Mar. 11, 1901, Taylor Papers, File 70H.
39 Interview with Robert P. A. Taylor, June 17, 1974; and Joseph Killorin, ed., *Selected Letters of Conrad Aiken* (New Haven, 1978), 4–5.
40 See Copley, *Taylor*, Vol. 2, Ch. 3–4. Boxly adjoined the estate of Joseph S. Clark, Taylor's old friend.
41 Ibid., 188.
42 Taylor to Morris L. Cooke, Dec. 2, 1910, Carl G. Barth Papers (Harvard Business School, Boston, Mass.), Drawer 2.
43 Copley, *Taylor*, Vol. 2, Chs. 3–4. See also patents 841,306; 944,522; 1,033,290; 1,171,558; 1,171,559; and 1,171,560.
44 See Copley, *Taylor*, Vol. 2, Ch. 5.
45 Ibid., 171–72.
46 See Taylor's correspondence with A. Falkenau, Taylor Papers, File 84.
47 Taylor to White, Mar. 20, 1907, Taylor Papers, File 84F.
48 Taylor to White, Feb. 17, 1906, Taylor Papers, File 84F.
49 Taylor to Goodrich, Feb. 21, 1908, Taylor Papers, File 60A3.
50 *U.S. Federal Reporter* 166 (1909): 880–97.
51 The Taylor Papers, File 84E, contain a copy of the agreement.
52 See H. K. Hathaway to Wilfred Lewis, Mar. 2, 1910, Taylor Papers, File 122A; and Taylor to Sidney Newbold, Mar. 23, 1910, Taylor Papers, File 84E.
53 Thompson to Taylor, July 21, 1902, Taylor Papers, File 125A; and Thompson to Taylor, Dec. 21, 1903, Taylor Papers, File 125B.
54 Taylor-Thompson correspondence, Taylor Papers, File 125.
55 Kempton P. A. Taylor Recollections, Taylor Papers, File 14Y.
56 Ibid.
57 Frederick W. Taylor, "Shop Management," American Society of Mechanical Engineers *Transactions* 24 (1903): 1364–65.
58 Ibid., 1342.
59 Ibid., 1415.

60 Ibid., 1354–56.

61 Ibid., 1408–0.

62 Ibid., 1454.

63 Ibid., 1448–51.

64 On Jan. 23, 1902, shortly before he began "Shop Management," Taylor wrote Sanford Thompson that he did not believe "our particular individual experiences at Bethlehem would have much value. It [*sic*] might have value as a warning, but it would be better to generalize rather than to state our particular troubles" (Taylor to Thompson, Jan. 22, 1902, Taylor Papers, File 125A).

65 Taylor, "Shop Management," 1456, 1463, 1471.

66 L. P. Alford, *Henry Laurence Gantt, Leader in Industry* (New York, 1934), Chs. 8–9.

67 Robert Hoxie, for example, described Gantt's methods as a distinct management system (Hoxie, *Scientific Management and Labor* (New York, 1918), 7).

68 See Alford, *Gantt*, Chs. 8–9; and Samuel Haber, *Efficiency and Uplift* (Chicago, 1964), 44–49.

69 H. L. Gantt to Taylor, Sept. 15, 1911, Taylor Papers, File 121B.

70 Harlow Person to Richard A. Feiss, Feb. 1, 1924, Morris L. Cooke Papers (Franklin D. Roosevelt Library, Hyde Park, N.Y.), Box 2, File 9.

71 Taylor to Barth, Mar. 27, 1913, Taylor Papers, File 113D.

72 Dwight V. Merrick to Kempton P. A. Taylor, Aug. 16, 1915, Taylor Papers, File 14T.

73 Taylor to Merrick, Jan. 19, 1915, Taylor Papers, File 63A.

74 Charles D. Wrege and Amedeo G. Perroni, "Taylor's Pig-Tale: A Historical Analysis of Frederick W. Taylor's Pig Iron Experiments," *Academy of Management Journal* 17 (1974): 8.

75 Interview with Robert P. A. Taylor, June 17, 1974.

76 C. Bertrand Thompson, *The Theory and Practice of Scientific Management* (Boston, 1917), 44.

77 Cooke to Taylor, Apr. 24, 1903, Taylor Papers, File 114A.

78 See the Taylor-Cooke Correspondence, 1906, Taylor Papers, File 114A. See also Frederick Remsen Hutton, *A History of the American Society of Mechanical Engineers from 1880 to 1915* (New York, 1915), 115–16; and Kenneth E. Trombley, *The Life and Times of a Happy Liberal* (New York, 1954), 8.

79 See Edwin T. Layton, Jr., *The Revolt of the Engineers* (Cleveland, 1971), Ch. 7.

80 Cooke to Taylor, Oct. 6, 1907, Taylor Papers, File 114B; and Taylor to Gantt, Dec. 27, 1906, Taylor Papers, File 120B.

81 Cooke to Taylor, Oct. 7, 1907, Taylor Papers, File 114B.

82 Cooke to Taylor, Nov. 1, 1907, Taylor Papers, File 114B.

83 Carl G. Barth, "Introduction," Taylor Papers, Notebook 1 (1933).

84 Taylor to Gantt, May 10, 1911, Taylor Papers, File 121B.

85 Taylor to Barth, Nov. 15, 1909, Taylor Papers, File 113B.

86 Taylor to Barth, Jan. 28, 1908, Taylor Papers, File 113A.

87 Taylor to Barth, Jan. 28, 1908, Taylor Papers, File 113A; and Taylor to Thompson, May 4, 1908, Taylor Papers, File 126C.

88 Taylor to Gantt, Apr. 13, 1908, Taylor Papers, File 120B.

89 Taylor to Barth, Nov. 25, 1910, Taylor Papers, File 113B.

90 Taylor to Gantt, Dec. 5, 1910, Taylor Papers, File 121A.

91 Alford, *Gantt*, 131; and Cooke to Barth, Jan. 21, 1929, Cooke Papers, Box 1, File 9.

92 Robert N. Manley, *Centennial History of the University of Nebraska I: Frontier University (1869–1919)* (Lincoln, 1969), 57, 64–65, 69–70.

93 Harrington Emerson to Samuel Emerson, Apr. 5, 1903, Harrington Emerson Papers (New York Public Library, New York, N.Y.).

94 Edwin Emerson to George Emerson, July 12, 1900, Apr. 3, 1905, Emerson Papers.

95 Harrington Emerson, "Discussion," ASME *Transactions* 25 (1903–4):73; U.S., Congress, Senate, *Evidence Taken by the Interstate Commerce Commission in the Matter of Proposed Advances in Freight Rates by Carriers, August to December, 1910*, 61st Cong., 3rd sess., 1911, Senate Document Vol. 50, 4:2324; Horace B. Drury, *Scientific Management, A History and Criticism* (New York, 1915), 113; and Harrington Emerson to Taylor, June 18, 1903, Taylor Papers, File 58C.

96 See Emerson's correspondence during 1899, Emerson Papers. See also Harrington Emerson, "The Proposed Pacific Cables," *Engineering Magazine* 18 (Nov. 1899):233–39; and Harrington Emerson, "The Engineer and the Road to the Gold Fields," *Engineering Magazine* 17 (Aug. 1899):750–77.

97 Harrington Emerson to Alfred Emerson, Dec. 4, 1899; and Harrington Emerson to Edwin Emerson, Dec. 19, 1899, May 15, 1900, Emerson Papers.

98 Harrington Emerson to Edwin Emerson, Apr. 1, 1900, Emerson Papers.

99 Harrington Emerson to Edwin Emerson, July 2, 1900, Emerson Papers.

100 Harrington Emerson to Taylor, June 18, 1903, Taylor Papers, File 58C.

101 Harrington Emerson to Edwin Emerson, Apr. 4, May 9, 1900, Emerson Papers.

102 Harrington Emerson to Edwin Emerson, Sept. 29, 1900, Emerson Papers.

103 Harrington Emerson to Edwin Emerson, Apr. 20, 1902, Emerson Papers.

104 Ibid.

105 Harrington Emerson to Samuel Emerson, Jan. 17, 1903, Emerson Papers.

106 Harrington Emerson to Taylor, June 18, 1903, Taylor Papers, File 58C.

107 Harrington Emerson to Samuel Emerson, Apr. 5, 1903, Emerson Papers.

108 Harrington Emerson to Edwin Emerson, Apr. 6, 1903, Emerson Papers.

109 Harrington Emerson to Taylor, June 18, 1903, Emerson Papers.

110 Harrington Emerson, "Discussion," ASME *Transactions* 24 (1903):1463. Mrs. Emerson wrote that "at Saratoga we met a number of pleasant people and enjoyed the week exceedingly" (Mary Emerson to Edwin Emerson, June 29, 1903, Emerson Papers).

111 Harrington Emerson to Samuel Emerson, Apr. 5, 1903, Emerson Papers.

112 Harrington Emerson to Edwin Emerson, Aug. 16, 1906, Emerson Papers.

113 Harrington Emerson to Edwin Emerson, Apr. 24, 1907, Emerson Papers.

114 Samuel Emerson to Edwin Emerson, Mar. 26, 1907, Emerson Papers.

115 Ibid. See also Samuel Emerson to Edwin Emerson, Sept. 9, 1906, Emerson Papers.

116 Thompson, *Theory and Practice*, 50.

117 Taylor to G. C. Thayer, Dec. 8, 1911, Taylor Papers, File 34.

118 Taylor to Henri Le Chatelier, Feb. 15, 1912, Taylor Papers, File 63B.

119 For a different interpretation of the Taylor-Gilbreth relationship see Milton J. Nadworny's interesting essay "Frederick Taylor and Frank Gilbreth; Competition in Scientific Management," *Business History Review* 31 (1957): 23–24. Nadworny takes Gilbreth more seriously, perhaps because he emphasizes the post-1911 period when Gilbreth became a prominent apostle of "efficiency."

120 For Gilbreth's early life see Edna Yost, *Frank and Lillian Gilbreth, Partners for Life* (New Brunswick, 1949).

121 Thompson to Taylor, Dec. 13, 1906, Taylor Papers, File 126B.

122 Ibid.

123 Taylor to Thompson, Dec. 9, 1907, Taylor Papers, File 126B. Gilbreth cherished his memory of the meeting. See Conrad N. Lauer to Lillian M. Gilbreth, Oct. 28, 1924, Gilbreth Papers (Purdue University, Lafayette, Ind.).

124 Taylor to Thompson, Jan. 6, 1908, Taylor Papers, File 126C.

125 Thompson to Taylor, Jan. 11, 1908, Jan. 16, 1908, Taylor Papers, File 126C.

126 Taylor to Thompson, Jan. 13, Feb. 6, 1908, Taylor Papers, File 126C.

127 Thompson to Taylor, Jan. 11, 1908, Taylor Papers, File 126C.

128 Gilbreth to Taylor, Feb. 21, Mar. 4, 1908, Taylor Papers, File 59A.

129 Gilbreth to Taylor, Feb. 6, 1908, Taylor Papers, File 59A.

130 Taylor to Gilbreth, Apr. 27, 1908, Taylor Papers, File 59A; and Thompson to Taylor, Apr. 27, 1908, Taylor Papers, File 126C.

131 Thompson to Gilbreth, May 22, 1908, Taylor Papers, File 59A.

132 Taylor to Gilbreth, May 21, 1908, Taylor Papers, File 59A.

133 Gilbreth to Taylor, May 1, 1908, Taylor Papers, File 59A.

134 Thompson to Taylor, Nov. 12, 1908, Taylor Papers, File 126D.

135 Thompson to Taylor, Nov. 24, 1908, Taylor Papers, File 126D.

136 Thompson to Hathaway, Nov. 29, 1908, Taylor Papers, File 59A.

137 See Gilbreth to Taylor, Oct. 27, 1908, Taylor Papers, File 59A. Gilbreth attempted to introduce some of Taylor's methods at the Union Bag & Paper Company in 1911, but encountered union opposition and abandoned his effort (Milton J. Nadworny, *Scientific Management and the Unions, 1900–1932* [Cambridge, Mass., 1955], 54–55).

138 See *Evidence Taken by the Interstate Commerce Commission*, 2777–78; Gilbreth-Hathaway correspondence, May–Aug. 1911, Gilbreth Papers; Merrick to Gilbreth, Dec. 29, 1910, Gilbreth Papers; and Gilbreth to Merrick, Dec. 31, 1910, Gilbreth Papers.

139 Gilbreth to Taylor, Oct. 27, 1909, Taylor Papers, File 59A.

140 See Robert Thurston Kent's introduction to Frank B. Gilbreth's *Motion Study* (New York, 1911).

141 See Yost, *Gilbreth*, 184, 198–204.

142 Gilbreth to Taylor, Oct. 27, 1911, Taylor Papers, File 59A. See also Gilbreth to Taylor, Aug. 25, 1911; and Taylor to Gilbreth, Oct. 23, 1911, Taylor Papers, File 59A.

143 Gilbreth to Joseph W. Roe, Mar. 4, 1912, Gilbreth Papers.

144 Gilbreth to Taylor, Apr. 7, 1912, Gilbreth Papers.
145 Gilbreth to Taylor, Apr. 18, 1912, Taylor Papers, File 59B.
146 Taylor to Gilbreth, July 23, 1912, Taylor Papers, File 59B. See Barth, "Discussion," ASME *Transactions* 34 (1912):1205, Gilbreth stated his position in Gilbreth to Cooke, Sept. 22, 1921, Gilbreth Papers. Kent continued to help Gilbreth. See "Micro-Motion Study," *Industrial Engineering and Engineering Digest* 13 (Jan. 1913):28.
147 Taylor to Gilbreth, Aug. 24, 1912, Taylor Papers, File 59B. See also Yost, *Gilbreth*, 219.
148 Taylor to Hathaway, Sept. 2, 1912, Taylor Papers, File 112B.
149 Hathaway to Taylor, Sept. 9, 1912, Taylor Papers, File 122B.
150 Taylor to Barth, Oct. 12, 21, 1912, Taylor Papers, File 113; Taylor to W. W. Keen, Mar. 6, 1913, Taylor Papers, File 5; and Taylor to Le Chatelier, May 5, 1912, Taylor Papers, File 63B.
151 Taylor to Gilbreth, Mar. 11, 1914, Taylor Papers, File 59A.
152 Taylor to Hathaway, Mar. 18, 1914, Taylor Papers, File 123A.
153 Taylor to Lionel S. Marks, Aug. 29, 1914, Taylor Papers, File 52E. The disciples continued to snub Gilbreth after Taylor's death, and Gilbreth became increasingly hostile to them. For the period from 1914 to 1919 see Nadworny, "Taylor and Gilbreth," 30–34.

Chapter 6
Scientific Management in Practice, 1901–1915

1 See C. Bertrand Thompson, *The Theory and Practice of Scientific Management* (Boston, 1917), 37–38, 98.
2 Horace K. Hathaway to Frederick W. Taylor, Sept. 18, 1911, Frederick W. Taylor Papers (Stevens Institute of Technology, Hoboken, N.J.), File 122A.
3 See Henry Roland, "Six Examples of Successful Shop Management," *Engineering Magazine* 12 (Feb. 1897):835–37.
4 Taylor to Holden A. Evans, Dec. 12, 1909, Taylor Papers, File 187D.
5 Taylor to Hathaway, March 11, 1913, Taylor Papers, File 132C.
6 George F. Steele to James Deering, Apr. 28, 1894, Taylor Papers, File 70G.
7 International Association of Machinists *Monthly Journal* 6 (Nov. 1894):431.
8 Charles Harrah, "Testimony," U.S. Industrial Commission *Report on the Relations and Conditions of Capital and Labor* (Washington, D.C., 1901), 14:349.
9 Taylor's testimony in *Hearings before Special Committee of the House of Representatives to Investigate the Taylor and Other Systems of Shop Management* (Washington, D.C., 1912). 3: Taylor's "Testimony" is more readily available in Frederick W. Taylor, *Scientific Management* (New York, 1920). (See 249).
10 Ibid., 1008–11.
11 Steele to Deering, Apr. 28, 1894, Taylor Papers, File 70G.

12 International Association of Machinists *Monthly Journal* 6 (Nov. 1894):432.

13 Hathaway to Taylor, Sept. 18, 1911, Taylor Papers, File 122A.

14 Ibid.

15 Ibid.

16 Taylor, "Shop Management," American Society of Mechanical Engineers *Transactions* 24 (1903):1380.

17 Roland, "Six Examples," 837.

18 U.S. Commission on Industrial Relations, *Final Report and Testimony*, 64th Cong., 1st sess., 1916, 3:2854–55.

19 Taylor to William Crozier, Apr. 20, 1910, Taylor Papers, File 185A.

20 L. L. Bruff to Crozier, May 6, 1910, Record Group 156, Box 267, File 213/200–49, National Archives.

21 *Hearings before Special Committee of the House of Representatives*, 3:1590.

22 C. Bertrand Thompson, *Theory and Practice*, 22–23.

23 H. B. Drury, *Scientific Management: A History and Criticism* (New York). 121–23

24 See Samuel Emerson to Edwin Emerson, Mar. 26, 1907, Harrington Emerson Papers (New York Public Library, New York, N.Y.); Robert A. Hessen, *Steel Titan: The Life of Charles M. Schwab* (New York, 1975), 167; and Bruff to Crozier, May 6, 1910, RG 156, Box 267, File 213/200–49, National Archives.

25 See Thompson, *Theory and Practice*; and Robert F. Hoxie, *Scientific Management and Labor* (New York, 1918).

26 For Dodge's career see "James Mapes Dodge," *Iron Age* 96 (Dec. 9, 1915): 1368–69; and "James Mapes Dodge," *Journal of the Franklin Institute* 181 (Jan.–June 1916):148–51.

27 *Hearings before Special Committee of the House of Representatives.* 3:1699; and U.S., Congress, Senate, *Evidence Taken by the Interstate Commerce Commission in the Matter of Proposed Advances in Freight Rates by Carriers, August to December, 1910*, 61st Cong., 3rd sess., 1911, Senate Document Vol. 50, 4:2737.

28 *Hearings before Special Committee of the House of Representatives*, 3:1545.

29 *Evidence Taken by the Interstate Commerce Commission*, 4:2692.

30 Louis Bell, "The Philanthropy of Self-Help," *Cassier's Magazine* 24 (Sept. 1903):455.

31 James Mapes Dodge, "A History of the Introduction of Shop Management," *ASME Transactions* 27 (1906):720–25; and *Evidence Taken by the Interstate Commerce Commission*, 4:2691–2740.

32 Quoted in Frank B. Copley, *Frederick W. Taylor, Father of Scientific Management*, 2 vols. (New York, 1923), 2:79.

33 *Evidence Taken by the Interstate Commerce Commission*, 4:2739.

34 Charles Day, "The Taylor-White Process of Treating Tool Steel and Its Influence on the Mechanic Art," *Iron Trade Review* 34 (Sept. 12, 1901):22.

35 *Hearings before Special Committee of the House of Representatives*, 3:1545.

36 Ibid.

37 Ibid.

38 Ibid., 1547.
39 See "Methods of Management that Made Money," *Industrial Engineering and the Engineering Index* 9 (Jan. 1911):21–27; Horace L. Arnold, *The Factory Manager and Accountant* (London, 1910), Ch. 3; *Hearings before Special Committee of the House of Representatives*, 3:1546–47; and Dwight Merrick and C. Willis Adams to James Mapes Dodge, Apr. 24, 1909, Ordnance Department, RG 156, Box 266, File 213/75–199, National Archives.
40 See Drury, *Scientific Management*, 135–36.
41 See L. P. Alford, "Scientific Management in Use," *American Machinist* 36 (Apr. 4, 1912):548–50.
42 Barcalo Manufacturing Company, "Report of Philadelphia Trip," Nov. 25, 1912, Taylor Papers, File 138B.
43 Ibid.
44 "Scientific Management as Viewed from the Workman's Standpoint," *Industrial Engineering and the Engineering Index* 8 (Nov. 1910):378. This statement is also an interesting commentary on scientific management at Midvale.
45 Ibid.
46 Alford, "Scientific Management in Use," 50.
47 Ibid., 548.
48 Barcalo Manufacturing Company, "Report of Philadelphia Trip," Nov. 25, 1912, Taylor, Papers, File 138.
49 "Methods of Management that Made Money," 26.
50 Arnold, *Factory Manager*, 31, 40.
51 Ibid., 28.
52 Dodge to Taylor, Feb. 18, 1915, Taylor Papers, File 58B.
53 For the early history of Tabor see "The Tabor Molding Machine," *American Machinist* 13 (July 31, 1890):1–2; and Wilfred Lewis, "An Object Lession in Efficiency," *Industrial Engineering and the Engineering Digest* 9 (May 1911):379–80.
54 *Evidence Taken by the Interstate Commerce Commission*, 4:2680.
55 Drury, *Scientific Management*, 131. In one statement Taylor claimed that there were 120 blue collar and 3 white collar employees (Taylor to J. Sellers Bancroft, Jan. 7, 1907, Taylor Papers, File 57B).
56 Lewis, "An Object Lesson," 380.
57 Ibid.; and Lewis to Taylor, Sept. 24, 1902, Taylor Papers, File 162B.
58 Lewis, "An Object Lesson," 380.
59 Taylor later arranged for Tabor to manufacture most of his inventions. By 1910 Taylor-Newbold saws were the company's second most popular product (*Evidence Taken by the Interstate Commerce Commission*, 4:2655; and Hathaway to Taylor, Jan. 20, 1906, Taylor Papers, File 122A).
60 *Evidence Taken by the Intetstate Commerce Commission*, 4:2660–70.
61 The Carl G. Barth Papers (Harvard Business School, Boston, Mass.), Drawer 2, include many of the forms.
62 Lewis, "An Object Lesson," 382.
63 *Hearings before Special Committee of the House of Representatives*, 3:1516.

64 Ibid., 1511.

65 Hathaway to Taylor, Mar. 13, 1910, Taylor Papers, File 122A.

66 *Evidence Taken by the Interstate Commerce Commission*, 4:2656; and Taylor to Hathaway, Feb. 21, 1908, Taylor Papers, File 122A.

67 Barcalo Manufacturing Company, "Report of Philadelphia Trip," Nov. 25, 1912, Taylor Papers, File and 138B; and Horace K. Hathaway, "Symposium," Dartmouth College Conferences, First Tuck School Conference, *Addresses and Discussions at the Conference on Scientific Management Held Oct. 12, 13, 14, 1911* (Hanover, 1912), 341–42.

68 There are conflicting reports on the exact number of employees (*Evidence Taken by the Interstate Commerce Commission*, 4:2660; Drury, *Scientific Management*, 131; and Taylor to J. Sellers Bancroft, Jan. 7, 1907, Taylor Papers, File 57B).

69 Lewis, "Fifty Years of Scientific Management," *Manufacturing Industries* 15 (Apr. 1928):282.

70 *Hearings before Special Committee of the House of Representatives*, 3:152.

71 Thompson, *Theory and Practice*, 37–38, 98.

72 Ibid., 98.

73 Thompson did not list the "successes." The following analysis is based on the Taylor papers and related secondary sources.

74 The 25 firms were the Stokes & Smith Company; Sayles Bleachery; Yale & Towne; Santa Fe Railroad; Brighton Mills; Ferracute Machine; H. H. Franklin; Canadian Pacific Railroad; Smith & Furbush; Joseph Bancroft & Sons; Plimpton Press; Remington Typewriter; Forbes Lithograph; Joseph & Feiss; S. L. Moore; Amoskeag Mills; Cheney Brothers; New England Butt; Lewis Manufacturing; Herrmann Aukam; Pullman Palace Car; Baird Machine; Eaton, Crane & Pike; Eastern Manufacturing; and Winchester Repeating Arms. The other 28 were Lewis F. Shoemaker Company; F. B. Stearns; Universal Winding; Franz Premier; Goldie & McCulloch; Burgess Sulphite; Williamson Brothers; Westinghouse Electric; Standard Roller Bearing; Bausch & Lomb; Lowell Machine; Barcalo Manufacturing; Acme Wire; F. R. Patch; Williams & Wilkins; Sewell Clapp; Plymouth Cordage; Robins Conveying Belt; American Locomotive; Manhattan Press; Chester Steel Castings; Erie Forge; Brockton Heel; L. F. Fales; Monotype; Passaic Metalware; Seth Thomas; and James & E. H. Wilson. The German-American Button Company is also occasionally cited, but I have found no direct evidence that Taylor's disciples worked there.

75 See Daniel Nelson, "Scientific Management, Systematic Management, and Labor, 1880–1915," *Business History Review* 48 (1974):488–500.

76 Taylor to Barth, Nov. 12, 1909, Taylor Papers, File 113B.

77 Thompson, *Theory and Practive*, 79.

78 They were the Sayles Bleachery, Joseph Bancroft & Sons Company, Amoskeag Manufacturing Company, and Forbes Lithograph Company.

79 Alfred D. Chandler, Jr., *The Visible Hand: The Managerial Revolution in American Business* (Cambridge, Mass., 1977), 277–78.

80 See Charles H. Fry, "Shop Betterment Work on the Santa Fe," *Railroad*

Gazette 41 (Nov. 30, 1906):479–80; and Charles Buxton Going, "Methods of the Santa Fe," *Engineering Magazine* 38 (Apr. 1909):9–36; (May 1909): 225–48; (June 1909):337–60.

81 Hathaway to Oberlin Smith, Oct. 30, 1906, Taylor Papers, File 148G; and Smith to Hathaway, Jan. 7, 1907, Taylor Papers, File 148G; and Frederick A. Parkhurst, *Applied Methods of Scientific Management* (New York, 1911).

82 Edna Yost, *Frank and Lillian Gilbreth, Partners for Life* (New Brunswick, 1949), 252; and Hathaway to Taylor, Sept. 9, 1912, Taylor Papers, File 122B.

83 Samuel Emerson to Edwin Emerson, Mar. 26, 1907, Emerson Papers.

84 See Thompson, *Theory and Practice*, 98.

85 Milton J. Nadworny, *Scientific Management and the Unions, 1900–1932* (Cambridge, Mass., 1955), 27–28.

86 H. N. Stronck, "A Report on the Operation of Scientific Management at New England Butt Co.," Oct. 18, 1913, Frank B. Gilbreth Papers (Purdue University).

87 Hathaway to Taylor, May 16, 1914, Taylor Papers, File 123A.

88 N. Major to Frank B. Gilbreth, May 2, 1919, Gilbreth Papers.

89 See William Crozier, *Ordnance and the World War* (New York, 1920), 23–24.

90 See Peter Karsten, *The Naval Aristocracy* (New York, 1972), 355–56.

91 Taylor, "Lecture on Government Efficiency," n.d., Taylor Papers, File 187D.

92 Holden A. Evans, *One Man's Fight for a Better Navy* (New York, 1940), 182–83.

93 Holden A. Evans, *Cost Keeping and Scientific Management* (New York, 1911), 187–207.

94 Ibid., 235.

95 Ibid., 236–37.

96 Ibid., 235.

97 H. M. Burnet, "Conditions in and about San Francisco," International Association of Machinists *Monthly Journal* 18 (Nov. 1906):1052.

98 Evans to Taylor, Apr. 19, 1907, Taylor Papers, File 187D; and Evans, *One Man's Fight*, 184–85.

99 Burnet, "Conditions in and about San Francisco," 1052.

100 See "Resolutions," International Association of Machinists *Monthly Journal* 18 (July 1906):658.

101 Burnet, "Conditions in and about San Francisco," 1052.

102 Evans to Washington Capps, Aug. 30, 1907, Taylor Papers, File 187D. He later testified that he had previously "determined standard tools" (*Hearings before Special Committee of the House of Representatives*, 3:1267). See also Evans to Taylor, Jan. 6, 1912, Taylor Papers, File 187G. Gillespie and Wolle had subtracted 40% at Bethlehem; see Ch. 4, above.

103 Evans to Capps, Aug. 30, 1907, Taylor Papers, File 187D. Taylor usually used 40% as the bonus that might have to be paid.

104 Evans, *Cost Keeping*, 234.

105 Evans, *One Man's Fight*, 204.

106 Taylor to Maunsel White, Mar. 26, 1908, Taylor Papers, File 84F.

107 Taylor to Caspar F. Goodrich, Dec. 24, 1908, Taylor Papers, File 60A3.

108 Goodrich to Taylor, Dec. 21, 1908, Taylor Papers, File 60A3.

109 Goodrich to Taylor, Feb. 18, 1909, Taylor Papers, File 60A3. There were few initiatives after this time. See *Hearings before Special Committee of the House of Representatives.* 3:1733–34.

110 Taylor to Goodrich, Dec. 17, 1908, Taylor Papers, File 60A3.

111 Taylor to Henry Pritchett, Apr. 19, 1909, Taylor Papers, File 5.

112 Taylor to Goodrich, May 28, 1909; Goodrich to Taylor, Aug. 8, 1909, Taylor Papers, File 60A3.

113 Taylor to Hathaway, Nov. 10, 1910, Taylor Papers, File 122A.

114 Taylor to Holden A. Evans, Jan. 31, 1911, Taylor Papers, File 187F.

115 Evans to Taylor, June 7, 1911, Taylor Papers, File 187F.

116 In early 1912 the committee submitted a report that was promptly forgotten. See U.S., Congress, House, Committee on Naval Affairs, *Report of Civilian Expert Board on Industrial Management of United States Navy Yards*, 62nd Cong., 2nd sess., 1912.

117 Taylor to Goodrich, Apr. 15, 1911, Taylor Papers, File 60A4.

118 Taylor to Evans, Apr. 15, 1911, Taylor Papers, File 187F.

119 For a list of Navy visitors see C. B. Wheeler to William Crozier, Dec. 2, 1911, Ordnance Department—Watertown, RG 156, Box 267, File 213/500–49, National Archives.

120 Holden A. Evans, *One Man's Fight*, 256–71. See also Evans to Taylor, June 12, July 29, 1911, Taylor Papers, File 187F.

121 Evans, *One Man's Fight*, 27381.

122 See Navy Department to Commandant, Navy Yard, Norfolk, Jan. 31, 1912, RG 80, Entry No. 58 in "Shop Management Data," National Archives.

123 Taylor to Walter L. Clark, Apr. 9, 1895, Taylor Papers, File 84B.

124 Taylor to H. L. Gantt, Jan. 3, 1907, Taylor Papers, File 120B.

125 See Hugh J. G. Aitken, *Taylorism at Watertown Arsenal* (Cambridge, Mass., 1960), 50–57. Though he succumbs to the Taylor-Copley tradition and devotes more attention to the Watertown labor dispute than it deserves, Aitken is an essential starting point for any discussion of Barth's activities at Watertown.

126 Taylor to Crozier, Dec. 10, 1906, Taylor Papers, File 185A.

127 Crozier selected Watertown rather than Rock Island or Springfield, both of which had piecework systems. See Fred H. Colvin, *60 Years with Men and Machines* (New York, 1947), 184.

128 Frank Hobbs to Crozier, Feb. 8, 1909, Taylor Papers, File 185A.

129 Ibid. For the workers' protests see *Hearings before Special Committee of the House of Representatives*, 2:838–45. 866–72.

130 Crozier to Taylor, Jan. 9, 1909, Taylor Papers, File 185A.

131 Crozier to Taylor, Feb. 13, 1909, Taylor Papers, File 185A.

132 Taylor to Crozier, Jan. 22, 1909, Taylor Papers, File 185A.

133 Taylor to Crozier, Apr. 15, 1909, Taylor Papers, File 185A.

134 Crozier to Taylor, Apr. 16, 1910, Taylor Papers, File 185A.

135 Crozier to Taylor, Jan. 25, 1909, Taylor Papers, File 185A.

136 Taylor to Crozier, Apr. 8, 1909, Taylor Papers, File 185A.

137 Taylor to Barth, May 28, 1909, Taylor Papers, File 113B.

138 C. B. Wheeler to Barth, Aug. 30, 1909, RG 156, Box 266, File 213/200–49, National Archives.

139 Hathaway to Taylor, June 1, 1910, Taylor Papers, File 122A.

140 Wheeler to Crozier, July 14, 1909, RG 156, Box 266, File 213/200–49, National Archives.

141 Wheeler to Crozier, Feb. 16, 1910, RG 146, Box 267, File 213/200–49, National Archives.

142 Wheeler to Crozier, Aug. 1, 1910, RG 145, Box 267, File 213/200–49, National Archives.

143 "Reports of Our Business Agents," International Association of Machinists *Monthly Journal* 22 (Jan. 1910):53; and C. C. Williams to W. B. Wilson, Nov. 1, 1911, RG 156, Box 267, File 213/400–49, National Archives.

144 "Proceedings of a Board of Officers," Dec. 20, 1910, RG 156, Box 267, File 213/250–99, National Archives.

145 Barth to Taylor, Dec. 27, 1910, Taylor Papers, File 113B.

146 "Proceedings of a Board of Officers," Dec. 20, 1910, RG 156, Box 267, File 213/250–99, National Archives.

147 Frank Jennings, "Reports of Our Business Agents," International Association of Machinists *Monthly Journal* 23 (July 1911):689; Crozier to Taylor, June 7, 1911, Taylor Papers, File 185B; and Nadworny, *Scientific Management and the Unions*, 56.

148 See Barth to Wheeler, June 1, 1914, RG 156, Box 268, File 213/800–49, National Archives.

149 Aitken, *Taylorism at Watertown Arsenal*, Ch. 4.

150 "Proceedings of a Board of Officers," Dec. 20, 1910, RG 156, Box 267, File 213/250–99, National Archives.

151 Nadworny, *Scientific Management and the Unions*, 57.

152 Ibid., Chs. 6–7.

153 See Barth to Wheeler, Oct. 21, 1911; Wheeler to Crozier, Jan. 25, 1912, RG 156, Box 267, File 213/400–49, National Archives.

154 C. B. Wheeler, "Questionnaire—Scientific Management," RG 156, Box 266, File 213, Schedule 1–3, Section 1, p. 11, National Archives.

155 For example, Fred H. Colvin, "Management at Watertown Arsenal," *American Machinist* 37 (Sept. 12, 1912):426; and *Hearings before Special Committee of the House of Representatives*, 3:1875–78.

156 *Hearings before Special Committee of the House of Representatives*, 3:1570.

157 Aitken, *Taylorism at Watertown Arsenal*, 207–8. The best contemporary source is Wheeler's answers to Robert Hoxie's 1915 questionaire ("Questionaire—Scientific Management," RG 156, Box 266, File 213, National Archives).

158 See W. W. Gibson to Wheeler, Nov. 20, 1913, RG 156, Box 268, File 213/745–49, National Archives.

159 Wheeler to C. C. Williams, Feb. 28, 1914, RG 156, Box 268, File 213/99, National Archives.

160 Hobbs to Crozier, Jan. 5, 1911; George Montgomery to Crozier, Dec. 31, 1910; S. L. Blunt to Crozier, Jan. 10, 1911, RG 156, Box 267, File 213/300–99, National Archives.

161 See Crozier to Taylor, Jan. 28, 1913, Taylor Papers, File 185D.

162 Barth to Crozier, Jan. 5, 1912, RG 156, Box 267, File 213/500–49, National Archives.

163 Crozier to Taylor, Feb. 28, 1913, Taylor Papers, File 185D.

164 Gantt worked there in 1916 and 1917. L. P. Alford, *Henry Laurence Gantt: Leader in Industry* (New York, 1934), 189, 194.

165 Crozier to Taylor, Feb. 10, 1912, Taylor Papers, File 185C.

166 *Hearings before Special Committee of the House of Representatives*, 2:956–58, 1082–83.

167 Ibid., 958, 1088–89; and Barth to Wheeler, Oct. 19, 1915. RG. 156, Box 269, File 213/922–74, National Archives.

168 W. W. Gibson to Crozier, Feb. 2, 1912, RG 156, Box 267, File 213/600–24, National Archives.

Chapter 7
Taylor and the Whole People, 1910–1915

1 See Robert H. Wiebe, *The Search for Order* (New York, 1967).

2 Ibid. For similar analyses of the progressive movement see Samuel P. Hays, *Conservation and the Gospel of Efficiency* (Cambridge, Mass., 1959); and Samuel Haber, *Efficiency and Uplift* (Chicago, 1964).

3 Frederick W. Taylor to H. L. Gantt, June 30, 1911, Taylor Papers (Stevens Institute of Technology, Hoboken, N.J.), File 121B.

4 Frank B. Gilbreth to Taylor, May 13, Sept. 23, 1909; and Taylor to Gilbreth, Jan. 25, 1910, Taylor Papers, File 59A.

5 For the assertion that Taylor advocated a science of engineering see Edwin T. Layton, Jr., *The Revolt of the Engineers* (Cleveland, 1971), Ch. 6; and Layton, "American Ideologies of Science and Engineering," *Technology and Culture* 17 (Oct. 1976):688–701.

6 Charles D. Wrege and Anne Marie Stotka, "Cooke Creates a Classic: The Story behind F. W. Taylor's *Principles of Scientific Management*," *Academy of Management Review* 3 (Oct. 1978):736–49.

7 Taylor to William Crozier, Apr. 17, 1911, Taylor Papers, File 185B.

8 Frederick W. Taylor, *The Principles of Scientific Management* (New York, 1911), 36–37.

9 "Report of Conversation," June 4, 1907, Taylor Papers, File 79I.

10 This statement is based on conversations with Professor Wrege.

11 Of the 133 pages of the book, 68 are devoted to illustrative incidents, including Gilbreth's brick-laying methods.

12 Taylor, *Principles*, 59.

13 William Crozier to Taylor, Nov. 21, 26, 1913; Taylor to Crozier, Dec. 4, 31, 1913, Taylor Papers, File 185D.

14 Edna Yost, *Frank and Lillian Gilbreth, Partners for Life* (New Brunswick, 1949), 184, 198–204.

15 Taylor's many errors are detailed in Daniel Nelson, "Taylorism and the Workers at Bethlehem Steel, 1898–1901," *Pennsylvania Magazine of History and Biography* 101 (Oct. 1977):487–505; and in Charles Wrege and Amedeo G. Perroni, "Taylor's Pig-Tale: A Historical Analysis of Frederick W. Taylor's Pig Iron Experiments," *Academy of Management Journal* 17 (1974): 6–27.

16 See Taylor to James Mapes Dodge, Jan. 27, 1915, Taylor Papers, File 58B; and Milton J. Nadworny, *Scientific Management and the Unions, 1900–1932* (Cambridge, Mass., 1955), Chs. 4–6.

17 See Nadworny, *Scientific Management and the Unions*, Chs. 4–6.

18 This was especially true of those who read the serialized version. See Ray Stannard Baker's introduction, "Frederick W. Taylor—Scientist in Business Management," *American Magazine* 71 (Mar. 1911):564–70.

19 Taylor, *Principles*, 127.

20 Ibid., 138–39, 142.

21 Taylor to Alexander C. Humphreys, Oct. 22, 1910, Taylor Papers, File 45B.

22 Taylor to Carl G. Barth, Jan. 9, 1911, Taylor Papers, File 113C.

23 Frank Barkley Copley, *Frederick W. Taylor, Father of Scientific Management*, 2 vols. (New York, 1923), 2:378–82.

24 See Haber, *Efficiency and Uplift*, Ch. 4; Alpheus Thomas Mason, *Brandeis, A Free Man's Life* (New York, 1946), 316. For a succinct summary of the hearings see "What is Scientific Management and What Does It Do?" *Industrial Engineering and the Engineering Digest* 9 (Jan. 1911):1–7.

25 Interview with Robert P. A. Taylor, Providence, Rhode Island, June 17, 1974. For a precise description of the disorder see Donald M. Hamilton and Warren A. Mann, "The Hospital Treatment of Involutional Psychoses," in Paul H. Hock and Joseph Zubin, eds., *Depression* (New York, 1954), 199–209.

26 Taylor to Dodge, Nov. 8, 1910, Taylor Papers, File 98J.

27 Taylor to Dodge, Nov. 4, 1910, Taylor Papers, File 58B.

28 Nadworny, *Scientific Management and the Unions*, 35; and Haber, *Efficiency and Uplift*, 51–55.

29 Taylor to Barth, Nov. 10, 1910, Taylor Papers, File 113.

30 Taylor to Louis Brandeis, Jan. 9, 1911, Taylor Papers, File 98J.

31 Taylor to Ray Stannard Baker, Nov. 8, 1910, Taylor Papers, File 4; Baker to Taylor, Dec. 14, 1910, Taylor Papers, File 4; Ida M. Tarbell, *All in the Day's Work* (New York, 1939), 292–95; and John E. Semonche, *Ray Stannard Baker* (Chapel Hill, 1969), Ch. 9.

32 Baker, "Scientist in Business Management," 570.

33 Interview with Robert P. A. Taylor, June 17, 1974.

34 For this suggestion I am indebted to Dr. John R. May, a clinical psychologist practicing in Columbia, Maryland.

35 Interview with Robert P. A. Taylor, June 17, 1974. Louise's temporary disfigurement was a reaction to medicines her doctor prescribed.

36 Taylor to Lionel S. Marks, Aug. 29, 1914, Taylor Papers, File 52E.

37 Taylor to Goodrich, July 13, 1912, Taylor Papers, File 60A4.

38 Taylor to Scudder Klyce, Feb. 10, 1913, Taylor Papers, File 62A2.

39 Ibid.; and Taylor to George F. Steele, Feb. 12, 1913, Taylor Papers, File 70H.

40 Taylor to Goodrich, Mar. 14, 1914, Taylor Papers, File 60A4.

41 Taylor to Frank L. Babbott, Apr. 8, 1914, Taylor Papers, File 57A.

42 Taylor to Babbott, Nov. 10, 1914, Taylor Papers File 57A.

43 See, for example, Yost, *Gilbreth*; Nadworny, *Scientific Management and the Unions*, Chs. 6–7; and Frank B. Copley, "Frederick W. Taylor, Revolutionist," *Outlook* 3 (Sept. 1, 1915):41–48.

44 A. Kauffman to Taylor, Mar. 9, 1914, Taylor Papers, File 58B. See also H. B. Drury, *Scientific Management, A History and Criticism* (New York, 1915), 134.

45 Frederick W. Taylor, "The Principles of Scientific Management," in Dartmouth College Conferences, First Tuck School Conference, *Addresses and Discussions at the Conference on Scientific Management Held October 12, 13, 14, 1911* (Hanover, 1917).

46 See Frederick W. Taylor, "Scientific Management," *Journal of the Efficiency Society* (Sept. 1914):13–35.

47 Copley, "Frederick W. Taylor, Revolutionist," 41–48; and "How It Works: What Manufacturers, and Workmen Are Getting Out of Scientific Management," *American Magazine* 75 (Apr. 1913):11–17.

48 Copley, *Taylor*, 1:417; and Henry Kendall to Taylor, Sept. 8, 1914, Taylor Papers, File 157D.

49 See Copley, "Taylor, Revolutionist"; and Taylor, "Scientific Management and the Unions," *Bulletin of the Society for the Promotion of the Science of Management* 1 (Dec. 1914):3.

50 See Taylor to Crozier, June 21, 1912, Taylor Papers, File 185C; and L. Urwick, ed., *The Golden Book of Management* (London, 1956), 56. See Aimée Moutet, "Les origines du système de Taylor en France: Le point de vue patronal (1907–1914)" *Le Mouvement Social* 93 (Oct.-Dec. 1975):15–49.

51 Taylor to Henri Le Chatelier, Mar. 20, 1913, Taylor Papers, File 63B.

52 Paul Devinat, *Scientific Management in Europe* (Geneva, 1927), 23. See also Charles S. Maier, "Between Taylorism and Technocracy: European Ideologies and the Vision of Industrial Productivity in the 1920's," *Journal of Contemporary History* 5 (1970):27–61.

53 Taylor to Goodrich, Nov. 18, 1911, Taylor Papers, File 60A4.

54 Taylor to Gantt, Dec. 4, 1914, Taylor Papers, File 121B.

55 Taylor to Klyce, Feb. 10, 1913, Taylor Papers, File 62A2.

56 Taylor to Dodge, Dec. 18, 1911, Taylor Papers, File 58B.

57 Taylor to Dodge, Dec. 26, 1911, Taylor Papers, File 58B.

58 Horace K. Hathaway to Taylor, Oct. 12, 1910, Taylor Papers, File 122A.

59 Hathaway to Taylor, Aug. 25, 1911, Taylor Papers, File 122A.

60 Hathaway to Taylor, Jan. 19, 1913, Taylor Papers, File 122C; and C. Bertrand Thompson to Frank B. Gilbreth, June 21, 1916, Frank B. Gilbreth Papers (Purdue University, Lafayette, Ind.).

61 See Taylor to Carl G. Barth, June 28, 1914, Taylor Papers, File 137D.

62 See Layton, *Revolt of the Engineers*, Ch. 7.

63 John Calder, "The Assembly of Small Interchangeable Parts," American Society of Mechanical Engineers *Transactions* 33 (1911):195; Calder, "Overvaluation of Management Science," *Iron Age* 9 (Mar. 6, 1913):605; and William J. Jaffe, *L. P. Alford and the Evolution of Modern Industrial Management* (New York, 1957), 39–40.

64 See L. P. Alford and A. H. Church, "Principles of Management," *American Machinist* 36 (May 30, 1912):857–62. See also Robert T. Kent's attack on Alford, "Slave Driving or Scientific Management?" *Industrial Engineering and the Engineering Digest* 9 (April 1911):309–10.

65 Jaffe, *L. P. Alford*, 36, 68–74; Layton, *Revolt of the Engineers*, 156; and Nadworny, *Scientific Management and the Unions*, 44–45.

66 Jaffe, *L. P. Alford*, 72–74.

67 Layton, *Revolt of the Engineers*, 154.

68 Robert T. Kent, "The Taylor Society Twenty Years Ago," *Bulletin of the Taylor Society* 17 (Feb. 1932):39. See also J. M. Blankenberg to Gilbreth, Oct. 27, 1910, Frank B. Gilbreth Papers. Gilbreth and Kent had gone to Canada in part to collect information for Louis Brandeis' presentation to the ICC.

69 Wilfred Lewis to Gilbreth, Nov. 14, 1910, Gilbreth Papers.

70 Ibid.

71 Taylor to Calvin Rice, Nov. 11, 1910, Taylor Papers, File 6.

72 Cooke to Kent, Mar. 28, 1911, Taylor Papers, File 6.

73 Sanford E. Thompson to Taylor, Apr. 21, 1911, Taylor Papers, File 6.

74 Kent, "The Taylor Society Twenty Years Ago," 40.

75 For the work of the society see Milton J. Nadworny, "The Society for the Promotion of the Science of Management," *Explorations in Entrepreneurial History* 5 (May 15, 1953):246.

76 See Frank B. and Lillian M. Gilbreth, "An Indictment of Stop-Watch Time Study," *Bulletin of the Taylor Society* 6 (June 1921):100–108.

77 See *Bulletin of the Society for the Promotion of the Science of Management* 1 Nov. 1915):3–5.

78 Horace K. Hathaway, "On the Field of Activity of the Society," June 28, 1912, p. 13, Taylor Papers, File 62.

79 H. F. J. Porter, "Discussion," ASME *Transactions* 41 (1919):192–93.

80 Porter to Taylor, Feb. 20, 1906, Taylor Papers, File 63C.

81 Porter to Taylor, Mar. 18, 1906, Taylor Papers, File 63C.

82 Taylor to Barth, Nov. 4, 1907, Taylor Papers, File 113A.

83 See the Taylor-Porter Correspondence, Sept.–Nov. 1911, Taylor Papers, File 5.

84 Taylor to B. Preston Clark, Feb. 12, 1912, Taylor Papers, File 5.

85 Taylor to E. C. Wolf, Mar. 11, 1915, Taylor Papers, File 6J.

86 "The Promotion of Efficiency," *Industrial Engineering and the Engineering Digest* 11 (Mar. 1912):284–85; and Charles Buxton Going, "The Efficiency Movement: An Outline," *Transactions of the Efficiency Society* 1 (1912):11–20.

87 Layton, *Revolt of the Engineers*, Ch. 7.
88 Taylor's only political involvement was in 1910 when he endorsed the candidacy of the Proper Philadelphian and progressive Rudolph Blankenburg for mayor of Philadelphia. See Layton, *Revolt of the Engineers*, Ch. 7; and Kenneth E. Trombley, *The Life and Times of a Happy Liberal* (New York, 1954), 14–30.
89 See Lawrence A. Cremin, *The Transformation of the School* (New York, 1968).
90 Taylor to George W. Hammond, Oct. 1, 1906, Taylor Papers, File 70E.
91 Ibid.; and "A Comparison of University and Industrial Methods and Discipline," 6–8, Taylor Papers, File 76A. Taylor, however, refused to send his son Robert to Phillips Exeter because of his recollection of the school's harsh discipline (Taylor to Babbott, July 12, 1912, Taylor Papers File 57A).
92 Taylor to Hammond, Oct. 1, 1906, Taylor Papers, File 70E.
93 Charles W. Eliot to Taylor, Mar. 7, 1907, Taylor Papers, File 52C.
94 Alexander C. Humphreys to Kempton P. A. Taylor, July 23, 1915, Taylor Papers, File 140. See also Taylor to Humphreys, Mar. 30, 1908, Taylor Papers, File 54B.
95 Taylor to Ira N. Hollis, Nov. 14, 1907, Taylor Papers, File 72J.
96 Hugo Diemer to Kempton P. A. Taylor, Sept. 8, 1915, Taylor Papers, File 14E.
97 C. Bertrand Thompson to Edwin F. Gay, Feb. 12, 1914, Taylor Papers, File 52D.
98 By 1915 Columbia, New York University, Syracuse, and Pennsylvania State College also had courses on scientific management. Many of the professors who taught the courses had attended Gilbreth's summer schools. See Drury, *Scientific Management*, 19; and Yost, *Frank and Lillian Gilbreth*, 238–39.
99 See Gay to Taylor, Dec. 7, 1909, Taylor Papers, File 52D.
100 Taylor Papers, File 77B4.
101 Taylor had enunciated the "exception principle" in "Shop Management," ASME *Transactions* 26 (1903):1408–9.
102 See Taylor to Barth, Feb. 8, 1909, Taylor Papers, File 113B.
103 Hathaway to Taylor, Oct. 11, 1913; and Taylor to Hathaway, Oct. 15, 1913, Taylor Papers, File 122C.
104 Taylor to Gay, May 26, 1913, Taylor Papers, File 52D.
105 Baker, "Scientist in Business Management," 567.
106 See Nadworny, *Scientific Management and the Unions*, Ch. 4.
107 For the union position see ibid.
108 Taylor to Gantt, Jan. 12, 1911 Taylor Papers, File 121B; and Taylor to Barth, Jan. 12, 1911, Taylor Papers, File 113C.
109 Taylor to Hathaway, Apr. 17, 1914, Taylor Papers, File 123A.
110 See Nadworny, *Scientific Management and the Unions*, 74; and H. B. Drury, "Organized Labor and Scientific Management," *Industrial Engineering and the Engineering Digest* 14 (Apr. 1914):145–47.
111 Taylor to Gantt, Sept. 6, 1911, Taylor Papers, File 121B; and Taylor to Dodge, Sept. 6, 1911, Taylor Papers, File 58B.

112 Taylor to Hollis Godfrey, Jan. 22, 1912, Taylor Papers, File 58B.
113 See Yost, *Frank and Lillian Gilbreth*, 211.
114 Taylor to Goodrich, Nov. 18, 1911, Taylor Papers, File 60A4.
115 Taylor to Dodge, June 20, 1912, Taylor Papers, File 58B.
116 See C. Bertrand Thompson to Taylor, Dec. 19, 1914, Taylor Papers, File 52G; Taylor to Barth, Dec. 30, 1914, Taylor Papers, File 113D; and Hathaway to Taylor, Dec. 31, 1914, Taylor Papers, File 123B.
117 Taylor to Crozier, Mar. 3, 1915, Taylor Papers, File 185D.
118 *Philadelphia North American*, Mar. 22, 1915.
119 Taylor to Goodrich, Sept. 14, 1914, Taylor Papers, File 60A4.
120 Taylor to Klyce, Nov. 10, 1914, Taylor Papers, File 62A2.
121 Interview with Robert P. A. Taylor, June 17, 1974.
122 Taylor to Babbott, Feb. 12, 1915, Taylor Papers, File 57A.
123 "Minutes of Meeting of Frederick W. Taylor Cooperators," Oct. 26, 1915, Taylor Papers, File 6L.
124 Frank B. Copley to Morris L. Cooke Jan. 25, 1917, Morris L. Cooke Papers (Franklin D. Roosevelt Library, Hyde Park, N.Y.), Box 5, File 46.
125 Copley to Cooke, Jan. 14, 28, 1917, Cooke Papers, Box 5, File 46.
126 Copley to Cooke, Mar. 15, 1917, Cooke Papers, Box 5, File 46.
127 Ibid.
128 Copley to Mrs. Morris L. Cooke, Mar. 23, 1917, Cooke Papers, Box 5, File 46.
129 Copley to Edward W. Clark, III, May 13, 1920, Cooke Papers, Box 19, File 170.
130 "Final Memorandum on Manuscript of Copley's Taylor," n.d., Cooke Papers, Box 19, File 170.
131 "General Criticism of Mr. Copley's Manuscript Made by Mrs. Taylor," n.d., Cooke Papers, Box 19, File 170.
132 "Comments on Taylor Biography by Sanford E. Thompson," May 26, 1920, Cooke Papers, Box 19, File 170.
133 Ibid.
134 See Henry G. Pearson, "Report of the Committee on the Biography of Frederick W. Taylor Proposing a Plan for the Completion of Mr. Copley's Work," Mar. 17, 1920, Cooke Papers, Box 19, File 170.
135 Copley to Clark, May 13, 1920, Cooke Papers, Box 19, File 170.
136 Ibid.
137 Ibid.
138 "Meetings of Biography Committee with Mr. Copley," Jan. 18, 1921, Cooke Papers, Box 19, File 170.
139 Sanford E. Thompson to Clark, Oct. 23, 1922, Cooke Papers, Box 19, File 170.
140 Ibid.

Chapter 8
Epilogue: Taylor and the Managerial Revolution

1 Frederick W. Taylor, "Shop Management," American Society of Mechanical Engineers *Transactions* 24 (1903):1417–18.

2 Majority Report of Sub-Committee on Administration, "The Present State of the Art of Industrial Management," ASME *Transactions* 34 (1912):1137.

3 Ray Stannard Baker, "Frederick W. Taylor—Scientist in Business Management," *American Magazine* 71 (Mar. 1911):570.

4 Horace B. Drury wrote in 1922 that "there are few important factories where the influence of scientific management has not been felt, to at least a·small extent" (Horace Bookwalter Drury, *Scientific Management, A History and Criticism*, 3rd ed., [New York, 1922], 187).

5 See Stanley Mathewson *Restriction of Output among Unorganized Workers* (New York, 1931).

6 My study of rubber tire manufacturing plants, perhaps the most "modern" American factories of the 1920's and 1930's, documents this statement in detail. Essentially, the workers' potential for restricting production depended on machine processes, not managerial systems. For a dissenting view see David Montgomery, "The 'New Unionism' and the Transformation of Workers' Consciousness in America, 1909–22," *Journal of Social History* 7 (Summer 1974):518.

7 National Industrial Conference Board, *Systems of Wage Payment* (New York, 1930), 8.

8 See Daniel Nelson, *Managers and Workers: Origins of the New Factory System in the United States 1880–1920* (Madison, 1975), Ch. 8.

9 Alfred D. Chandler, Jr., *The Visible Hand: The Managerial Revolution in American Business* (Cambridge, Mass., 1977), 412.

10 See Edwin T. Layton, *The Revolt of the Engineers* (Cleveland, 1971), Ch. 10.

11 Milton J. Nadworny, *Scientific Management and the Unions, 1900–1932* (Cambridge, Mass., 1955), Ch. 8.

Bibliographical Note

This book is based on two bodies of materials, both voluminous. The first is the unpublished papers of Frederick W. Taylor (Samuel C. Williams Library, Stevens Institute of Technology, Hoboken, N.J.) and his followers, Carl G. Barth (Harvard Business School, Baker Library, Boston, Mass.), Morris L. Cooke (Franklin D. Roosevelt Library, Hyde Park, N.Y.), Frank B. Gilbreth (Purdue University Library, Lafayette, Ind.), and Harrington Emerson (New York Public Library, New York, N.Y.). The huge Taylor archive is by far the most important of these collections. Taylor apparently kept every scrap of paper related to his career, and the bulk of his holdings are available at the Stevens Institute. Exactly what is not available is unclear. The papers passed through so many hands between 1915 and 1951 and have been used by so many people (often with minimal supervision) that it is impossible to ascertain what, if anything of consequence, is missing. Barth charged in 1933 that certain technical materials had disappeared, and a major weeding of the collection occurred after Louise Taylor's death in 1949. It is my guess that many forms, engineering reports, and other seemingly low value documents related to Taylor's consulting jobs were discarded. Since 1951, when the collection was opened to the public, some material seems to have been misplaced. Robert P. A. Taylor provided valuable information about the collection, as well as other facets of Taylor's personal life.

The papers of Taylor's disciples were much less valuable for my purposes. The Barth collection is sparse and unrevealing; Cooke's papers, on the other hand, are abundant, but also generally unrevealing. Gilbreth's papers are helpful on some points, and the Emerson collection documents the turbulent early career of that most flamboyant of scientific management practitioners. Professor Charles Wrege graciously provided me with copies of other Emerson materials from the Thomas Burke collection at the University of Washington, Seattle. The DuPont Collection (Eleutherian Mills Historical Library, Wilmington, Del.) includes useful information on the Johnson Company. The William C. Whitney Papers (Library of Congress), the arsenal records (National Archives), and the Joseph Wharton Papers (Friends Library at Swarthmore College, Swarthmore, Pa.) were also helpful. Harris Ebenbach guided me through the records of the Unitarian Society of Germantown, Pa., and Edward A. Coates supplied biographical data on Atherton B. Wadleigh. Bayard S. Clark and Frederick W. Clark provided various materials on the Taylor-Clark tie.

My second essential resource was the vast published literature of American manufacturing between 1880 and 1915. I had earlier surveyed much of this material for my *Managers and Workers: Origins of the New Factory System in the*

United States, 1880–1920. For the present work I also carefully reviewed *Iron Age, Iron Trade Review, Industrial Engineering and the Engineering Digest,* and the U.S. Patent Office publications relevant to Taylor's inventions. In addition, I read most of the popular magazine articles on Taylor that appeared after 1910 and the equally voluminous scholarly literature of scientific management. When these works proved helpful, they are cited in the notes.

Index

Midvale Steel Company (continued)
  with men, 123, 171; management after
  Taylor, 138—40; mentioned, 21, 29, 102,
  151, 154, 206n8, 232n44
Miller, Emlen Hare: makes time studies,
  41; surveys literature, 43; Thompson
  reviews time studies, 60; mentioned,
  212n73
Miller, Fred J., 222n60
Mitchell, John, 190—91
Mitscherlich patent: used by Manufactur-
  ing Investment Company, 48—49;
  problems, 49, 52; mentioned, 214n11
Mnemonic system, 57, 85
Monroe, Paul, 209n65
Montgomery, David, 207n24, 243n6
Montgomery, George, 166
Morgan, Anne, 190
Morgan, J. P., 48
Morrow, J. T., 110
Motion study: Gilbreth develops, 131—35;
  introduced at New England Butt, 153
Motion Study (1911), 133
Mott, Lucretia, 23
Moutet, Aimée, 239n50
Moxham, Arthur J.: Johnson partner, 62;
  Taylor's superior, 64; sells Johnson to
  Federal Steel, 69; mentioned, 67
Mullaney, John E., 72
Mushet self-hardening tool steel, 57

Nadworny, Milton J., 209n60, 229n119,
  234n85, 236n147, 236n151, 238n16,
  238n28, 240n65, 240n75, 241n106,
  241n110, 243n11
National Cash Register Company: welfare
  work, 17—18; strike, 18; Taylor criti-
  cizes, 118—19
National Civic Federation: defines welfare
  work, 16; welfare department, 19
Nebraska, University of, 127
Nelson, Daniel, 205n5, 207n14, 207n18,
  208n38, 209n61, 209n63, 209n67,
  233n75, 238n15, 243n8
Nelson Valve Company, 185
Nerst Lamp Company, 185
"New factory system," 3—4, 10—20
Newberry, Truman, 159
Newbold, Sidney: Taylor assistant, 90;
  Taylor-White patents, 114; Tabor em-

ployee, 121
New England Butt Company: Gilbreth
  client, 134, 153—54; mentioned, 149,
  153, 233n74
"New Era" economy, 10
New Nationalism, 169
New York Navy Yard, 158—59
New York University, 241n98
Niles-Bement-Pond Company, 114
Noble, David, 205n4
Noll, Henry: pig iron loader, 94; problems,
  98; in *Principles*, 172; mentioned, 142,
  190, 224n112
Norfolk Navy Yard: Evans's base, 155;
  Evans manages, 160; strike, 160
Northern Electric Manufacturing Com-
  pany, 62
Norton, Charles D., 160
Norton, Thomas L., 207n21
"Notes on Belting" (1893), 58, 119, 216n53

O'Connell, James, 209n59
"On the Art of Cutting Metals" (1906), 114,
  123
Ordnance Department, Army, 155, 161,
  190
Outlook, 179

Packard Motor Company: contacts Taylor,
  124; Taylor lectures at, 180
Panhard Auto Works, 179
Paper Mill Journal, 61
Paris Exhibition (1900), 88
Parkhurst, Frederick A., 153, 234
Passer, Harold C., 207n32
Patterson, John H.: work at NCR, 17—18;
  Taylor criticizes, 118—19; mentioned,
  186, 200
Paullin, Charles Oscar, 220n6, 220n17,
  220n20
Payne, Oliver H., 48, 52
Payson, F. C., 128
Pearson, Henry G., 195—96
Pennsylania, University of, 24, 122, 186
Pennsylvania Railroad, 32
Pennsylvania State College: Taylor lec-
  tures at, 180; mentioned, 187, 241n98
Pepper, Irwin S., 165
Perlman, Mark, 209n59
Perroni, Amedeo G., 96, 223n80, 223n82,

COMPOSED BY FIVE STAR PHOTO TYPESETTING, INC.
NEENAH, WISCONSIN
MANUFACTURED BY THOMSON-SHORE, INC.
DEXTER, MICHIGAN
TEXT IS SET IN TIMES ROMAN, DISPLAY LINES IN BASKERVILLE

Library of Congress Cataloging in Publication Data
Nelson, Daniel, 1941 –
Frederick W. Taylor and the rise of scientific management.
Includes bibliographical references and index.
1. Taylor, Frederick Winslow, 1856 – 1915.
2. Industrial management—United States—History.
3. Industrial engineers—United States—Biography.
I. Title.
T55.85.T38N44   658.5′0092′4 [B]   79-5411
ISBN 0-299-08160-5